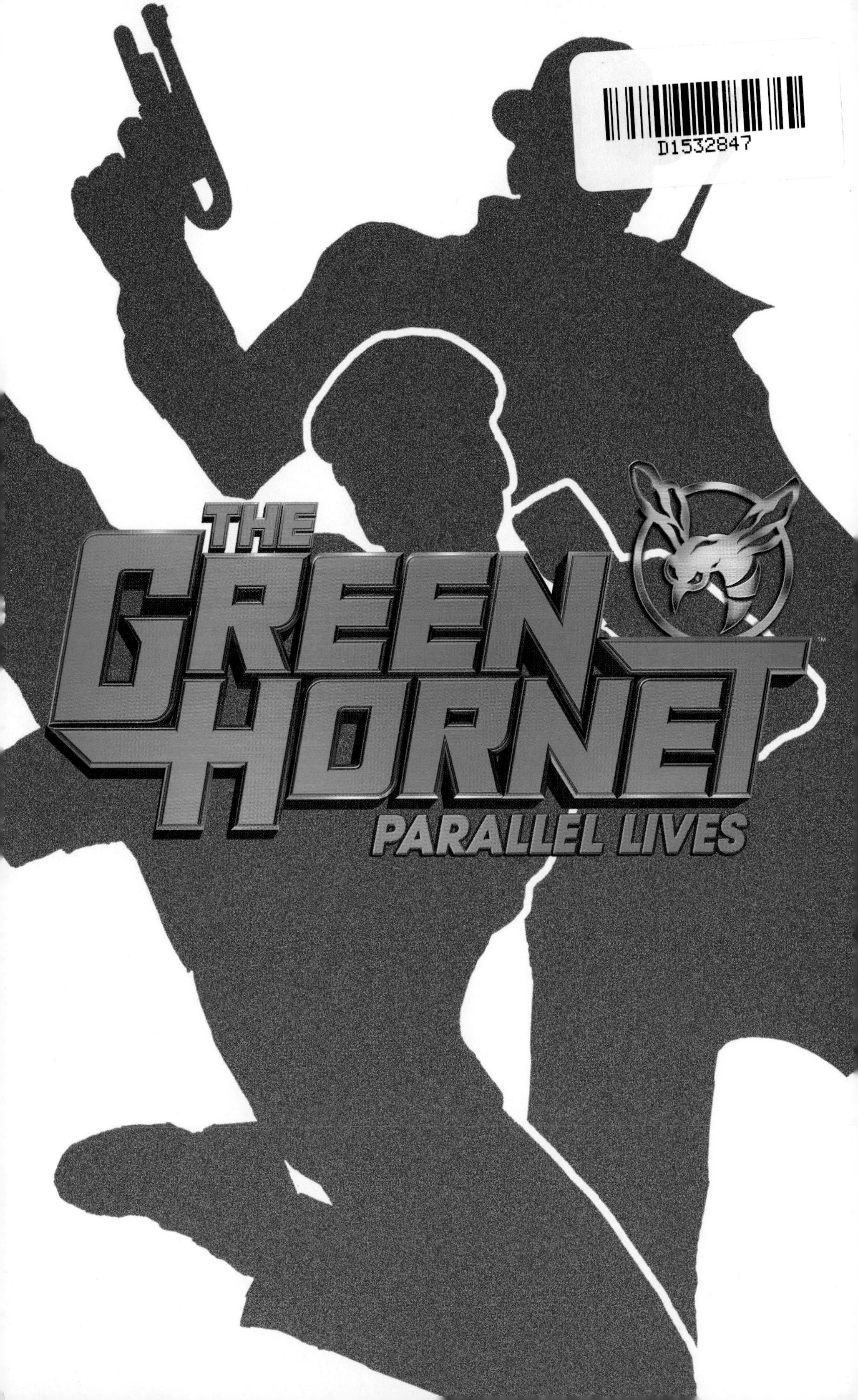
THE
GREEN
HORNET
PARALLEL LIVES

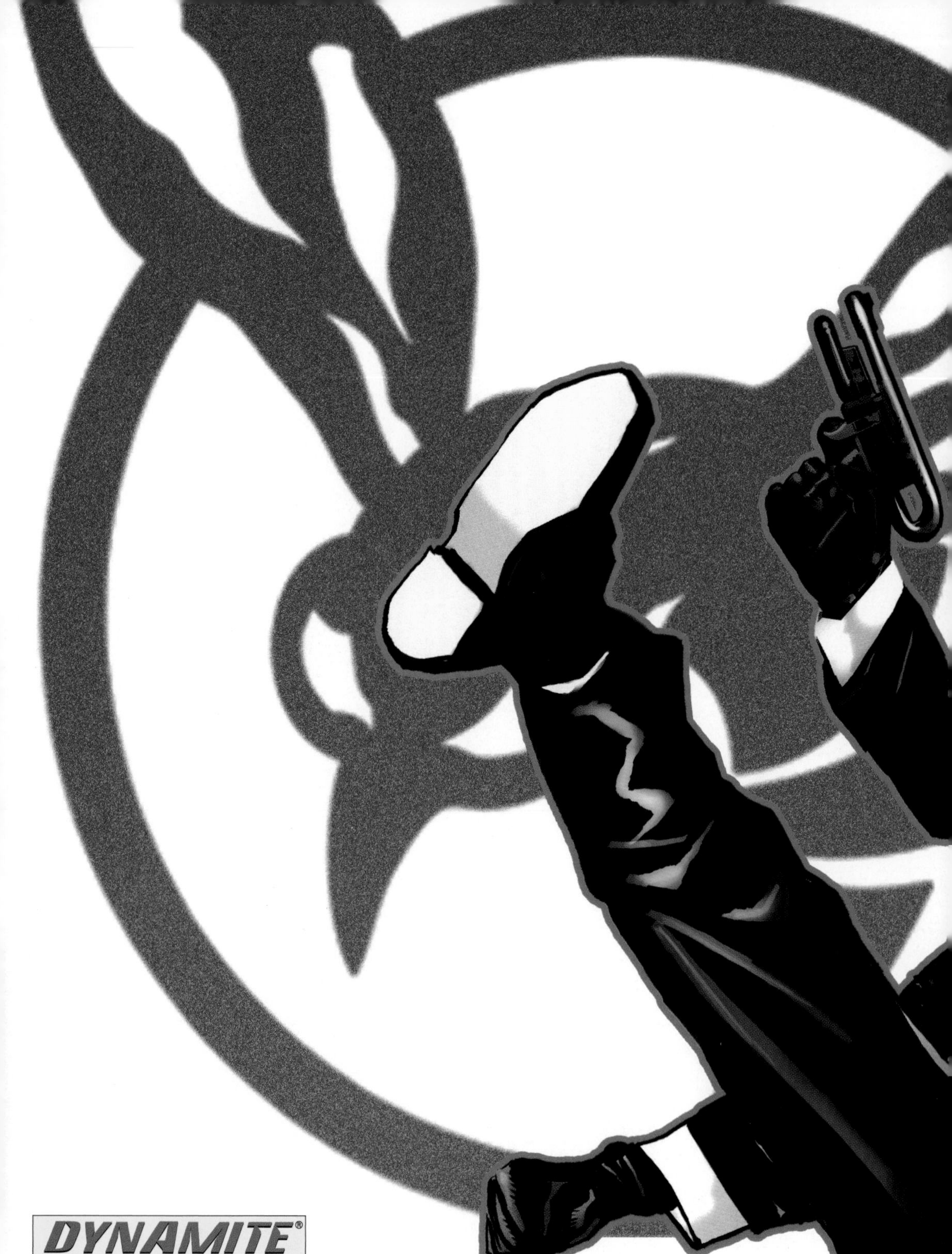

DYNAMITE® ENTERTAINMENT

WWW.DYNAMITEENTERTAINMENT.COM

NICK BARRUCCI • PRESIDENT
JUAN COLLADO • CHIEF OPERATING OFFICER
JOSEPH RYBANDT • EDITOR
JOSH JOHNSON • CREATIVE DIRECTOR
RICH YOUNG • DIRECTOR OF BUSINESS DEVELOPMENT
JASON ULLMEYER • GRAPHIC DESIGNER

ISBN-10: 1-60690-148-6 ISBN-13: 978-1-60690-148-9 First Printing 10 9 8 7 6 5 4 3 2 1

THE GREEN HORNET™: PARALLEL LIVES, VOLUME ONE. First printing. Contains materials originally published in The Green Hornet: Parallel Lives #1-5. Published by Dynamite Entertainment. 155 Ninth Ave. Suite B, Runnemede, NJ 08078. Printed in Canada.

For media rights, foreign rights, promotions, licensing, and advertising: marketing@dynamiteentertainment.com.

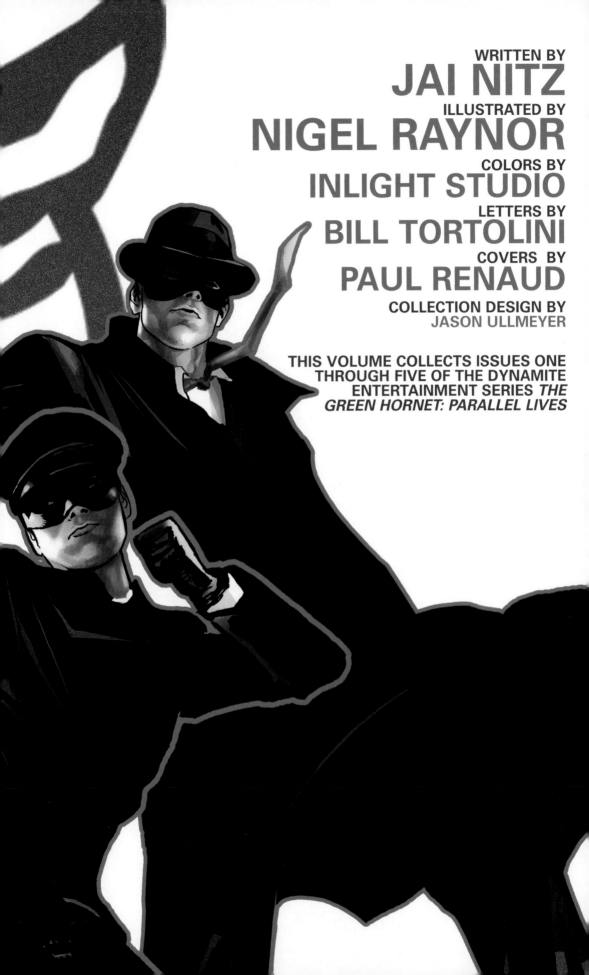

WRITTEN BY
JAI NITZ
ILLUSTRATED BY
NIGEL RAYNOR
COLORS BY
INLIGHT STUDIO
LETTERS BY
BILL TORTOLINI
COVERS BY
PAUL RENAUD
COLLECTION DESIGN BY
JASON ULLMEYER

THIS VOLUME COLLECTS ISSUES ONE
THROUGH FIVE OF THE DYNAMITE
ENTERTAINMENT SERIES *THE
GREEN HORNET: PARALLEL LIVES*

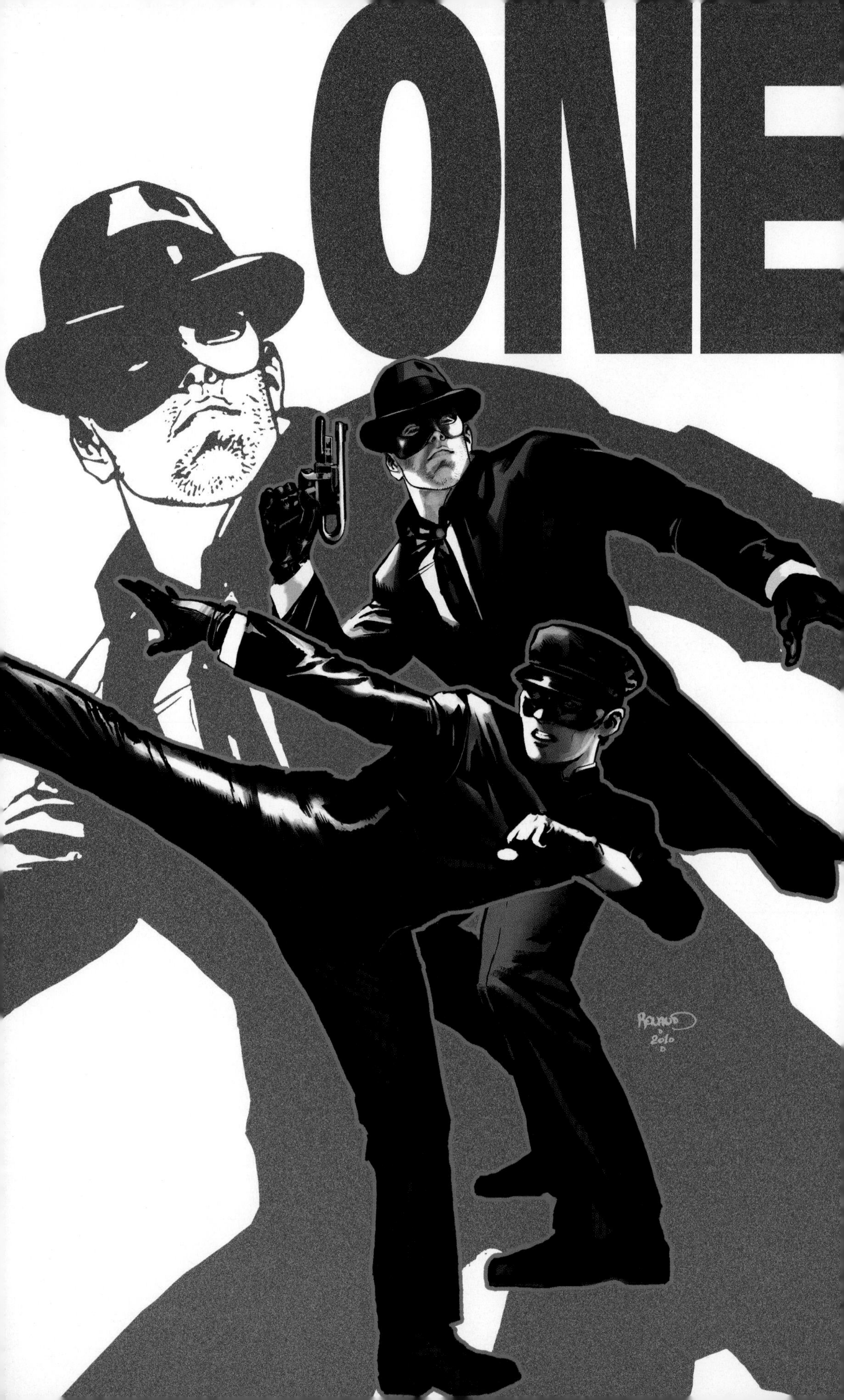
ONE

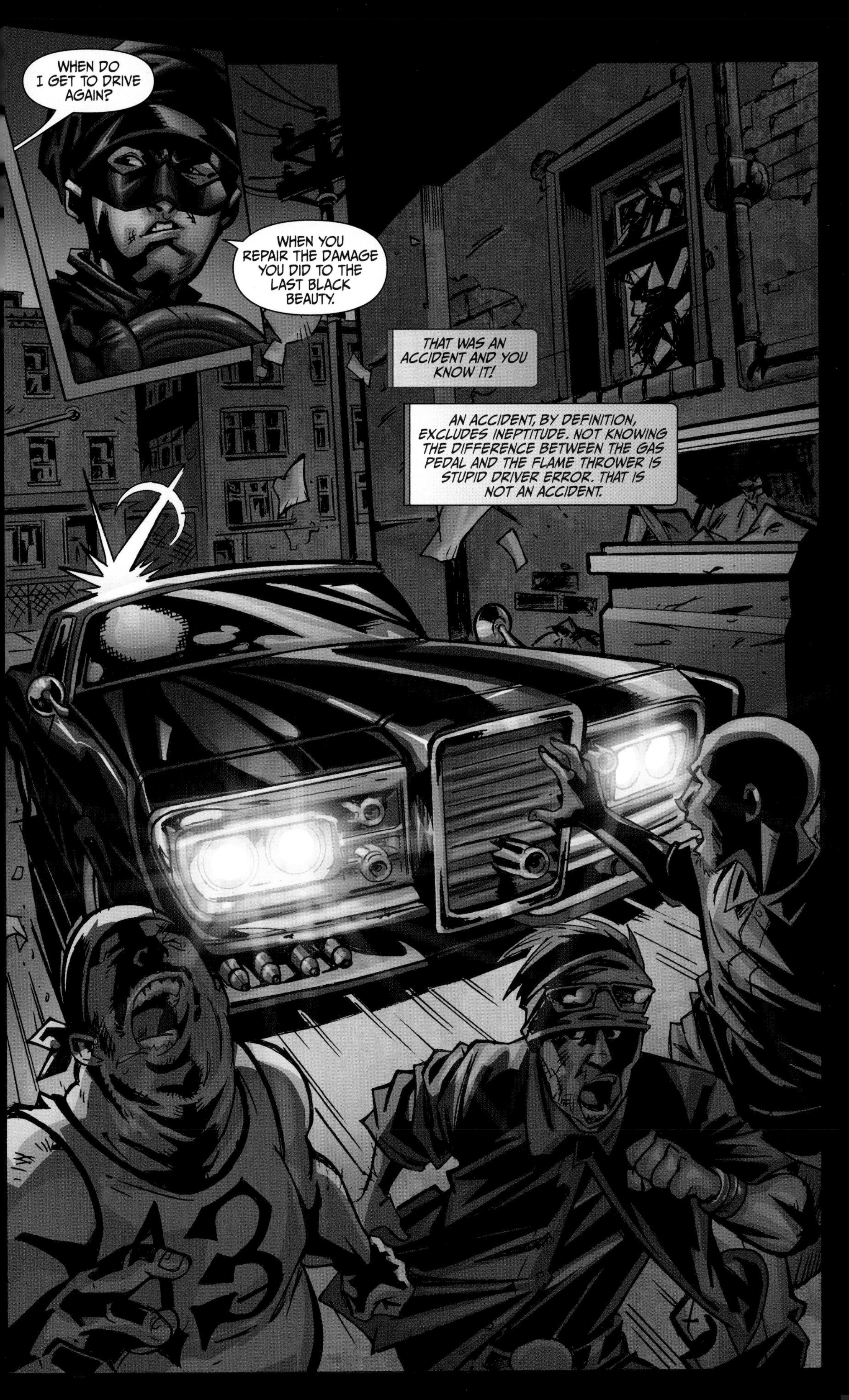
WHEN DO I GET TO DRIVE AGAIN?
WHEN YOU REPAIR THE DAMAGE YOU DID TO THE LAST BLACK BEAUTY.
THAT WAS AN ACCIDENT AND YOU KNOW IT!
AN ACCIDENT, BY DEFINITION, EXCLUDES INEPTITUDE. NOT KNOWING THE DIFFERENCE BETWEEN THE GAS PEDAL AND THE FLAME THROWER IS STUPID DRIVER ERROR. THAT IS NOT AN ACCIDENT.

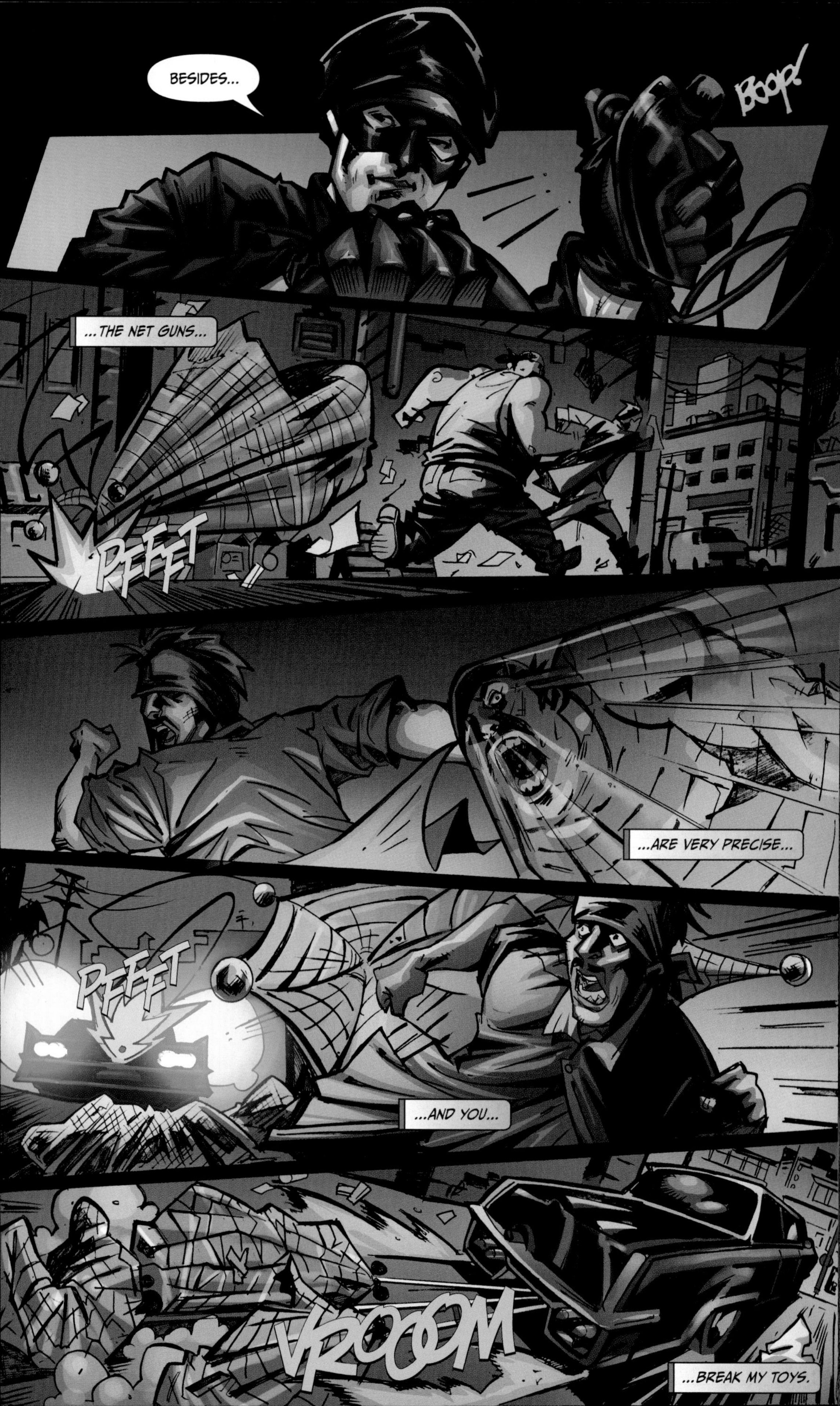
BESIDES...
BOOP!
...THE NET GUNS...
PFFFT
...ARE VERY PRECISE...
PFFFT
...AND YOU...
VROOOM
...BREAK MY TOYS.

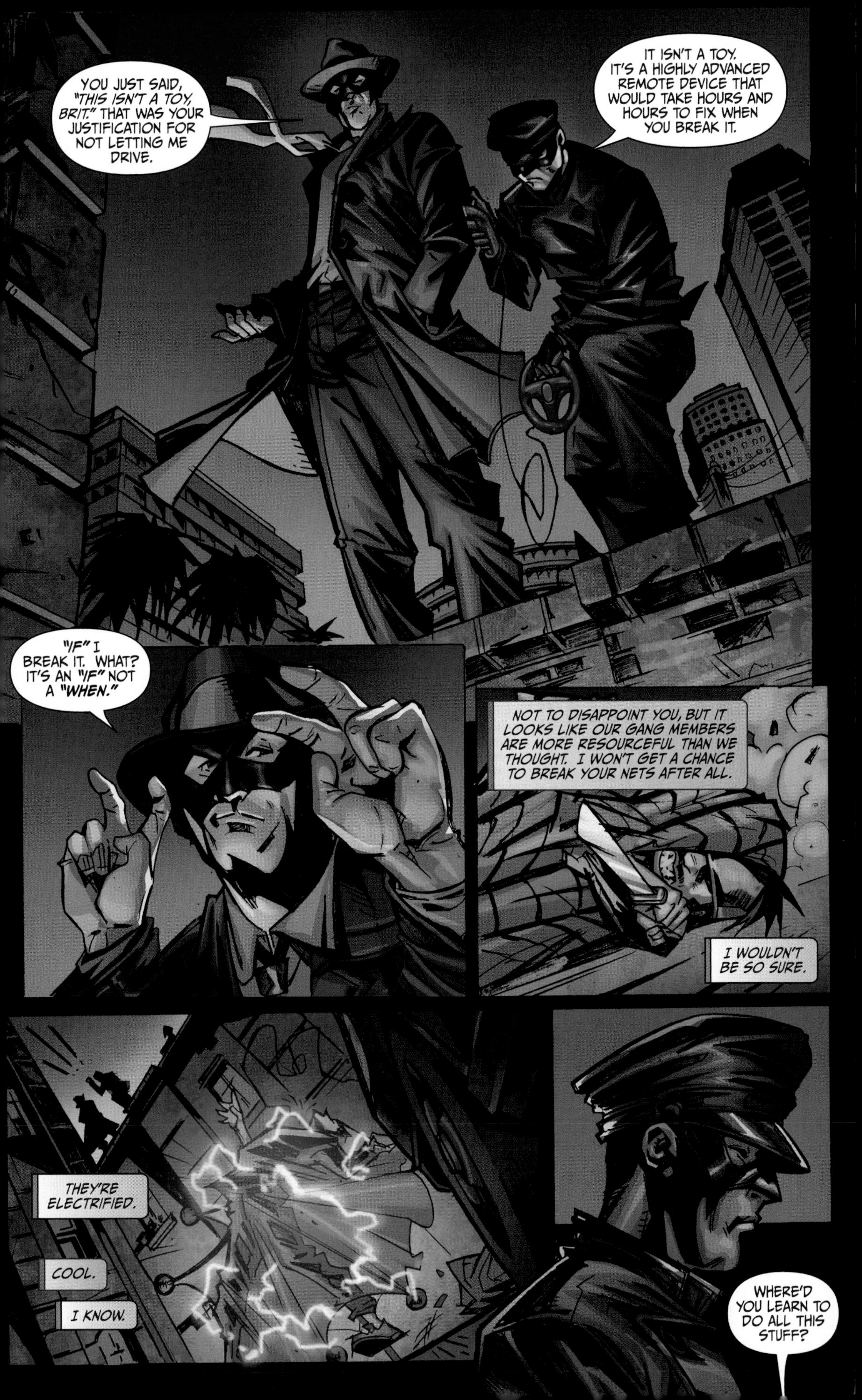

YOU JUST SAID, "THIS ISN'T A TOY, BRIT." THAT WAS YOUR JUSTIFICATION FOR NOT LETTING ME DRIVE.
IT ISN'T A TOY. IT'S A HIGHLY ADVANCED REMOTE DEVICE THAT WOULD TAKE HOURS AND HOURS TO FIX WHEN YOU BREAK IT.
"IF" I BREAK IT. WHAT? IT'S AN "IF" NOT A "WHEN."
NOT TO DISAPPOINT YOU, BUT IT LOOKS LIKE OUR GANG MEMBERS ARE MORE RESOURCEFUL THAN WE THOUGHT. I WON'T GET A CHANCE TO BREAK YOUR NETS AFTER ALL.
I WOULDN'T BE SO SURE.
THEY'RE ELECTRIFIED.
COOL.
I KNOW.
WHERE'D YOU LEARN TO DO ALL THIS STUFF?

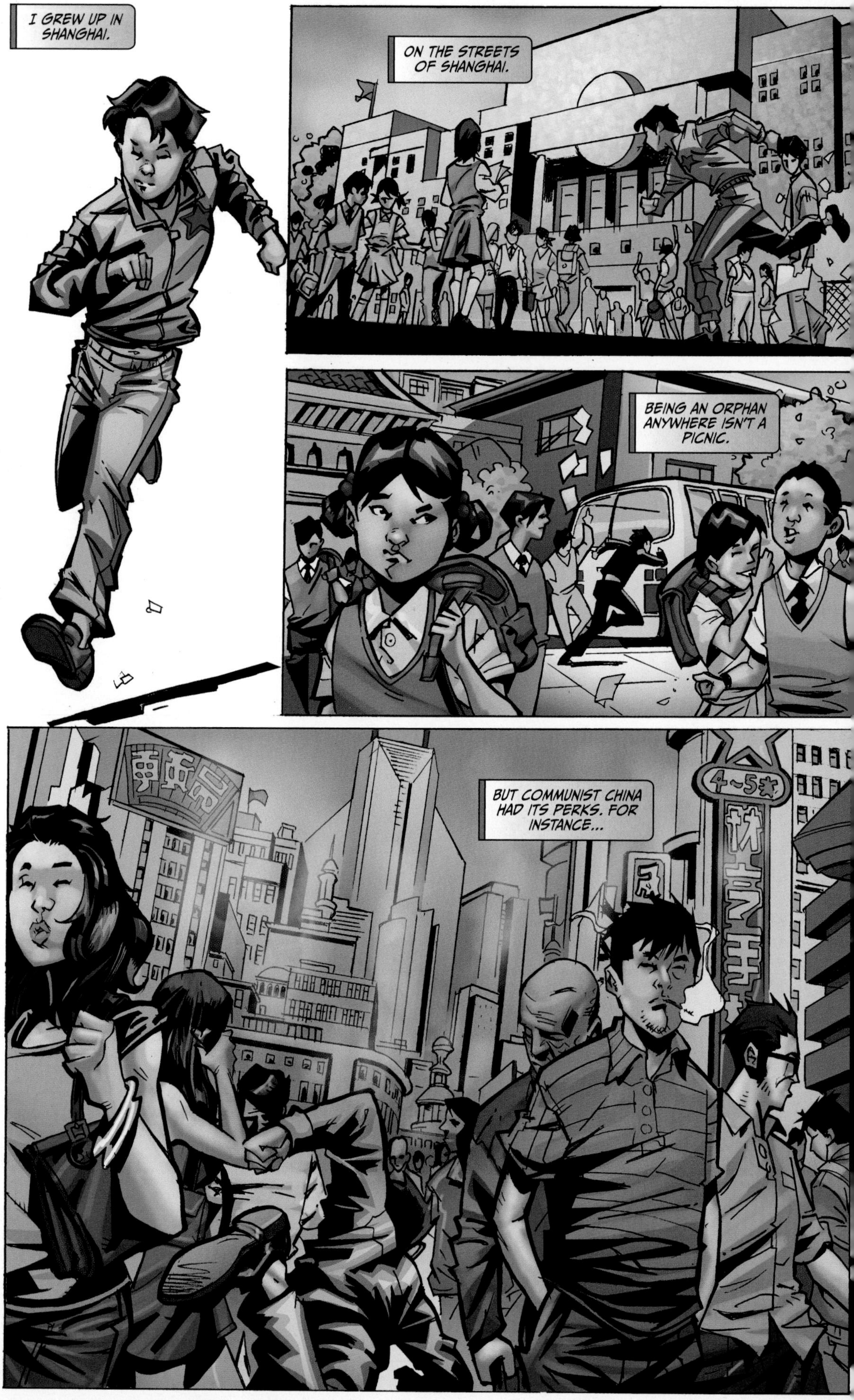
I GREW UP IN SHANGHAI.
ON THE STREETS OF SHANGHAI.
BEING AN ORPHAN ANYWHERE ISN'T A PICNIC.
BUT COMMUNIST CHINA HAD ITS PERKS. FOR INSTANCE...

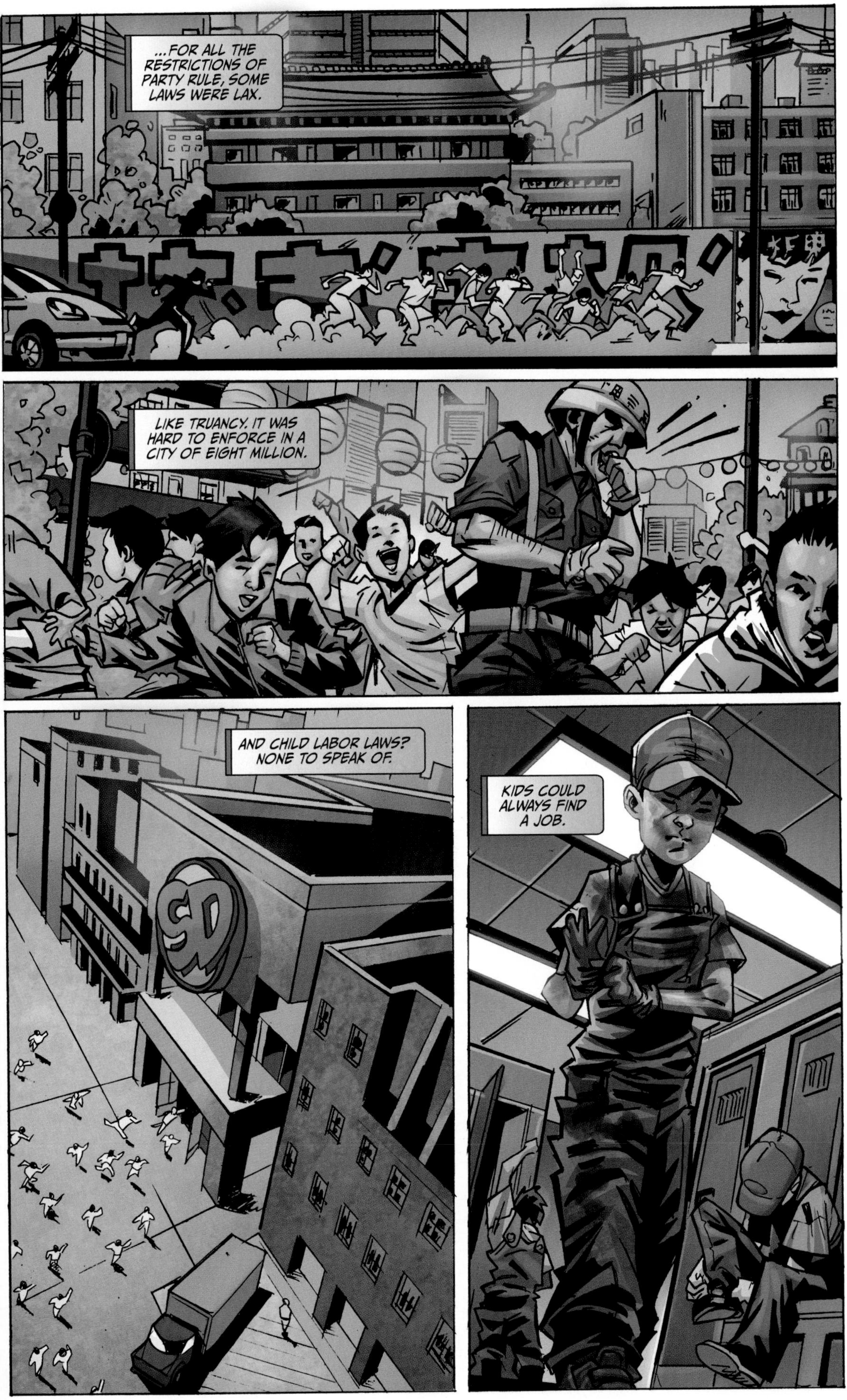

...FOR ALL THE RESTRICTIONS OF PARTY RULE, SOME LAWS WERE LAX.
LIKE TRUANCY. IT WAS HARD TO ENFORCE IN A CITY OF EIGHT MILLION.
AND CHILD LABOR LAWS? NONE TO SPEAK OF.
KIDS COULD ALWAYS FIND A JOB.

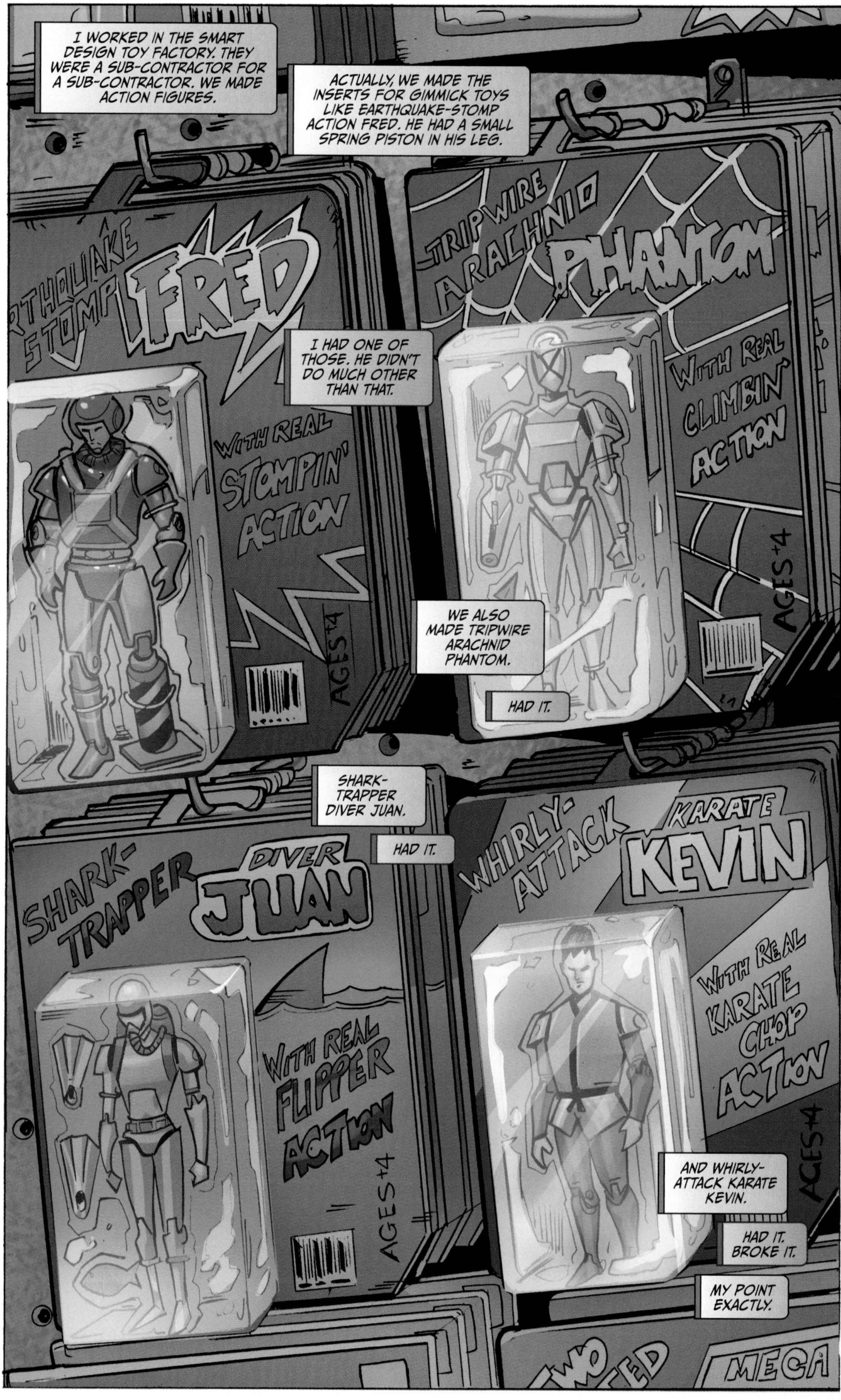

I WORKED IN THE SMART DESIGN TOY FACTORY. THEY WERE A SUB-CONTRACTOR FOR A SUB-CONTRACTOR. WE MADE ACTION FIGURES.
ACTUALLY, WE MADE THE INSERTS FOR GIMMICK TOYS LIKE EARTHQUAKE-STOMP ACTION FRED. HE HAD A SMALL SPRING PISTON IN HIS LEG.
STOMP FRED
WITH REAL STOMPIN' ACTION
AGES +4
TRIPWIRE ARACHNID PHANTOM
WITH REAL CLIMBIN' ACTION
AGES +4
I HAD ONE OF THOSE. HE DIDN'T DO MUCH OTHER THAN THAT.
WE ALSO MADE TRIPWIRE ARACHNID PHANTOM.
HAD IT.
SHARK-TRAPPER DIVER JUAN.
HAD IT.
SHARK-TRAPPER DIVER JUAN
WITH REAL FLIPPER ACTION
AGES +4
WHIRLY-ATTACK KARATE KEVIN
WITH REAL KARATE CHOP ACTION
AGES +4
AND WHIRLY-ATTACK KARATE KEVIN.
HAD IT. BROKE IT.
MY POINT EXACTLY.
MEGA

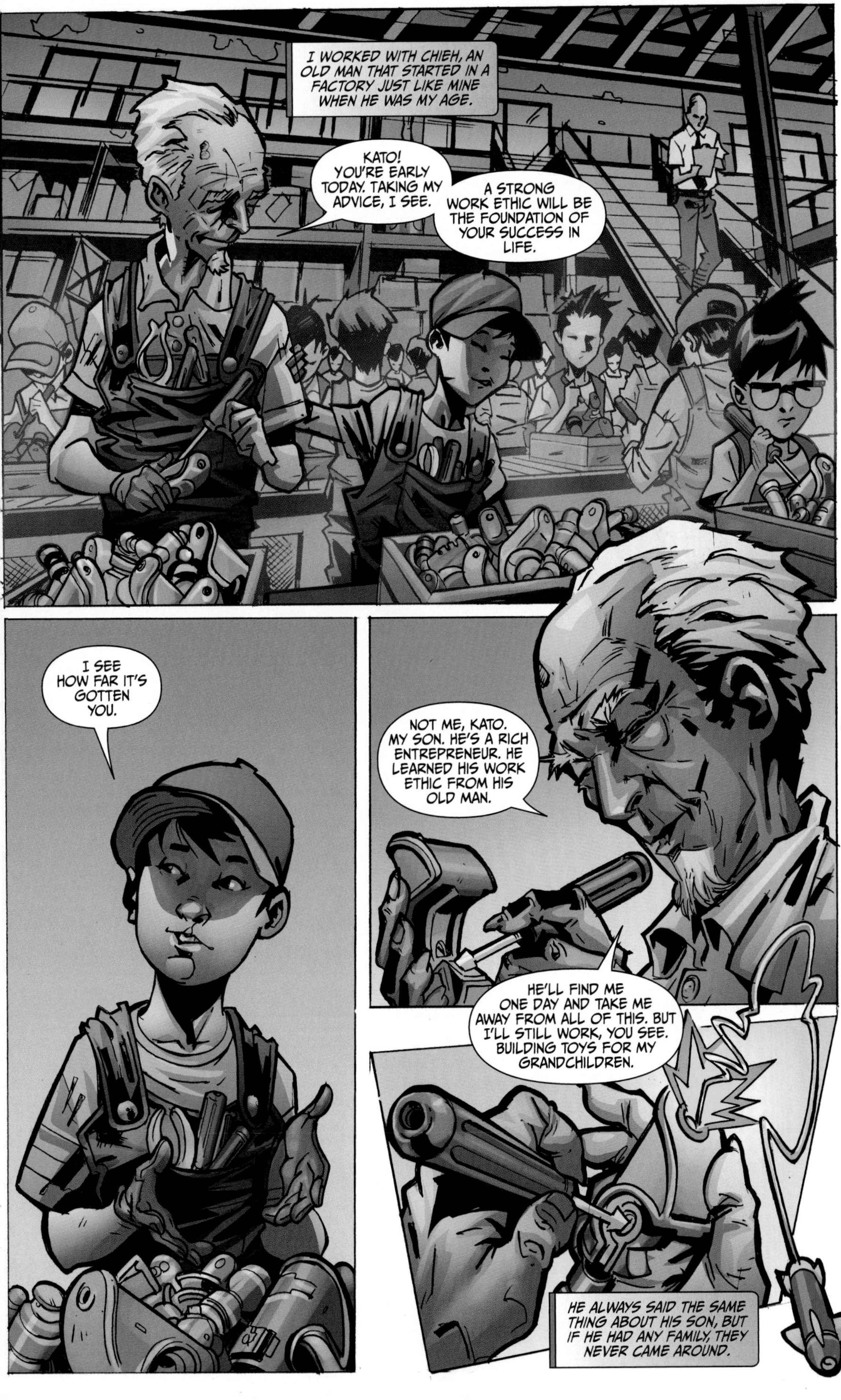

I WORKED WITH CHIEH, AN OLD MAN THAT STARTED IN A FACTORY JUST LIKE MINE WHEN HE WAS MY AGE.
KATO! YOU'RE EARLY TODAY. TAKING MY ADVICE, I SEE.
A STRONG WORK ETHIC WILL BE THE FOUNDATION OF YOUR SUCCESS IN LIFE.
I SEE HOW FAR IT'S GOTTEN YOU.
NOT ME, KATO. MY SON. HE'S A RICH ENTREPRENEUR. HE LEARNED HIS WORK ETHIC FROM HIS OLD MAN.
HE'LL FIND ME ONE DAY AND TAKE ME AWAY FROM ALL OF THIS. BUT I'LL STILL WORK, YOU SEE. BUILDING TOYS FOR MY GRANDCHILDREN.
HE ALWAYS SAID THE SAME THING ABOUT HIS SON, BUT IF HE HAD ANY FAMILY, THEY NEVER CAME AROUND.

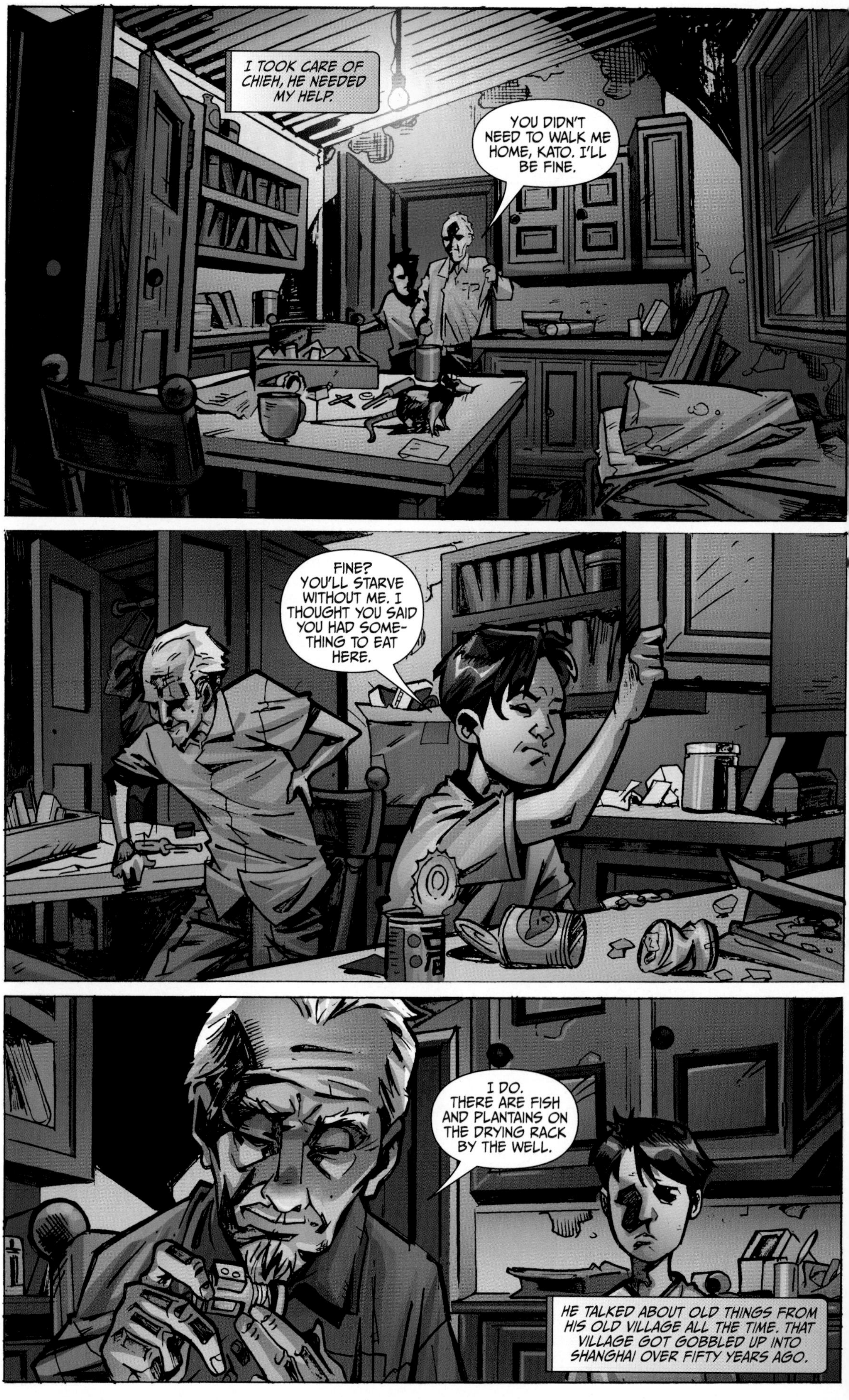
I TOOK CARE OF CHIEH, HE NEEDED MY HELP.
YOU DIDN'T NEED TO WALK ME HOME, KATO. I'LL BE FINE.
FINE? YOU'LL STARVE WITHOUT ME. I THOUGHT YOU SAID YOU HAD SOME-THING TO EAT HERE.
I DO. THERE ARE FISH AND PLANTAINS ON THE DRYING RACK BY THE WELL.
HE TALKED ABOUT OLD THINGS FROM HIS OLD VILLAGE ALL THE TIME. THAT VILLAGE GOT GOBBLED UP INTO SHANGHAI OVER FIFTY YEARS AGO.

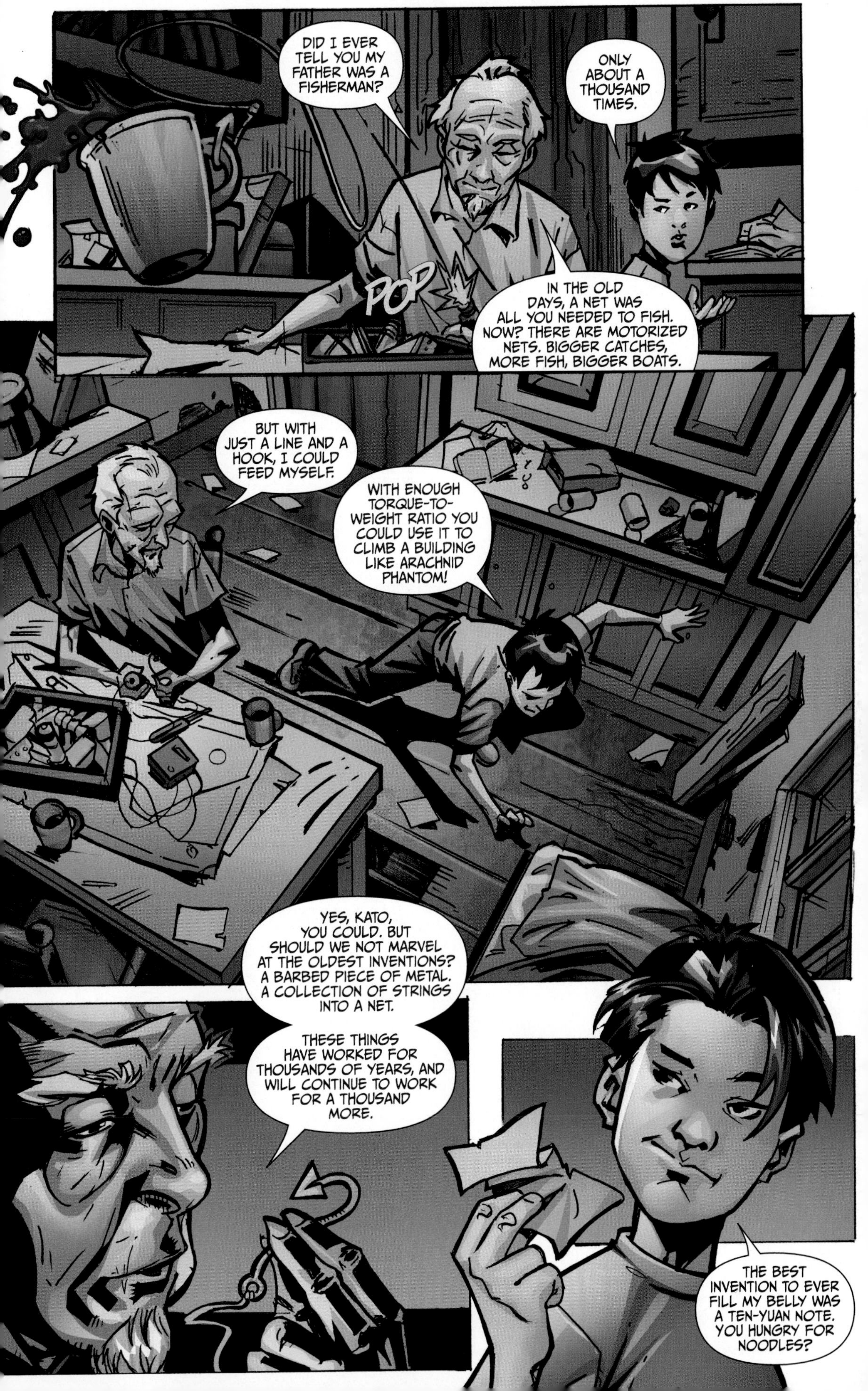
DID I EVER TELL YOU MY FATHER WAS A FISHERMAN?
ONLY ABOUT A THOUSAND TIMES.
POP
IN THE OLD DAYS, A NET WAS ALL YOU NEEDED TO FISH. NOW? THERE ARE MOTORIZED NETS. BIGGER CATCHES, MORE FISH, BIGGER BOATS.
BUT WITH JUST A LINE AND A HOOK, I COULD FEED MYSELF.
WITH ENOUGH TORQUE-TO-WEIGHT RATIO YOU COULD USE IT TO CLIMB A BUILDING LIKE ARACHNID PHANTOM!
YES, KATO, YOU COULD. BUT SHOULD WE NOT MARVEL AT THE OLDEST INVENTIONS? A BARBED PIECE OF METAL. A COLLECTION OF STRINGS INTO A NET.
THESE THINGS HAVE WORKED FOR THOUSANDS OF YEARS, AND WILL CONTINUE TO WORK FOR A THOUSAND MORE.
THE BEST INVENTION TO EVER FILL MY BELLY WAS A TEN-YUAN NOTE. YOU HUNGRY FOR NOODLES?

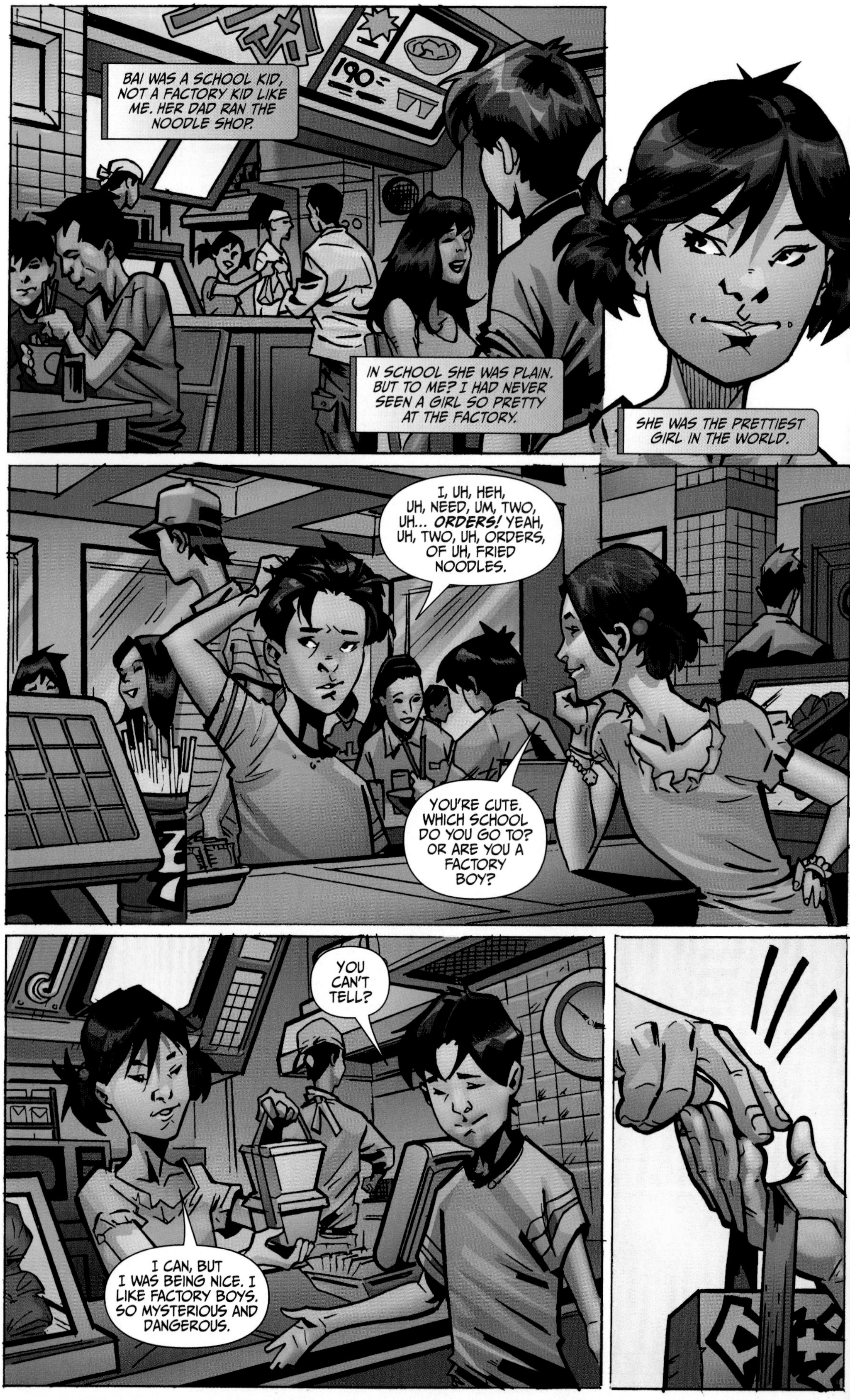
190
BAI WAS A SCHOOL KID, NOT A FACTORY KID LIKE ME. HER DAD RAN THE NOODLE SHOP.
IN SCHOOL SHE WAS PLAIN. BUT TO ME? I HAD NEVER SEEN A GIRL SO PRETTY AT THE FACTORY.
SHE WAS THE PRETTIEST GIRL IN THE WORLD.
I, UH, HEH, UH, NEED, UM, TWO, UH... ORDERS! YEAH, UH, TWO, UH, ORDERS, OF UH, FRIED NOODLES.
YOU'RE CUTE. WHICH SCHOOL DO YOU GO TO? OR ARE YOU A FACTORY BOY?
YOU CAN'T TELL?
I CAN, BUT I WAS BEING NICE. I LIKE FACTORY BOYS. SO MYSTERIOUS AND DANGEROUS.

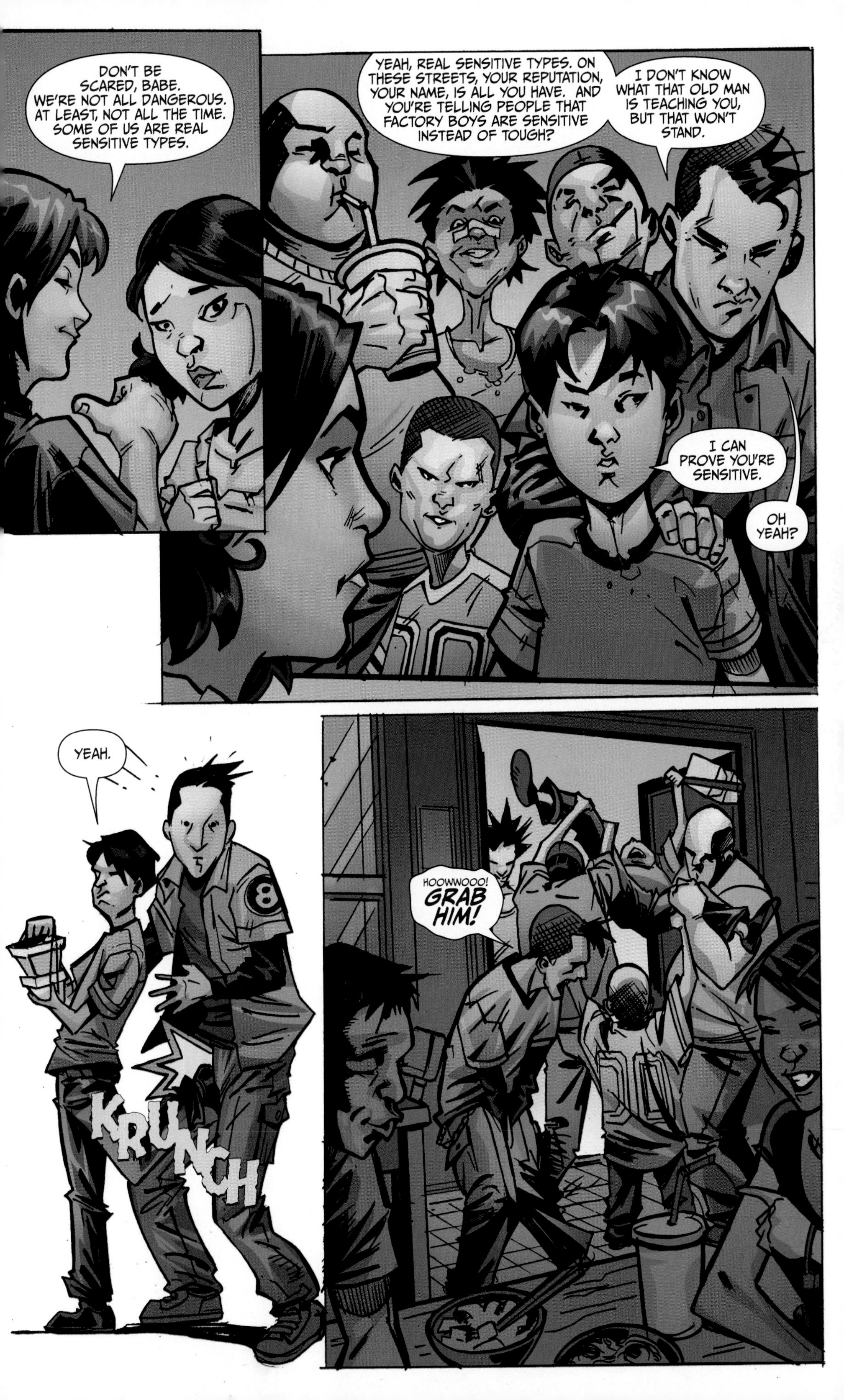
DON'T BE SCARED, BABE. WE'RE NOT ALL DANGEROUS. AT LEAST, NOT ALL THE TIME. SOME OF US ARE REAL SENSITIVE TYPES.
YEAH, REAL SENSITIVE TYPES. ON THESE STREETS, YOUR REPUTATION, YOUR NAME, IS ALL YOU HAVE. AND YOU'RE TELLING PEOPLE THAT FACTORY BOYS ARE SENSITIVE INSTEAD OF TOUGH?
I DON'T KNOW WHAT THAT OLD MAN IS TEACHING YOU, BUT THAT WON'T STAND.
I CAN PROVE YOU'RE SENSITIVE.
OH YEAH?
YEAH.
KRUNCH
HOOWWOOO! GRAB HIM!

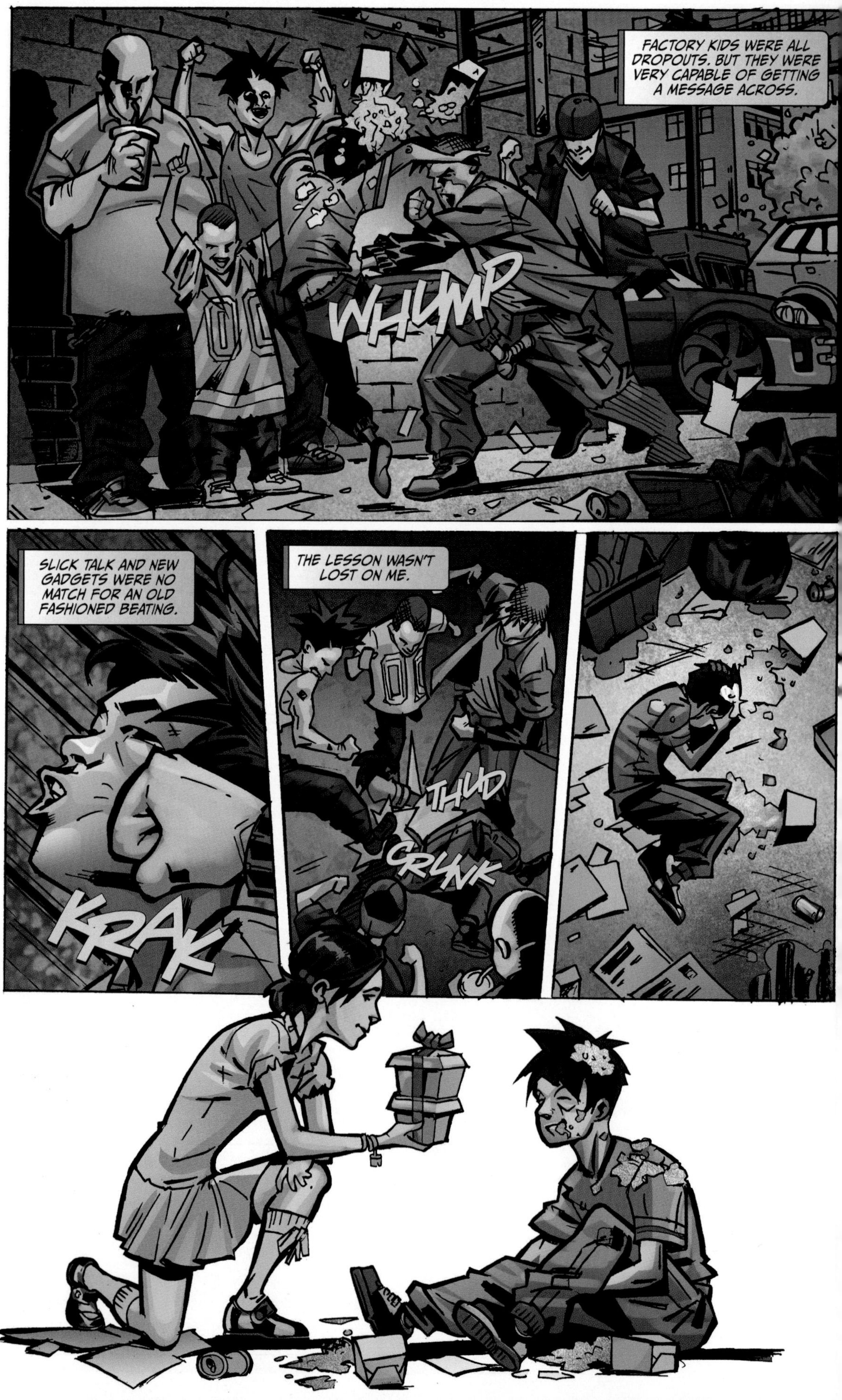
FACTORY KIDS WERE ALL DROPOUTS. BUT THEY WERE VERY CAPABLE OF GETTING A MESSAGE ACROSS.
WHUMP
SLICK TALK AND NEW GADGETS WERE NO MATCH FOR AN OLD FASHIONED BEATING.
KRAK
THE LESSON WASN'T LOST ON ME.
THUD
CRUNK

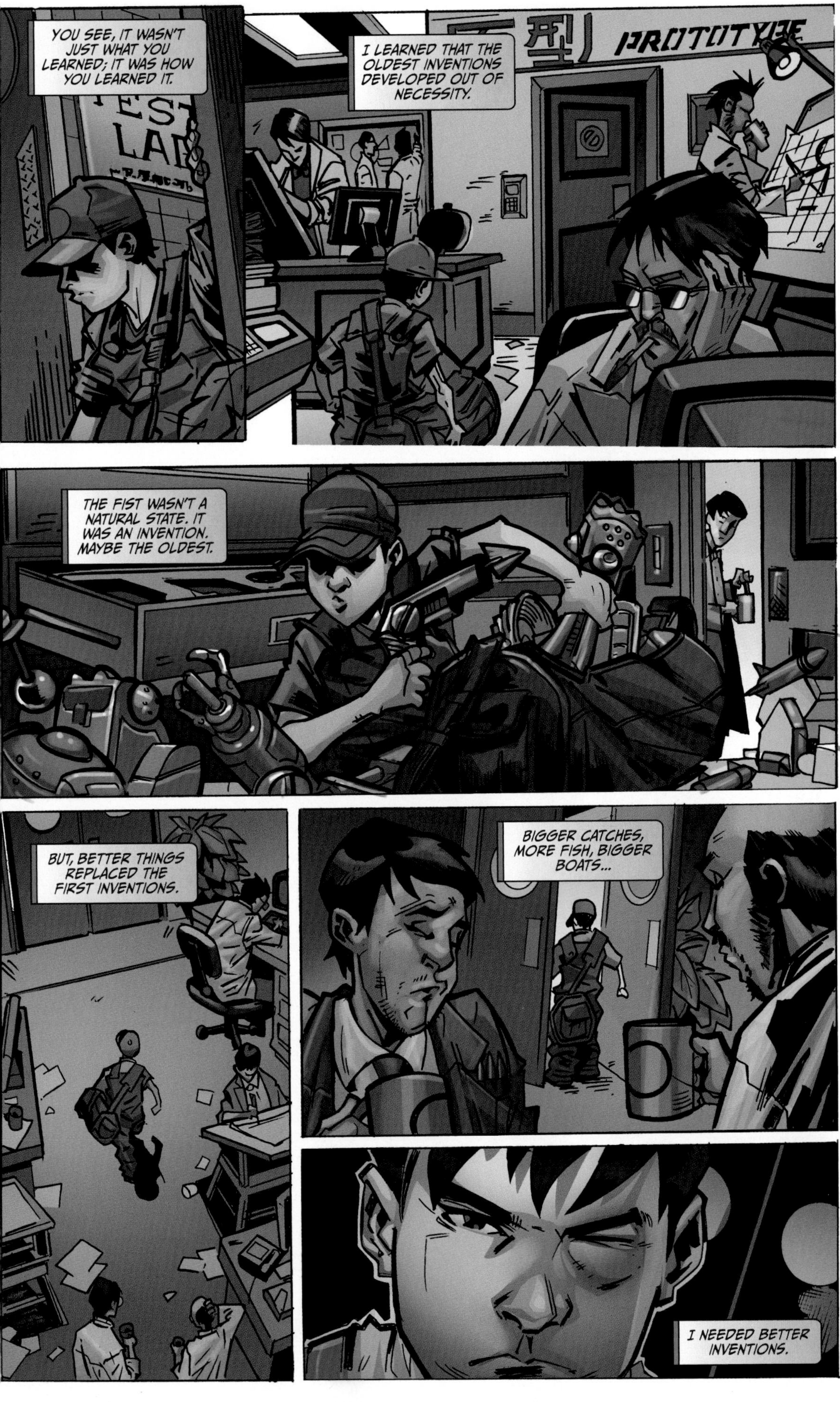
YOU SEE, IT WASN'T JUST WHAT YOU LEARNED; IT WAS HOW YOU LEARNED IT.
I LEARNED THAT THE OLDEST INVENTIONS DEVELOPED OUT OF NECESSITY.
PROTOTYPE
THE FIST WASN'T A NATURAL STATE. IT WAS AN INVENTION. MAYBE THE OLDEST.
BUT, BETTER THINGS REPLACED THE FIRST INVENTIONS.
BIGGER CATCHES, MORE FISH, BIGGER BOATS...
I NEEDED BETTER INVENTIONS.

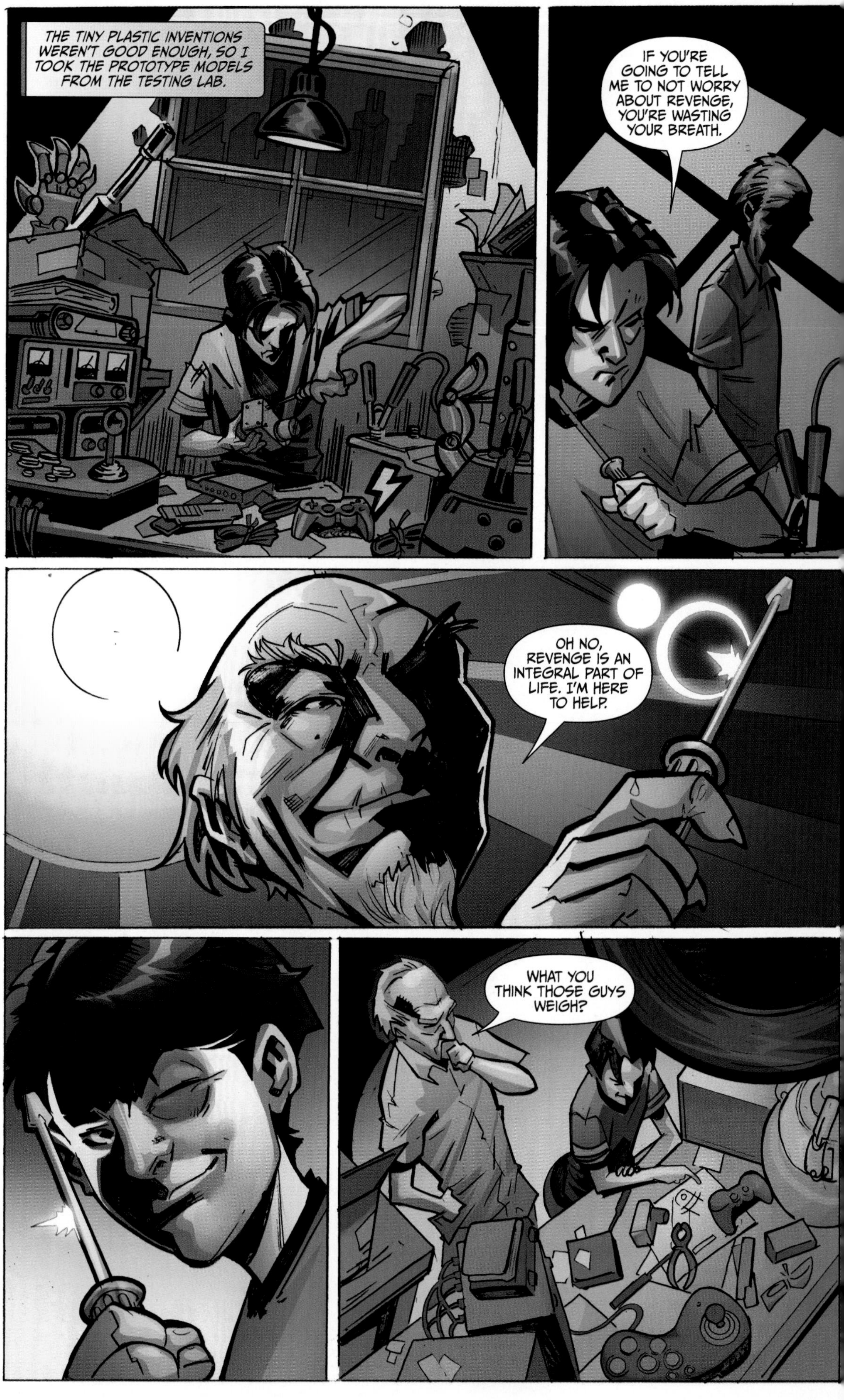
THE TINY PLASTIC INVENTIONS WEREN'T GOOD ENOUGH, SO I TOOK THE PROTOTYPE MODELS FROM THE TESTING LAB.
IF YOU'RE GOING TO TELL ME TO NOT WORRY ABOUT REVENGE, YOU'RE WASTING YOUR BREATH.
OH NO, REVENGE IS AN INTEGRAL PART OF LIFE. I'M HERE TO HELP.
WHAT YOU THINK THOSE GUYS WEIGH?

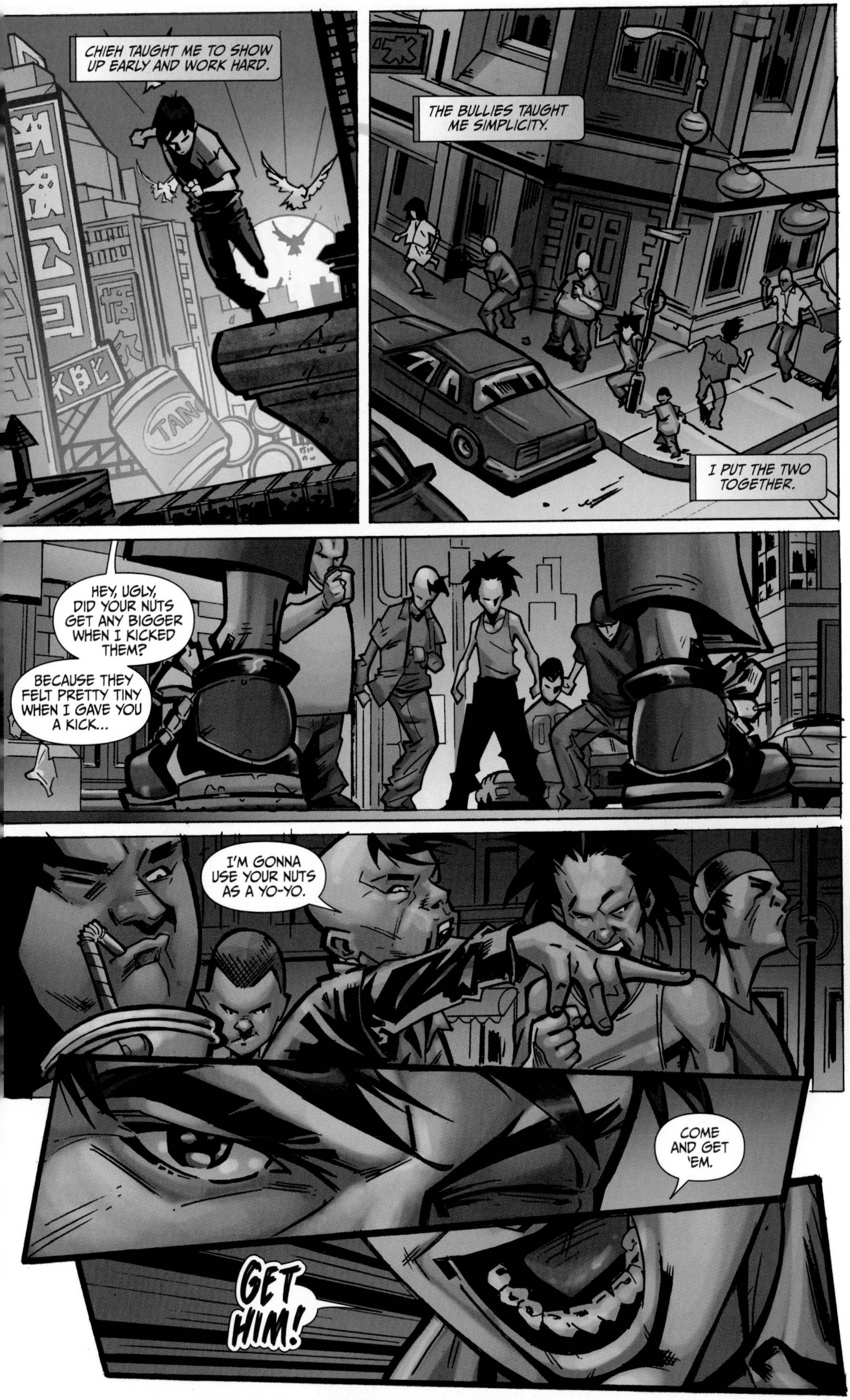
CHIEH TAUGHT ME TO SHOW UP EARLY AND WORK HARD.
THE BULLIES TAUGHT ME SIMPLICITY.
I PUT THE TWO TOGETHER.
HEY, UGLY, DID YOUR NUTS GET ANY BIGGER WHEN I KICKED THEM?
BECAUSE THEY FELT PRETTY TINY WHEN I GAVE YOU A KICK...
I'M GONNA USE YOUR NUTS AS A YO-YO.
COME AND GET 'EM.
GET HIM!

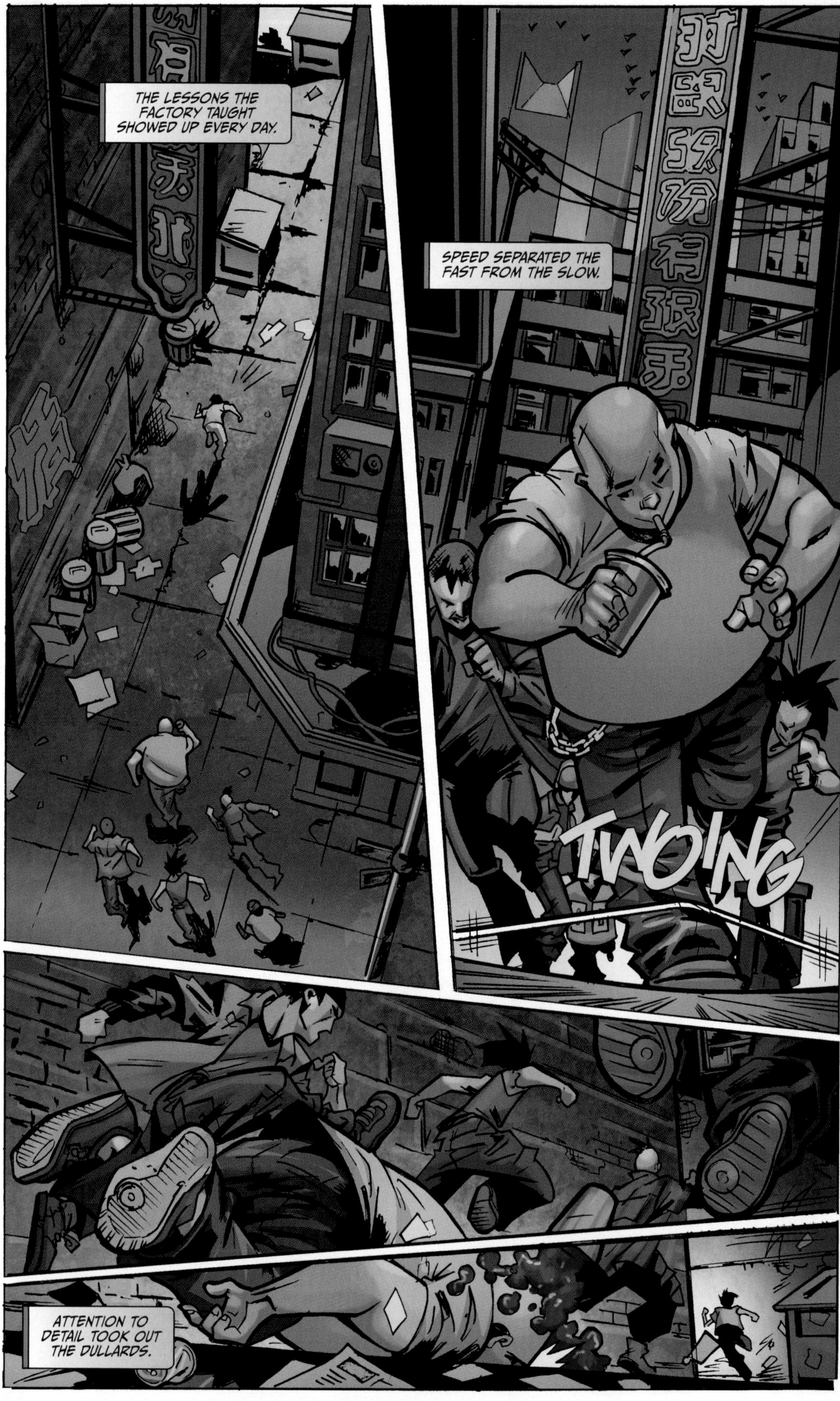
THE LESSONS THE FACTORY TAUGHT SHOWED UP EVERY DAY.
SPEED SEPARATED THE FAST FROM THE SLOW.
TWOING
ATTENTION TO DETAIL TOOK OUT THE DULLARDS.

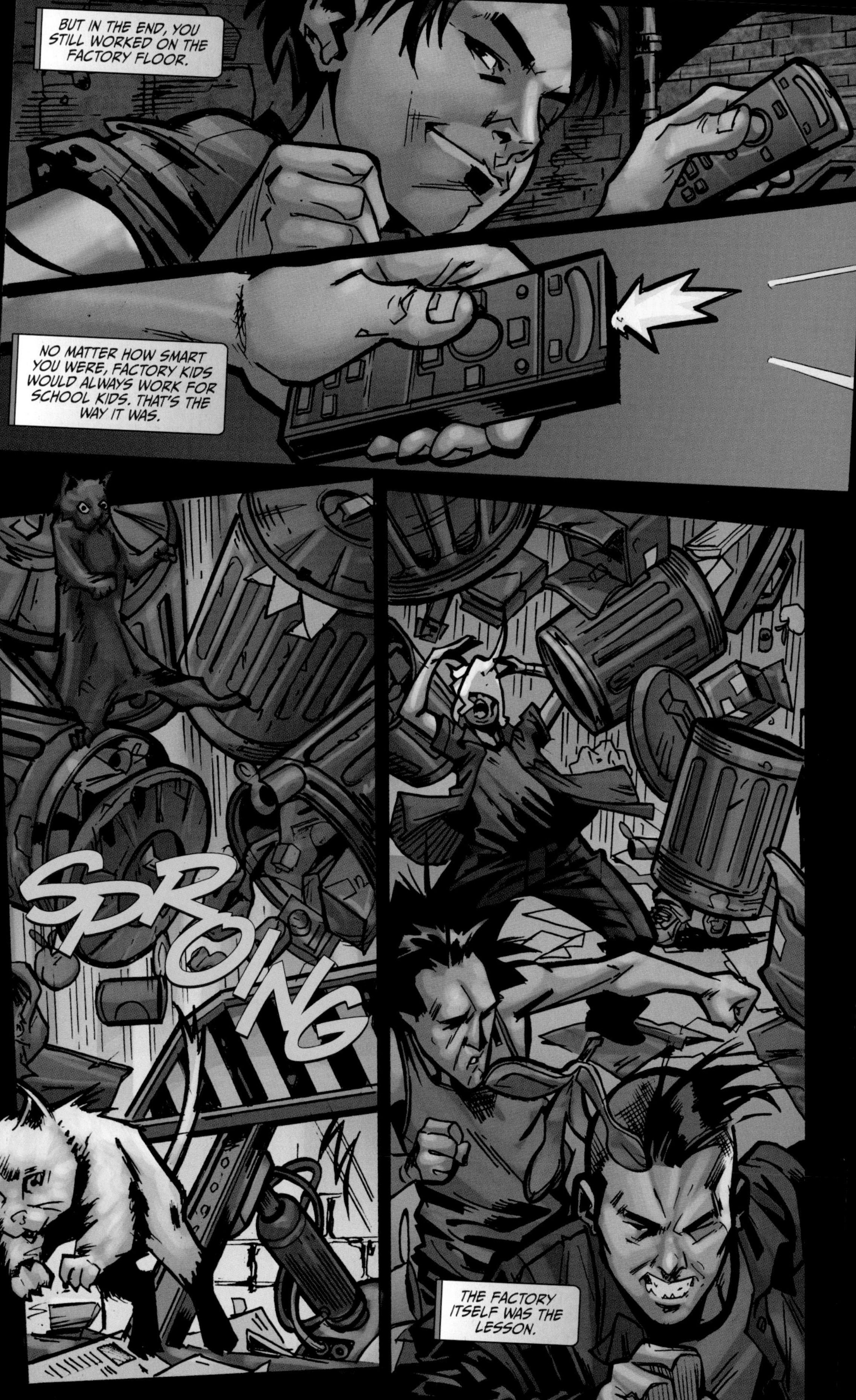
BUT IN THE END, YOU STILL WORKED ON THE FACTORY FLOOR.
NO MATTER HOW SMART YOU WERE, FACTORY KIDS WOULD ALWAYS WORK FOR SCHOOL KIDS. THAT'S THE WAY IT WAS.
SPROING
THE FACTORY ITSELF WAS THE LESSON.

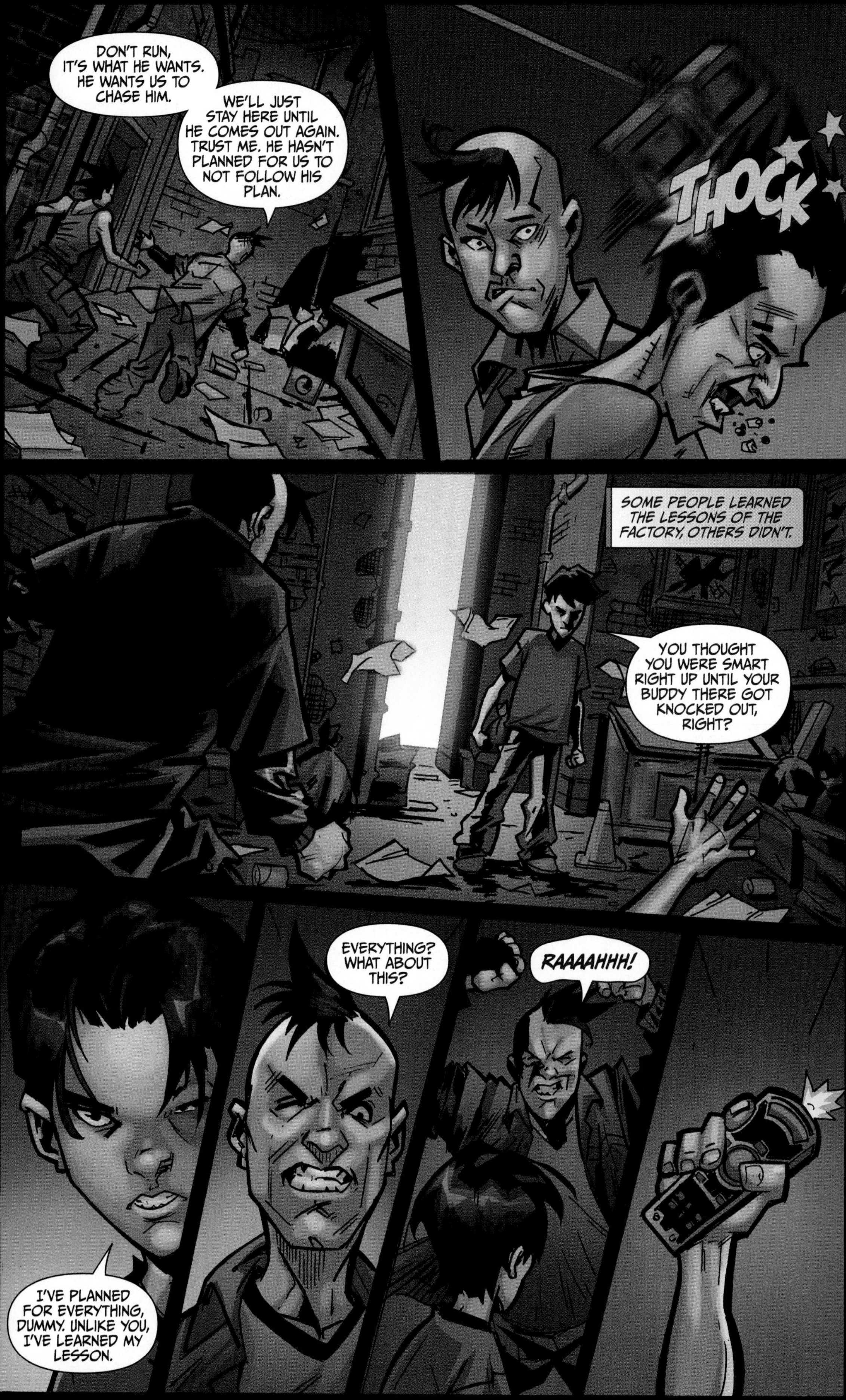
DON'T RUN, IT'S WHAT HE WANTS. HE WANTS US TO CHASE HIM.
WE'LL JUST STAY HERE UNTIL HE COMES OUT AGAIN. TRUST ME. HE HASN'T PLANNED FOR US TO NOT FOLLOW HIS PLAN.
THOCK
SOME PEOPLE LEARNED THE LESSONS OF THE FACTORY, OTHERS DIDN'T.
YOU THOUGHT YOU WERE SMART RIGHT UP UNTIL YOUR BUDDY THERE GOT KNOCKED OUT, RIGHT?
I'VE PLANNED FOR EVERYTHING, DUMMY. UNLIKE YOU, I'VE LEARNED MY LESSON.
EVERYTHING? WHAT ABOUT THIS?
RAAAAHHH!

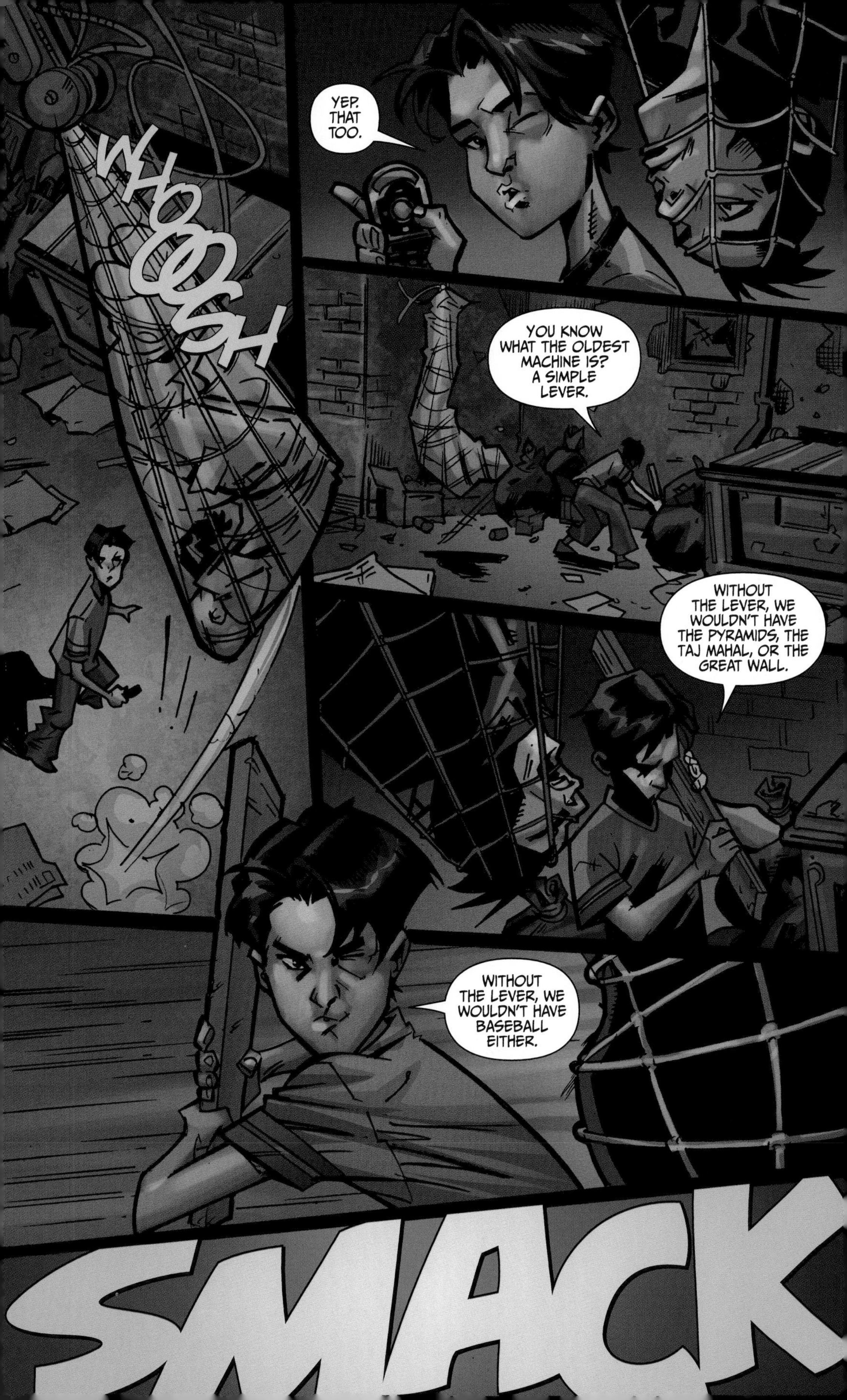
WHOOOSH
YEP. THAT TOO.
YOU KNOW WHAT THE OLDEST MACHINE IS? A SIMPLE LEVER.
WITHOUT THE LEVER, WE WOULDN'T HAVE THE PYRAMIDS, THE TAJ MAHAL, OR THE GREAT WALL.
WITHOUT THE LEVER, WE WOULDN'T HAVE BASEBALL EITHER.
SMACK

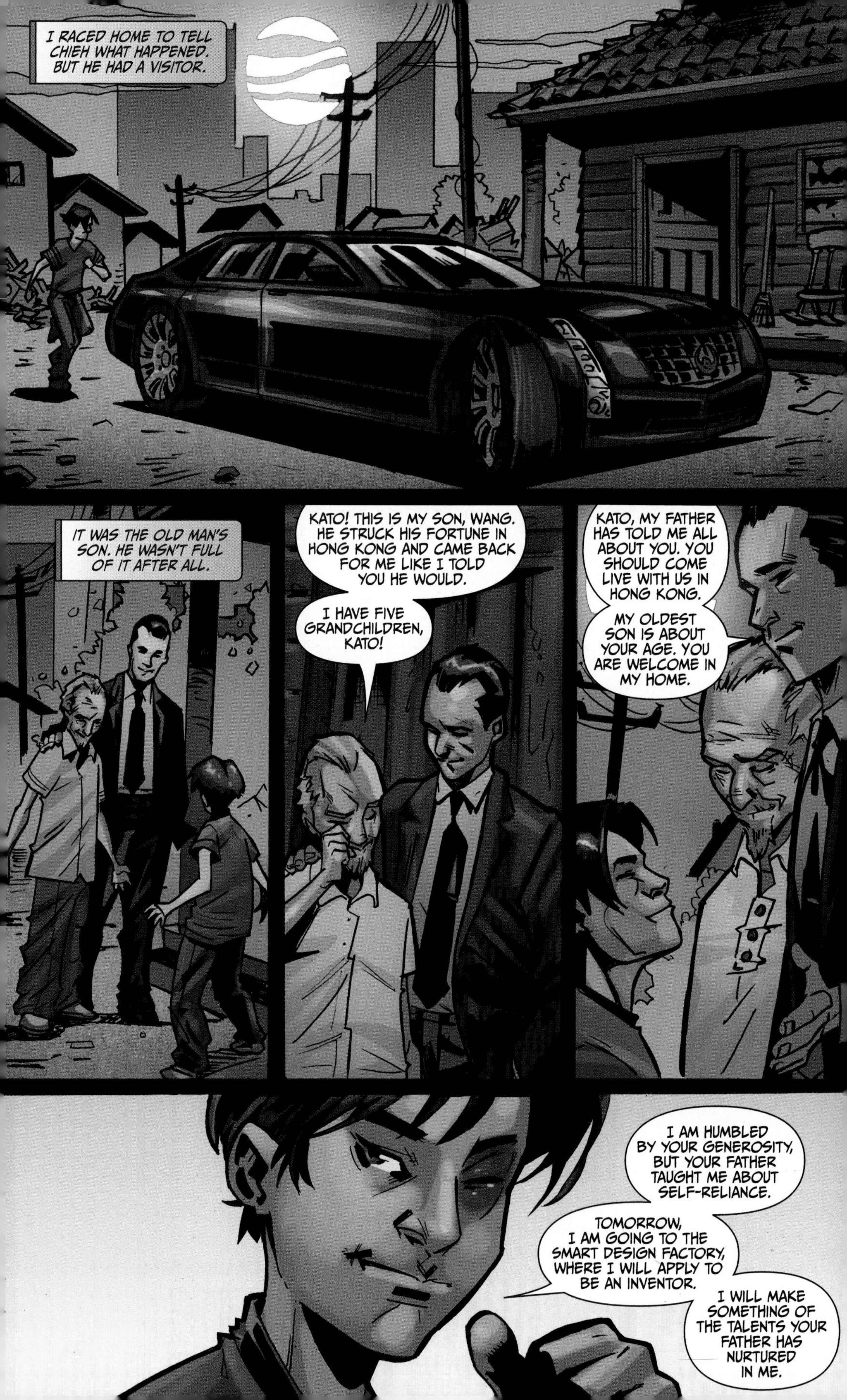
I RACED HOME TO TELL CHIEH WHAT HAPPENED. BUT HE HAD A VISITOR.
IT WAS THE OLD MAN'S SON. HE WASN'T FULL OF IT AFTER ALL.
KATO! THIS IS MY SON, WANG. HE STRUCK HIS FORTUNE IN HONG KONG AND CAME BACK FOR ME LIKE I TOLD YOU HE WOULD.
I HAVE FIVE GRANDCHILDREN, KATO!
KATO, MY FATHER HAS TOLD ME ALL ABOUT YOU. YOU SHOULD COME LIVE WITH US IN HONG KONG.
MY OLDEST SON IS ABOUT YOUR AGE. YOU ARE WELCOME IN MY HOME.
I AM HUMBLED BY YOUR GENEROSITY, BUT YOUR FATHER TAUGHT ME ABOUT SELF-RELIANCE.
TOMORROW, I AM GOING TO THE SMART DESIGN FACTORY, WHERE I WILL APPLY TO BE AN INVENTOR.
I WILL MAKE SOMETHING OF THE TALENTS YOUR FATHER HAS NURTURED IN ME.

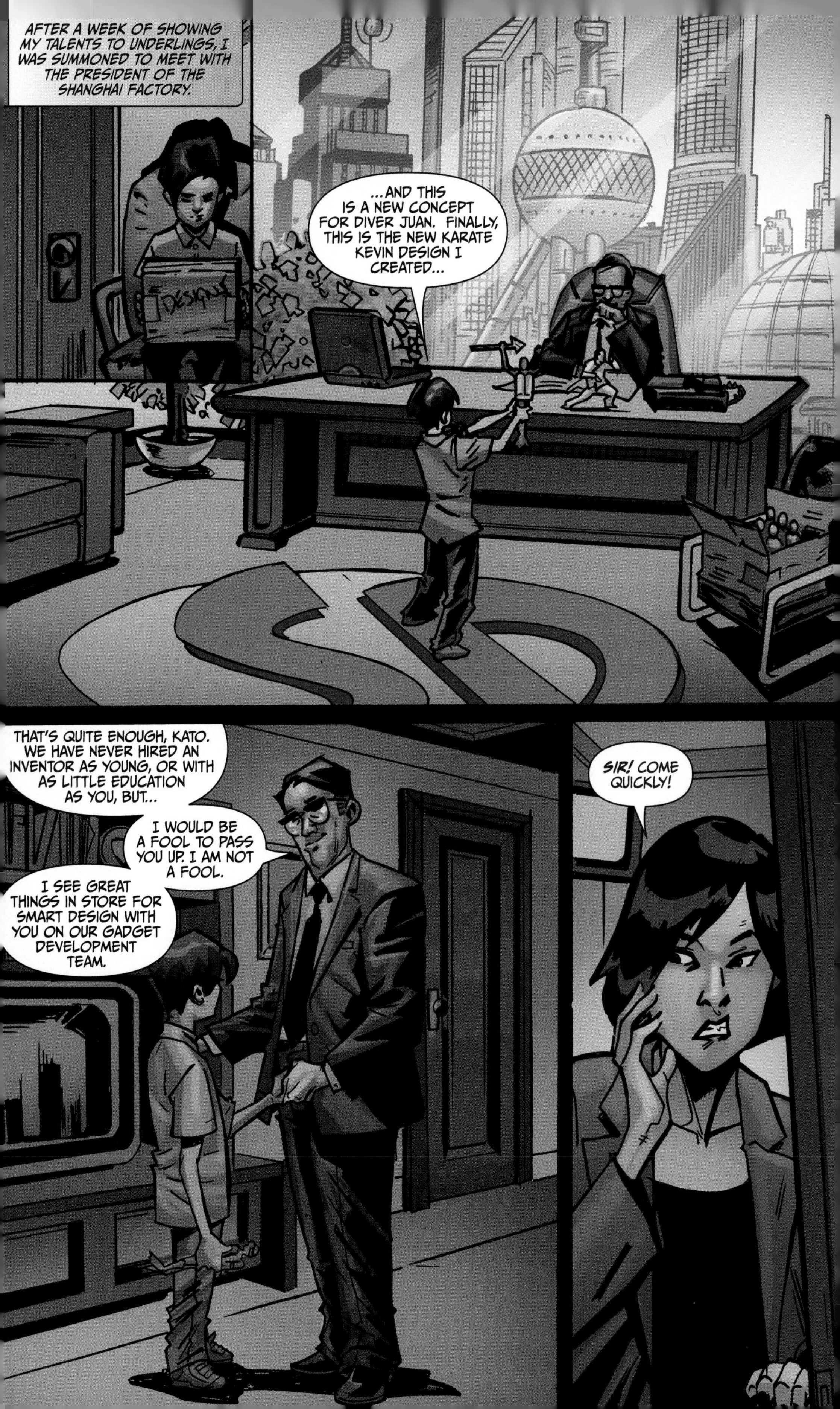
AFTER A WEEK OF SHOWING MY TALENTS TO UNDERLINGS, I WAS SUMMONED TO MEET WITH THE PRESIDENT OF THE SHANGHAI FACTORY.
...AND THIS IS A NEW CONCEPT FOR DIVER JUAN. FINALLY, THIS IS THE NEW KARATE KEVIN DESIGN I CREATED...
THAT'S QUITE ENOUGH, KATO. WE HAVE NEVER HIRED AN INVENTOR AS YOUNG, OR WITH AS LITTLE EDUCATION AS YOU, BUT...
I WOULD BE A FOOL TO PASS YOU UP. I AM NOT A FOOL.
I SEE GREAT THINGS IN STORE FOR SMART DESIGN WITH YOU ON OUR GADGET DEVELOPMENT TEAM.
SIR! COME QUICKLY!

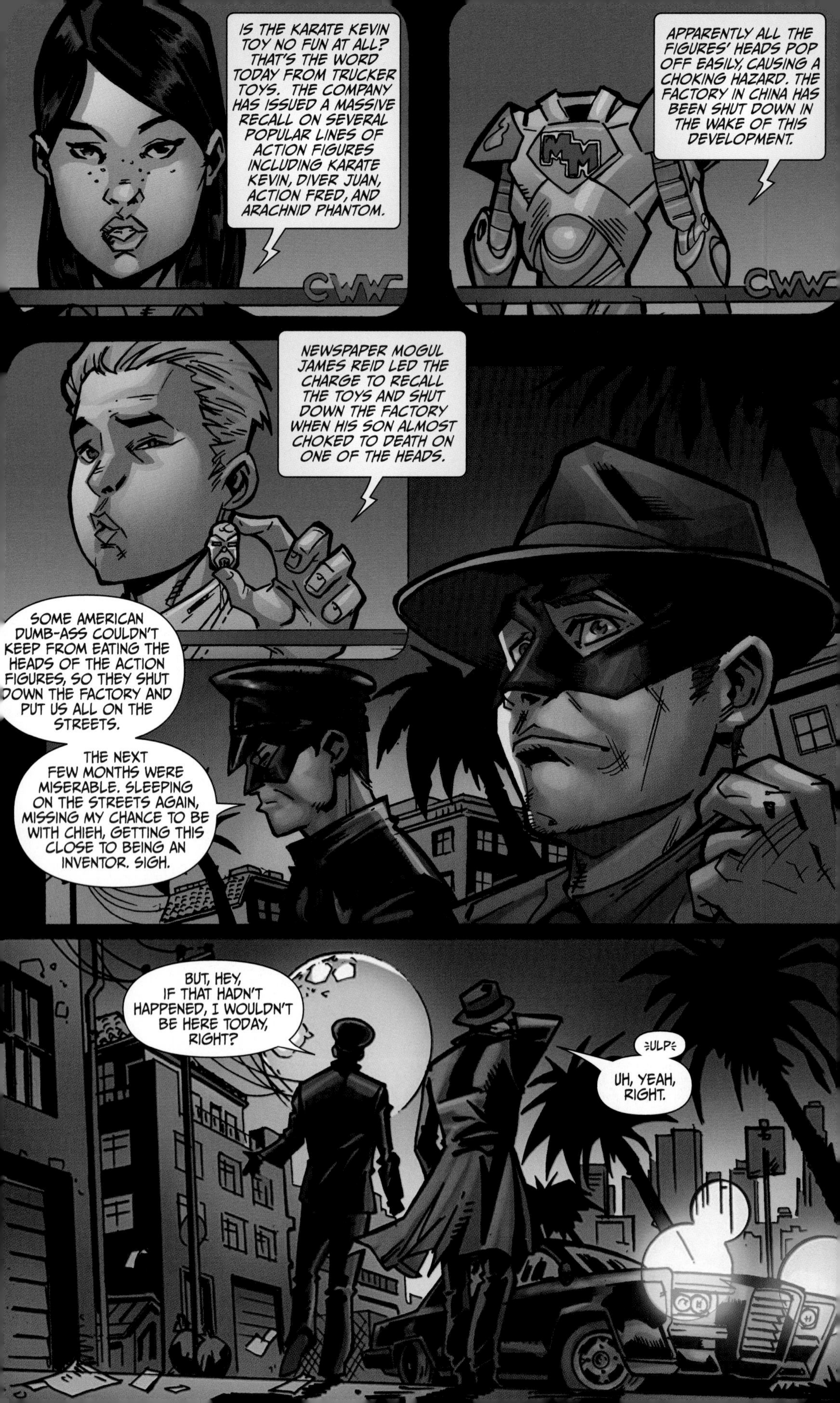
IS THE KARATE KEVIN TOY NO FUN AT ALL? THAT'S THE WORD TODAY FROM TRUCKER TOYS. THE COMPANY HAS ISSUED A MASSIVE RECALL ON SEVERAL POPULAR LINES OF ACTION FIGURES INCLUDING KARATE KEVIN, DIVER JUAN, ACTION FRED, AND ARACHNID PHANTOM.
CWW
APPARENTLY ALL THE FIGURES' HEADS POP OFF EASILY, CAUSING A CHOKING HAZARD. THE FACTORY IN CHINA HAS BEEN SHUT DOWN IN THE WAKE OF THIS DEVELOPMENT.
CWW
NEWSPAPER MOGUL JAMES REID LED THE CHARGE TO RECALL THE TOYS AND SHUT DOWN THE FACTORY WHEN HIS SON ALMOST CHOKED TO DEATH ON ONE OF THE HEADS.
SOME AMERICAN DUMB-ASS COULDN'T KEEP FROM EATING THE HEADS OF THE ACTION FIGURES, SO THEY SHUT DOWN THE FACTORY AND PUT US ALL ON THE STREETS.
THE NEXT FEW MONTHS WERE MISERABLE. SLEEPING ON THE STREETS AGAIN, MISSING MY CHANCE TO BE WITH CHIEH, GETTING THIS CLOSE TO BEING AN INVENTOR. SIGH.
BUT, HEY, IF THAT HADN'T HAPPENED, I WOULDN'T BE HERE TODAY, RIGHT?
ULP
UH, YEAH, RIGHT.

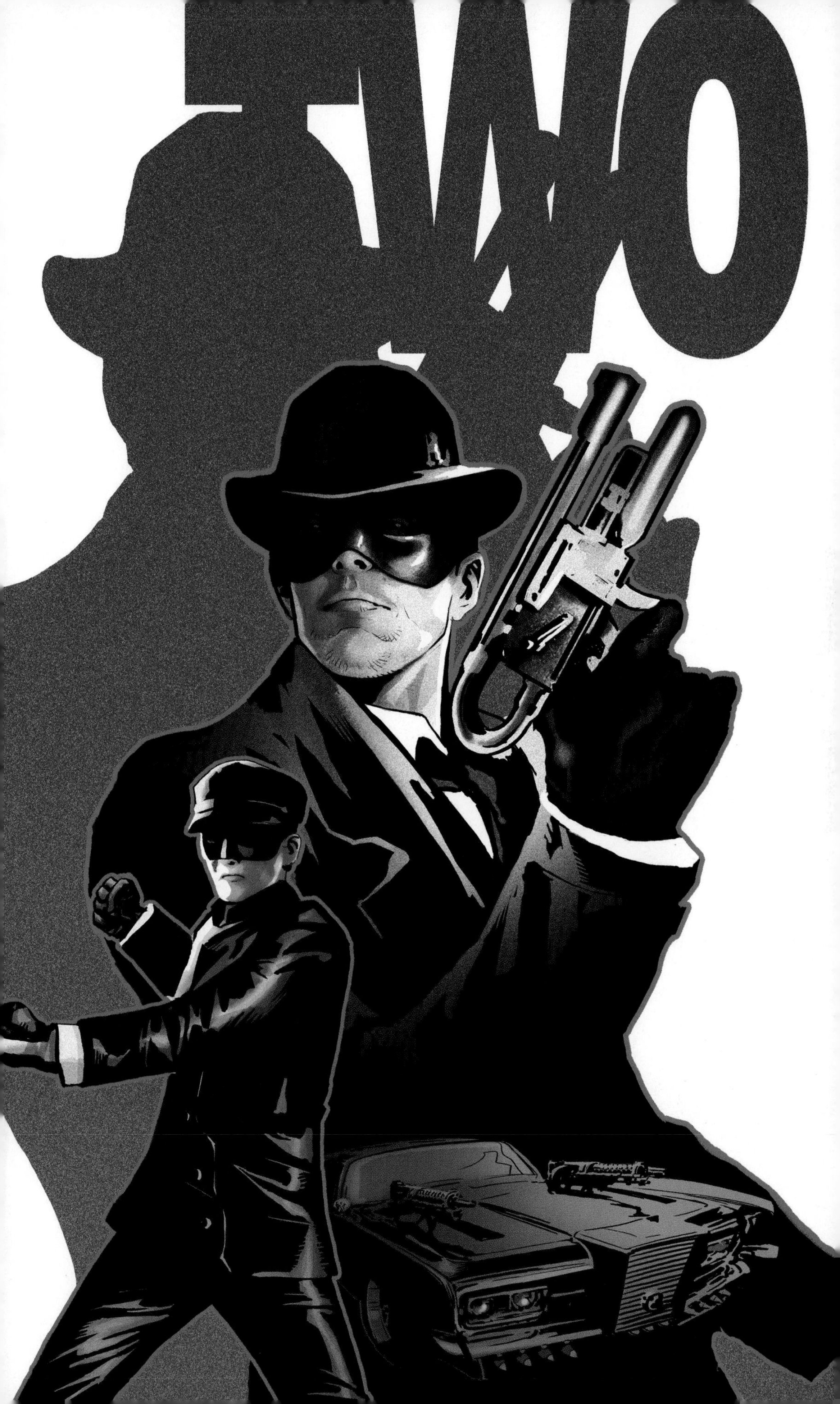
TWO

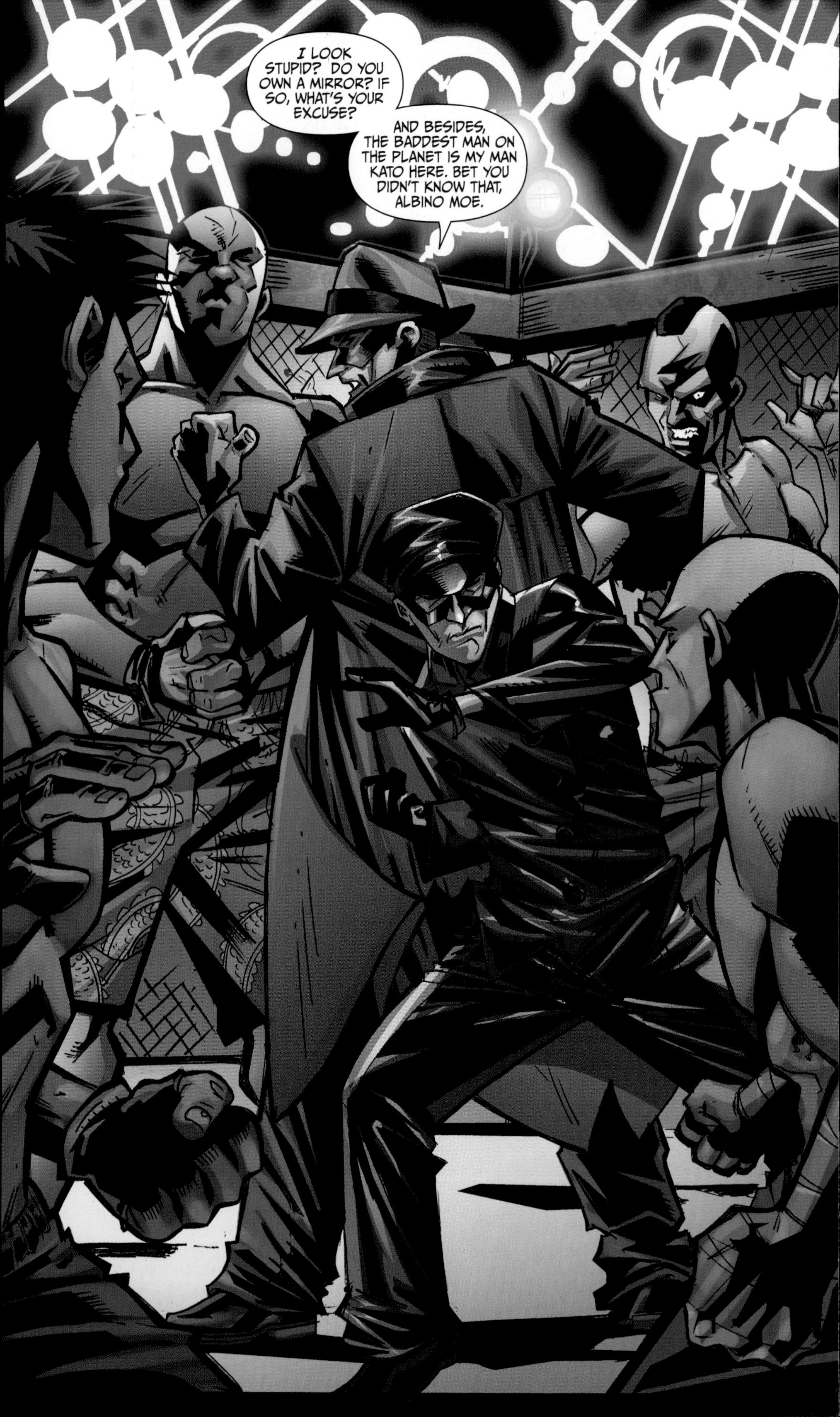
I LOOK STUPID? DO YOU OWN A MIRROR? IF SO, WHAT'S YOUR EXCUSE?
AND BESIDES, THE BADDEST MAN ON THE PLANET IS MY MAN KATO HERE. BET YOU DIDN'T KNOW THAT, ALBINO MOE.

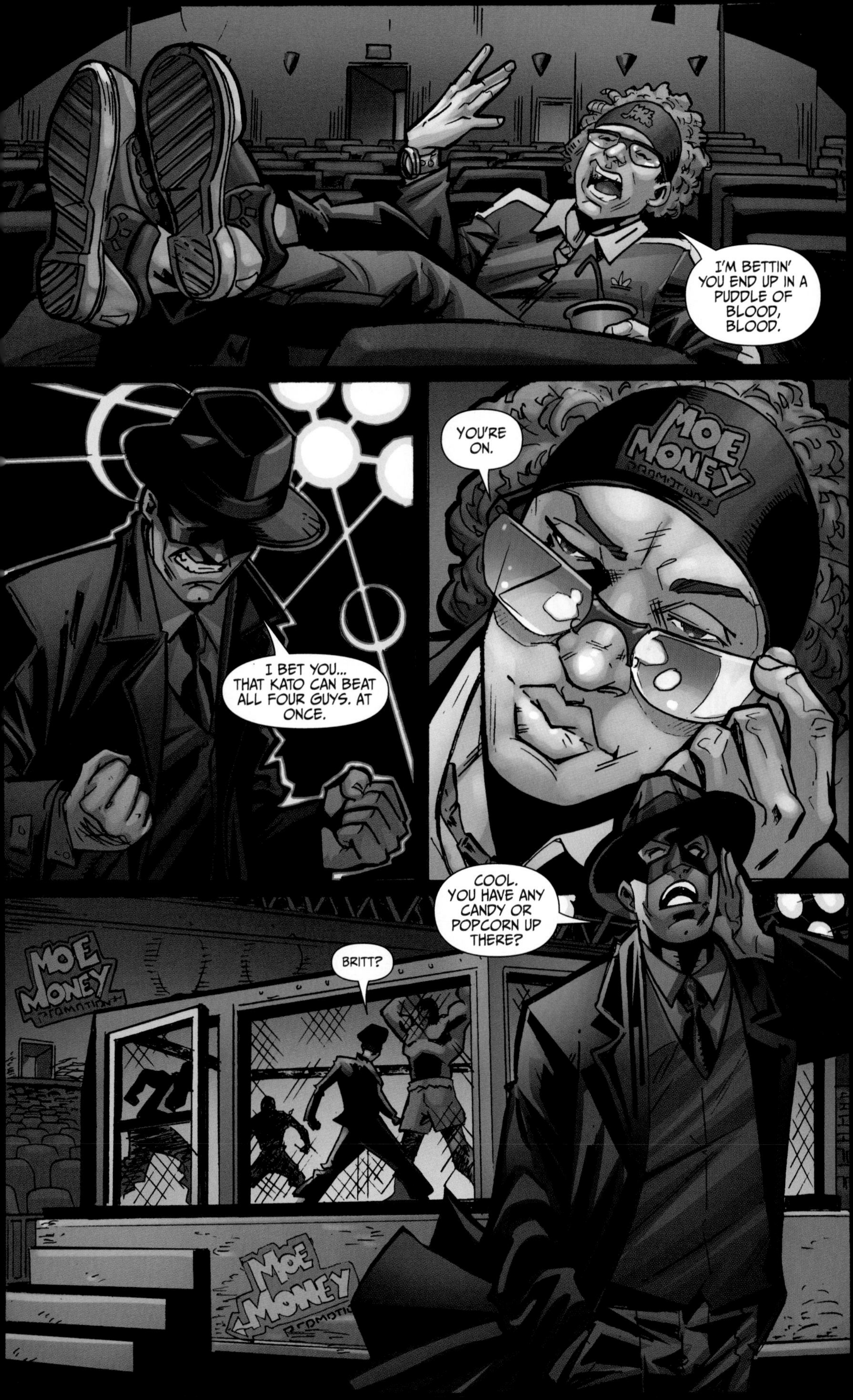
I'M BETTIN' YOU END UP IN A PUDDLE OF BLOOD, BLOOD.
I BET YOU... THAT KATO CAN BEAT ALL FOUR GUYS. AT ONCE.
MOE MONEY PROMOTIONS
YOU'RE ON.
COOL. YOU HAVE ANY CANDY OR POPCORN UP THERE?
BRITT?
MOE MONEY
MOE MONEY

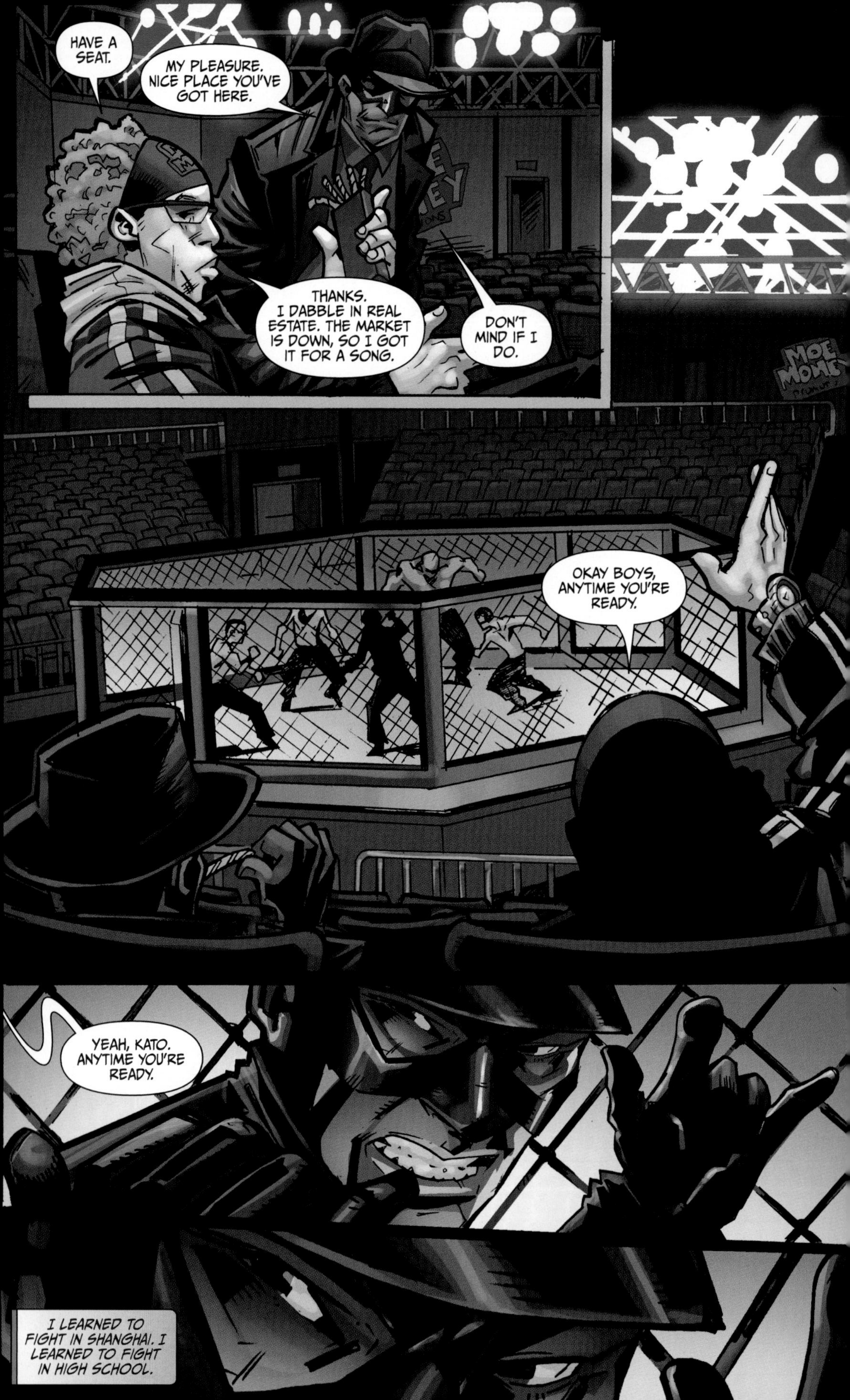
HAVE A SEAT.
MY PLEASURE. NICE PLACE YOU'VE GOT HERE.
THANKS. I DABBLE IN REAL ESTATE. THE MARKET IS DOWN, SO I GOT IT FOR A SONG.
DON'T MIND IF I DO.
OKAY BOYS, ANYTIME YOU'RE READY.
YEAH, KATO. ANYTIME YOU'RE READY.
I LEARNED TO FIGHT IN SHANGHAI. I LEARNED TO FIGHT IN HIGH SCHOOL.

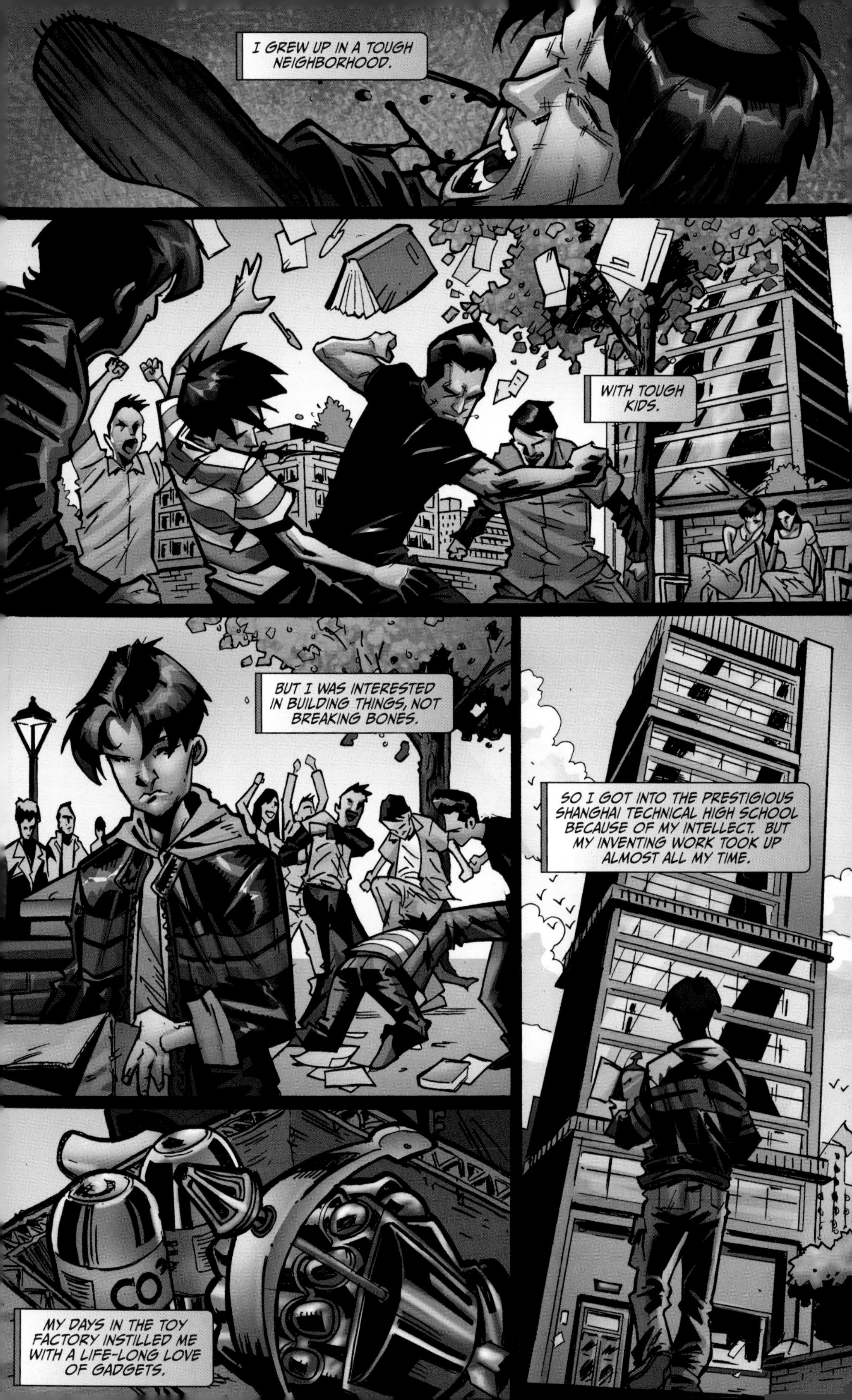
I GREW UP IN A TOUGH NEIGHBORHOOD.
WITH TOUGH KIDS.
BUT I WAS INTERESTED IN BUILDING THINGS, NOT BREAKING BONES.
MY DAYS IN THE TOY FACTORY INSTILLED ME WITH A LIFE-LONG LOVE OF GADGETS.
SO I GOT INTO THE PRESTIGIOUS SHANGHAI TECHNICAL HIGH SCHOOL BECAUSE OF MY INTELLECT. BUT MY INVENTING WORK TOOK UP ALMOST ALL MY TIME.

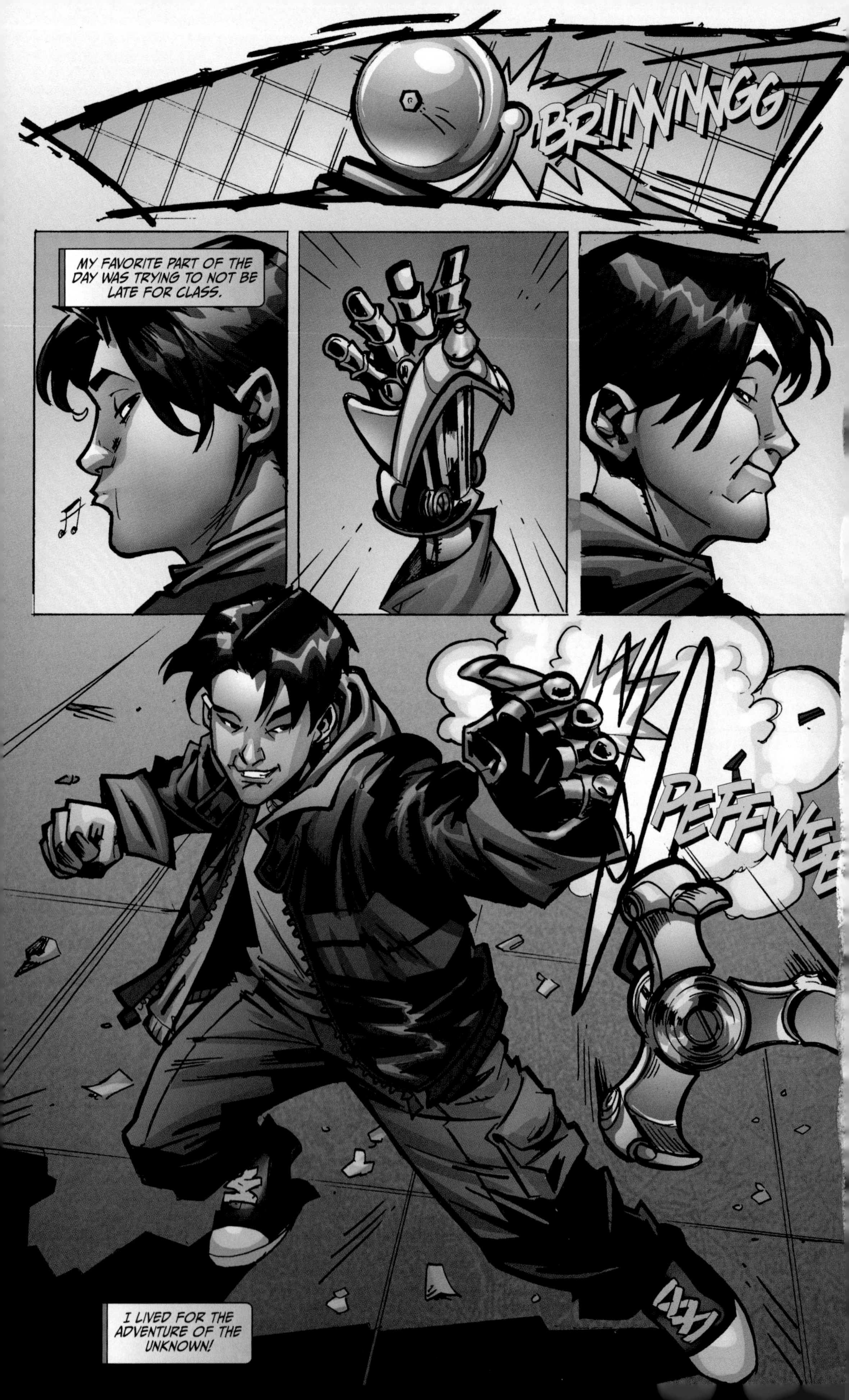
BRIIIINNNGG
MY FAVORITE PART OF THE DAY WAS TRYING TO NOT BE LATE FOR CLASS.
PEFFWEE
I LIVED FOR THE ADVENTURE OF THE UNKNOWN!

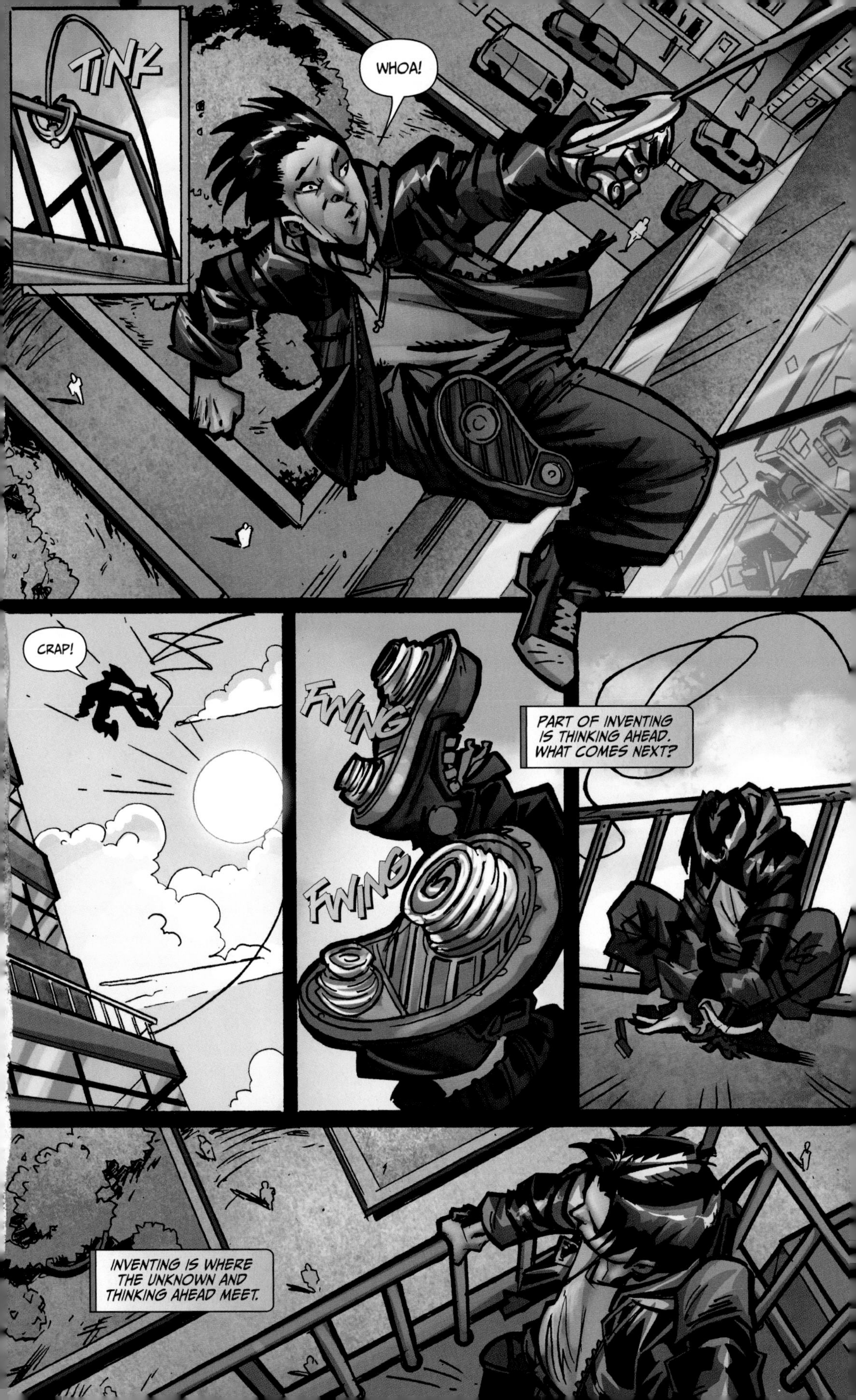
TINK
WHOA!
CRAP!
FWING
FWING
PART OF INVENTING IS THINKING AHEAD. WHAT COMES NEXT?
INVENTING IS WHERE THE UNKNOWN AND THINKING AHEAD MEET.

YOUTH SCIENCE ORGANIZATION

I THOUGHT I WOULD FIND THAT SPIRIT IN THE SCIENCE CLUB.

INSTEAD, I FOUND A BUNCH OF KIDS WHO ARGUED ABOUT GEORGE LUCAS AND STEPHEN HAWKING.

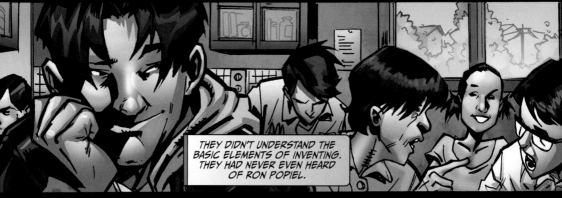

THEY DIDN'T UNDERSTAND THE BASIC ELEMENTS OF INVENTING. THEY HAD NEVER EVEN HEARD OF RON POPIEL.

KATO, I SEE YOU JUST MADE IT TO CLASS. AGAIN.

NEXT TIME, ADJUST THE TORQUE ON THE SPOOL MOTOR. THEN YOU WON'T NEED THE SHOES.

YOUR SECRET IDENTITY IS SAFE WITH ME, KATO.

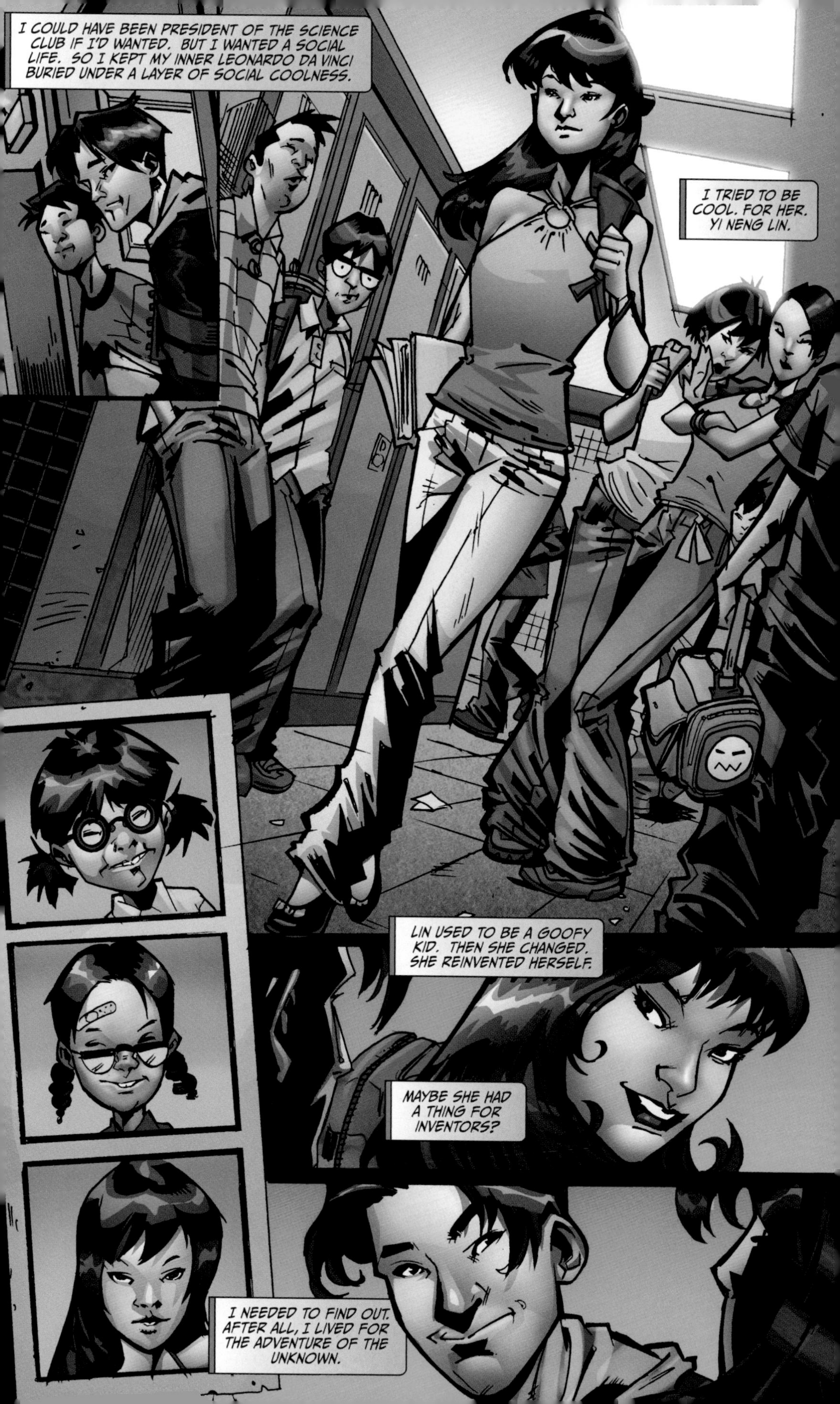
I COULD HAVE BEEN PRESIDENT OF THE SCIENCE CLUB IF I'D WANTED. BUT I WANTED A SOCIAL LIFE. SO I KEPT MY INNER LEONARDO DA VINCI BURIED UNDER A LAYER OF SOCIAL COOLNESS.
I TRIED TO BE COOL. FOR HER. YI NENG LIN.
LIN USED TO BE A GOOFY KID. THEN SHE CHANGED. SHE REINVENTED HERSELF.
MAYBE SHE HAD A THING FOR INVENTORS?
I NEEDED TO FIND OUT. AFTER ALL, I LIVED FOR THE ADVENTURE OF THE UNKNOWN.

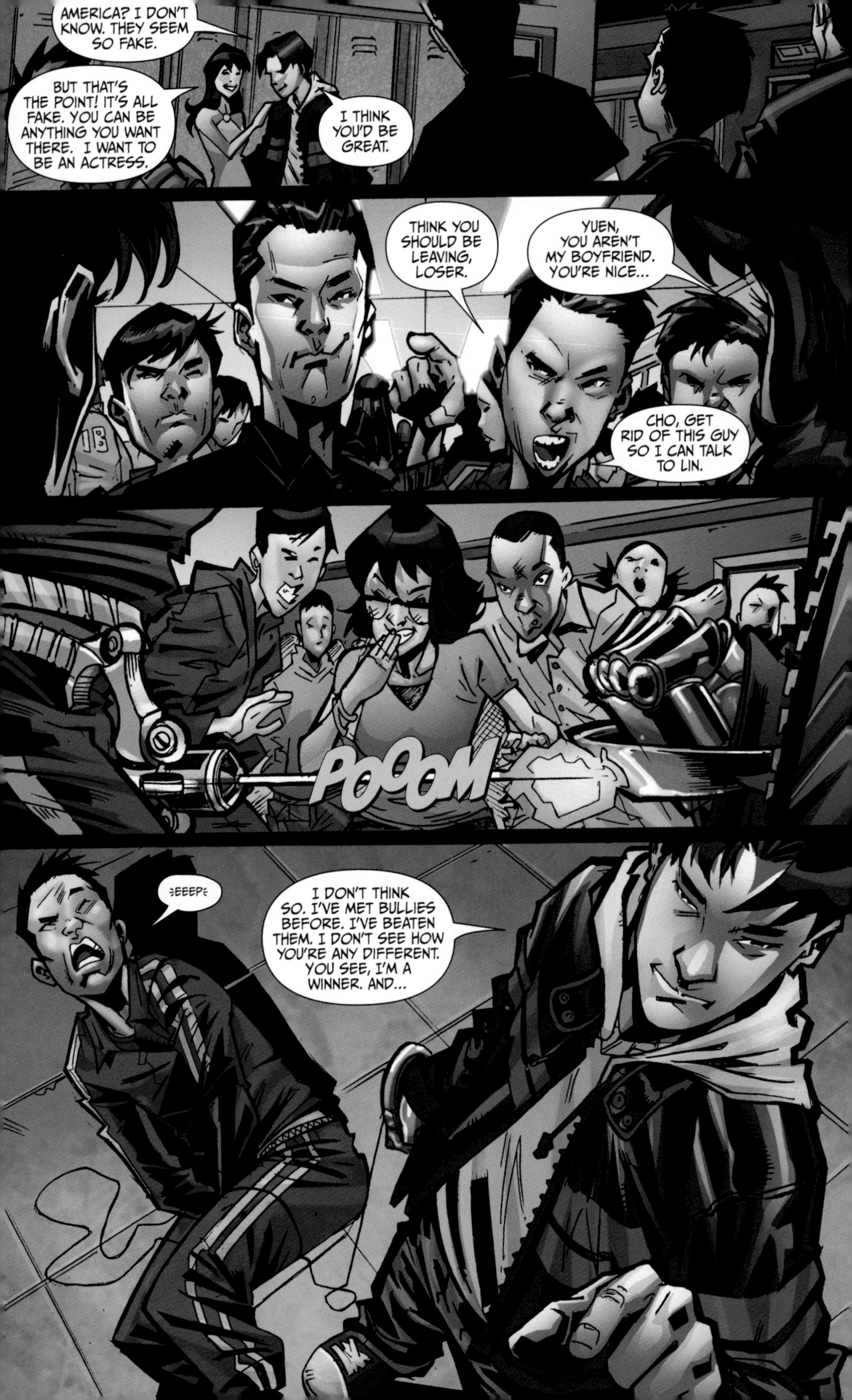
AMERICA? I DON'T KNOW. THEY SEEM SO FAKE.
BUT THAT'S THE POINT! IT'S ALL FAKE. YOU CAN BE ANYTHING YOU WANT THERE. I WANT TO BE AN ACTRESS.
I THINK YOU'D BE GREAT.
THINK YOU SHOULD BE LEAVING, LOSER.
YUEN, YOU AREN'T MY BOYFRIEND. YOU'RE NICE...
CHO, GET RID OF THIS GUY SO I CAN TALK TO LIN.
POOOM
EEEEP
I DON'T THINK SO. I'VE MET BULLIES BEFORE. I'VE BEATEN THEM. I DON'T SEE HOW YOU'RE ANY DIFFERENT. YOU SEE, I'M A WINNER. AND...

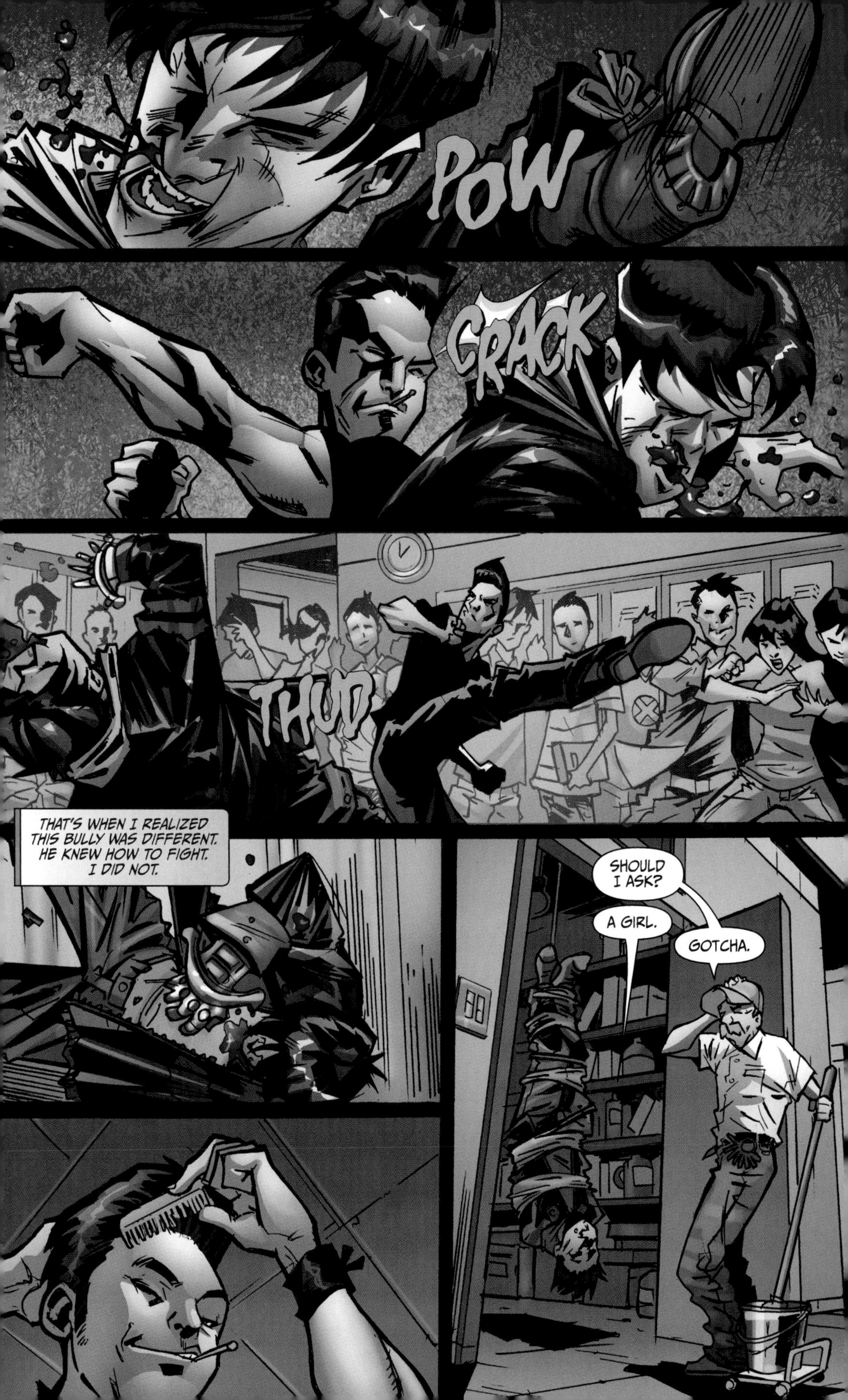
POW
CRACK
THUD
THAT'S WHEN I REALIZED THIS BULLY WAS DIFFERENT. HE KNEW HOW TO FIGHT. I DID NOT.
SHOULD I ASK?
A GIRL.
GOTCHA.

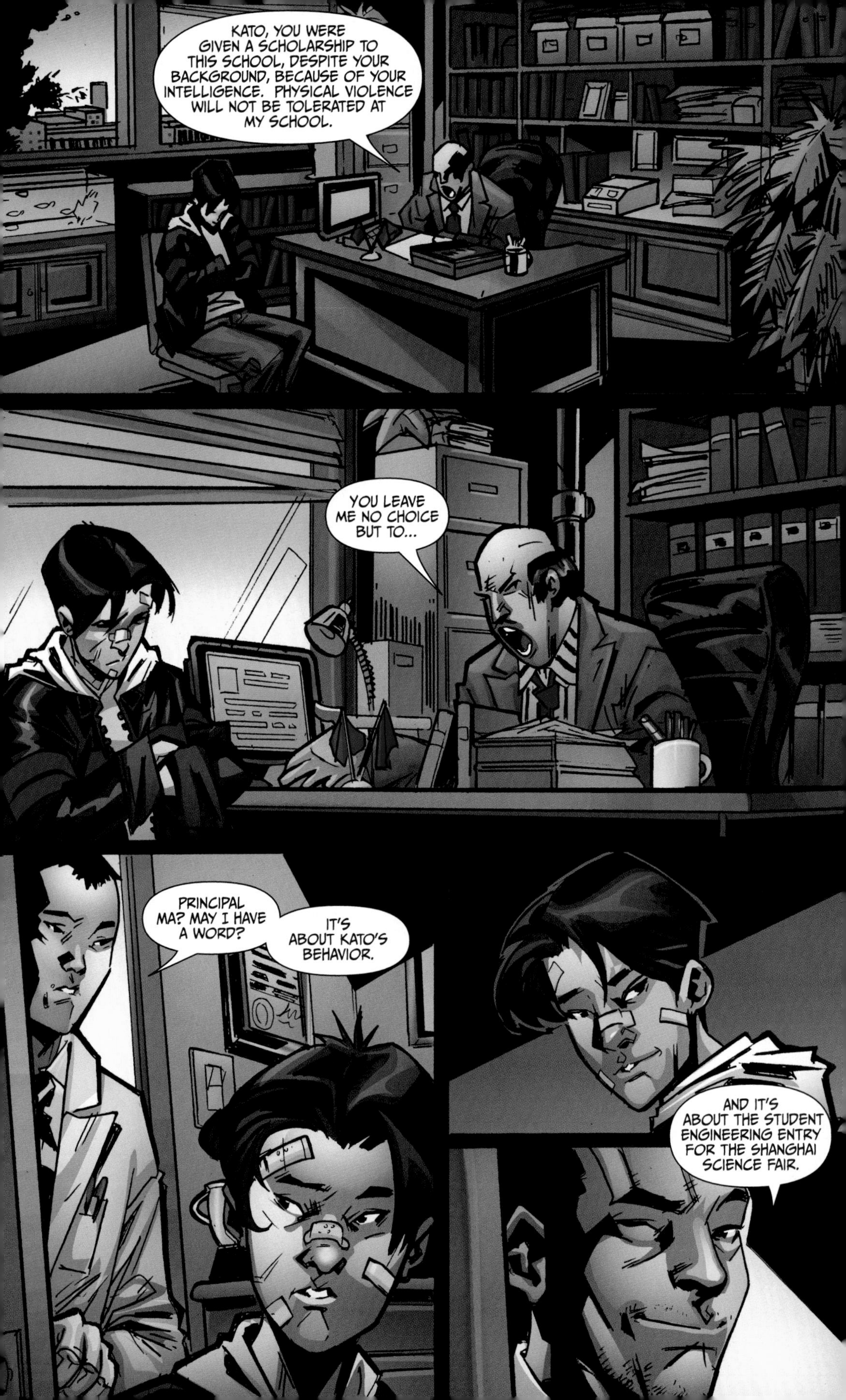
KATO, YOU WERE GIVEN A SCHOLARSHIP TO THIS SCHOOL, DESPITE YOUR BACKGROUND, BECAUSE OF YOUR INTELLIGENCE. PHYSICAL VIOLENCE WILL NOT BE TOLERATED AT MY SCHOOL.
YOU LEAVE ME NO CHOICE BUT TO...
PRINCIPAL MA? MAY I HAVE A WORD?
IT'S ABOUT KATO'S BEHAVIOR.
AND IT'S ABOUT THE STUDENT ENGINEERING ENTRY FOR THE SHANGHAI SCIENCE FAIR.

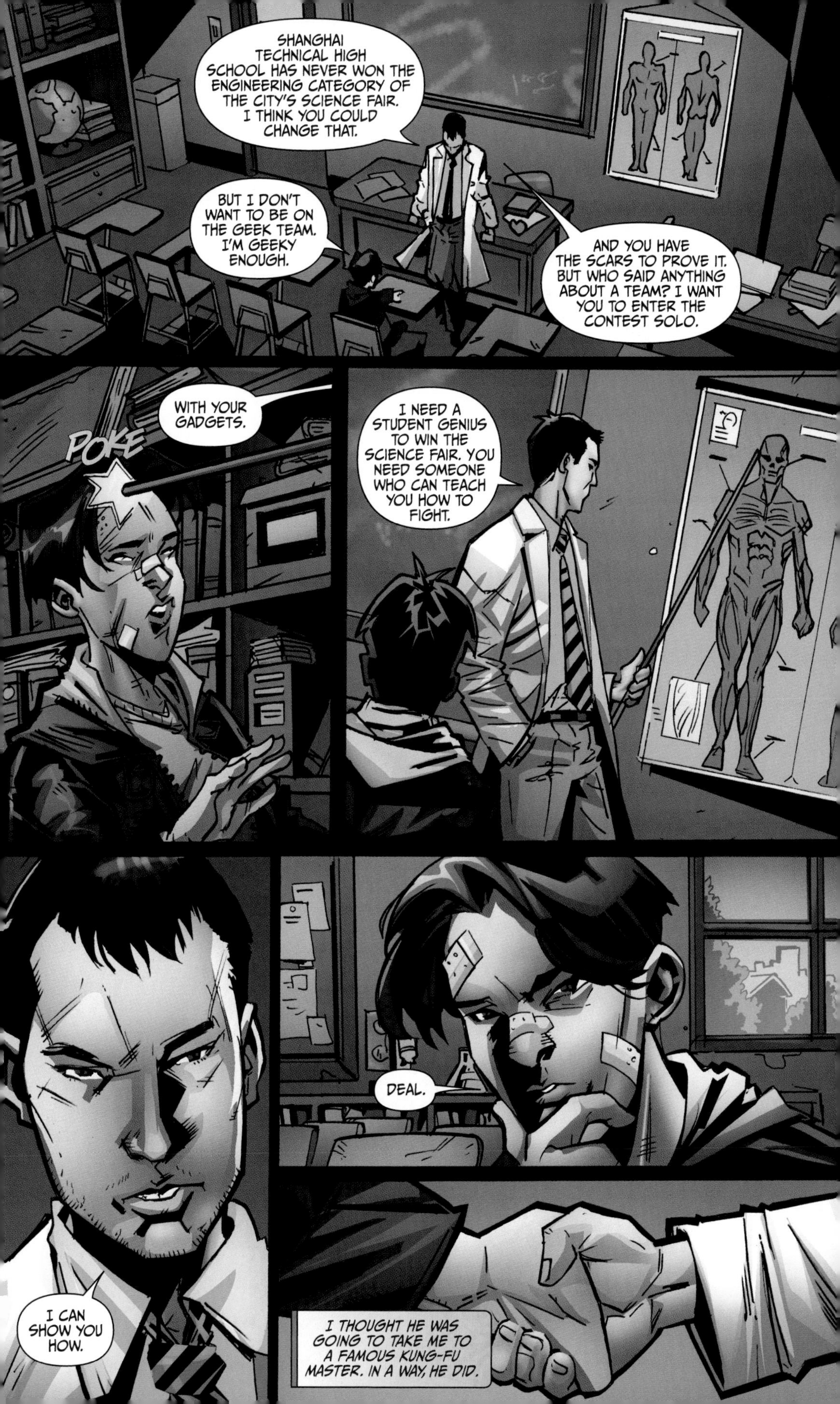
SHANGHAI TECHNICAL HIGH SCHOOL HAS NEVER WON THE ENGINEERING CATEGORY OF THE CITY'S SCIENCE FAIR. I THINK YOU COULD CHANGE THAT.
BUT I DON'T WANT TO BE ON THE GEEK TEAM. I'M GEEKY ENOUGH.
AND YOU HAVE THE SCARS TO PROVE IT. BUT WHO SAID ANYTHING ABOUT A TEAM? I WANT YOU TO ENTER THE CONTEST SOLO.
WITH YOUR GADGETS.
POKE
I NEED A STUDENT GENIUS TO WIN THE SCIENCE FAIR. YOU NEED SOMEONE WHO CAN TEACH YOU HOW TO FIGHT.
I CAN SHOW YOU HOW.
DEAL.
I THOUGHT HE WAS GOING TO TAKE ME TO A FAMOUS KUNG-FU MASTER. IN A WAY, HE DID.

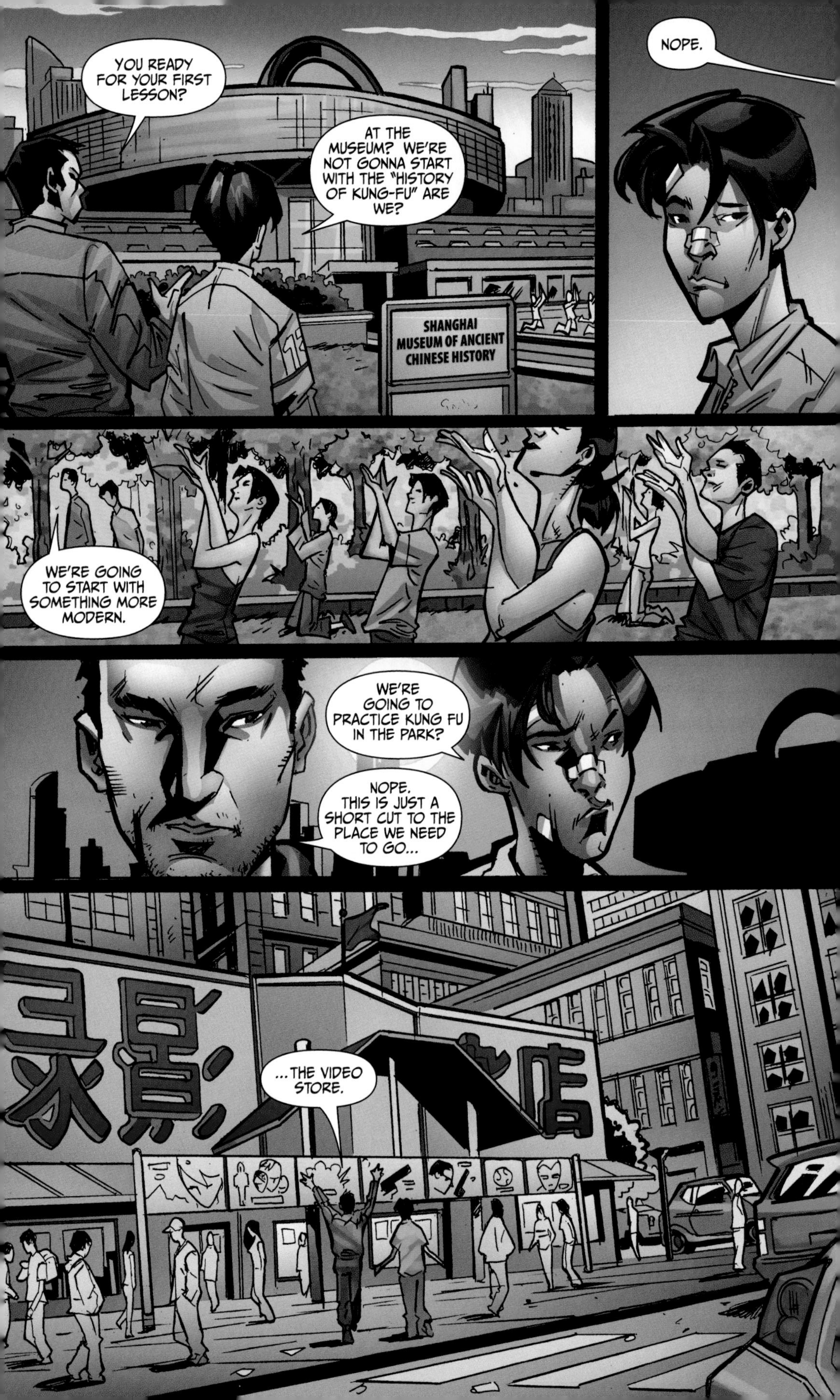
YOU READY FOR YOUR FIRST LESSON?
AT THE MUSEUM? WE'RE NOT GONNA START WITH THE "HISTORY OF KUNG-FU" ARE WE?
SHANGHAI MUSEUM OF ANCIENT CHINESE HISTORY
NOPE.
WE'RE GOING TO START WITH SOMETHING MORE MODERN.
WE'RE GOING TO PRACTICE KUNG FU IN THE PARK?
NOPE. THIS IS JUST A SHORT CUT TO THE PLACE WE NEED TO GO...
...THE VIDEO STORE.
店

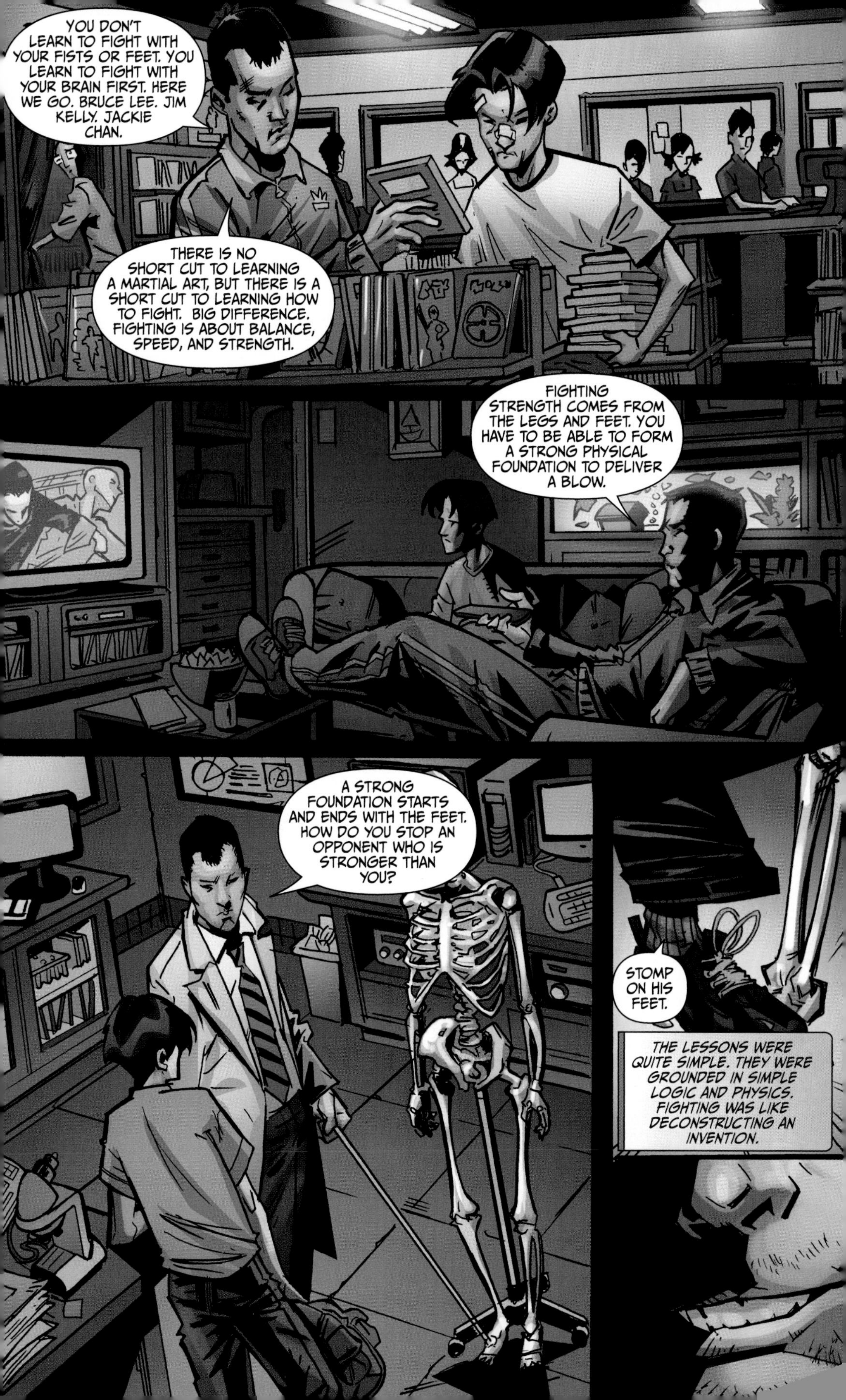
YOU DON'T LEARN TO FIGHT WITH YOUR FISTS OR FEET. YOU LEARN TO FIGHT WITH YOUR BRAIN FIRST. HERE WE GO. BRUCE LEE. JIM KELLY. JACKIE CHAN.
THERE IS NO SHORT CUT TO LEARNING A MARTIAL ART, BUT THERE IS A SHORT CUT TO LEARNING HOW TO FIGHT. BIG DIFFERENCE. FIGHTING IS ABOUT BALANCE, SPEED, AND STRENGTH.
FIGHTING STRENGTH COMES FROM THE LEGS AND FEET. YOU HAVE TO BE ABLE TO FORM A STRONG PHYSICAL FOUNDATION TO DELIVER A BLOW.
A STRONG FOUNDATION STARTS AND ENDS WITH THE FEET. HOW DO YOU STOP AN OPPONENT WHO IS STRONGER THAN YOU?
STOMP ON HIS FEET.
THE LESSONS WERE QUITE SIMPLE. THEY WERE GROUNDED IN SIMPLE LOGIC AND PHYSICS. FIGHTING WAS LIKE DECONSTRUCTING AN INVENTION.

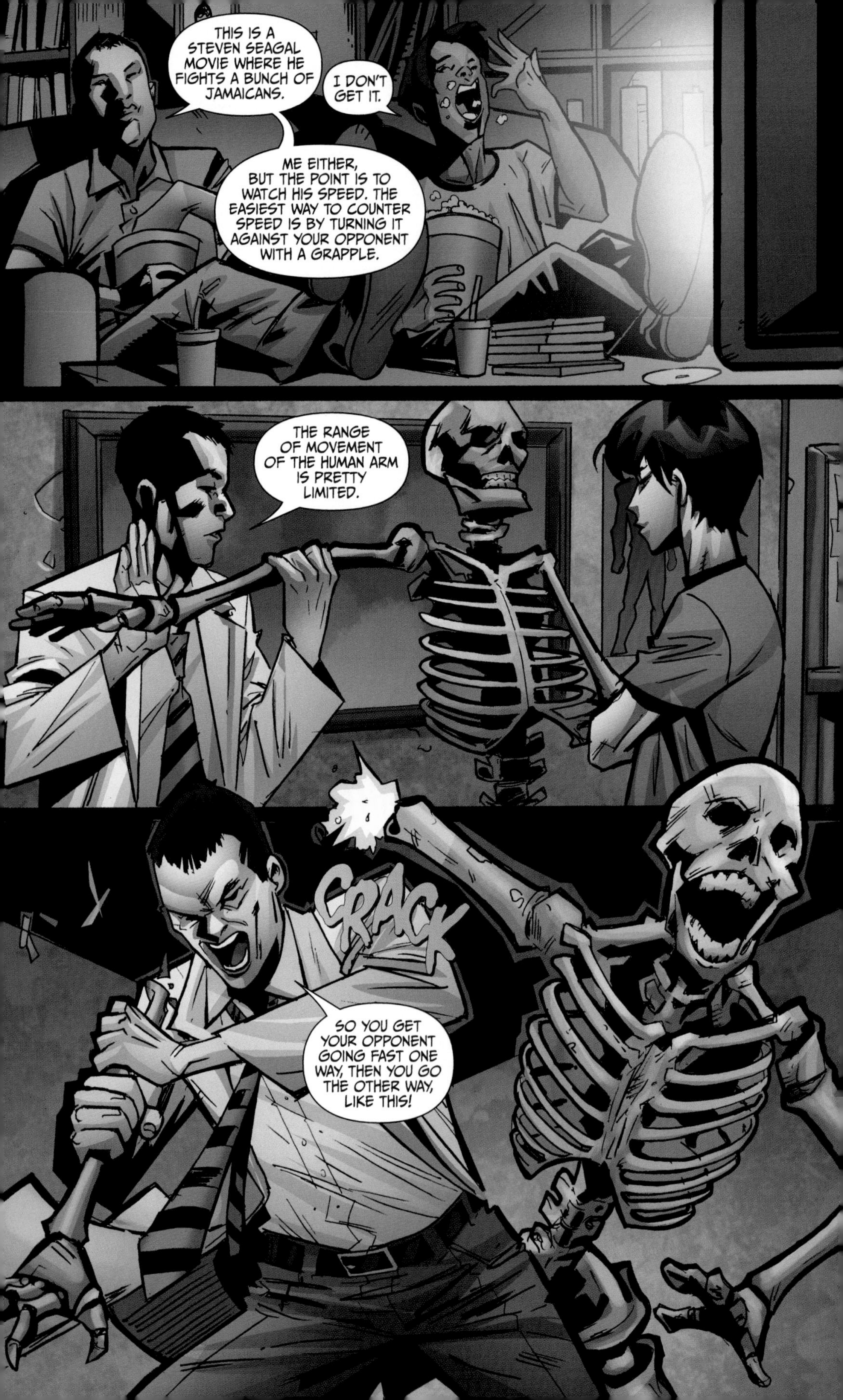
THIS IS A STEVEN SEAGAL MOVIE WHERE HE FIGHTS A BUNCH OF JAMAICANS.
I DON'T GET IT.
ME EITHER, BUT THE POINT IS TO WATCH HIS SPEED. THE EASIEST WAY TO COUNTER SPEED IS BY TURNING IT AGAINST YOUR OPPONENT WITH A GRAPPLE.
THE RANGE OF MOVEMENT OF THE HUMAN ARM IS PRETTY LIMITED.
CRACK
SO YOU GET YOUR OPPONENT GOING FAST ONE WAY, THEN YOU GO THE OTHER WAY, LIKE THIS!

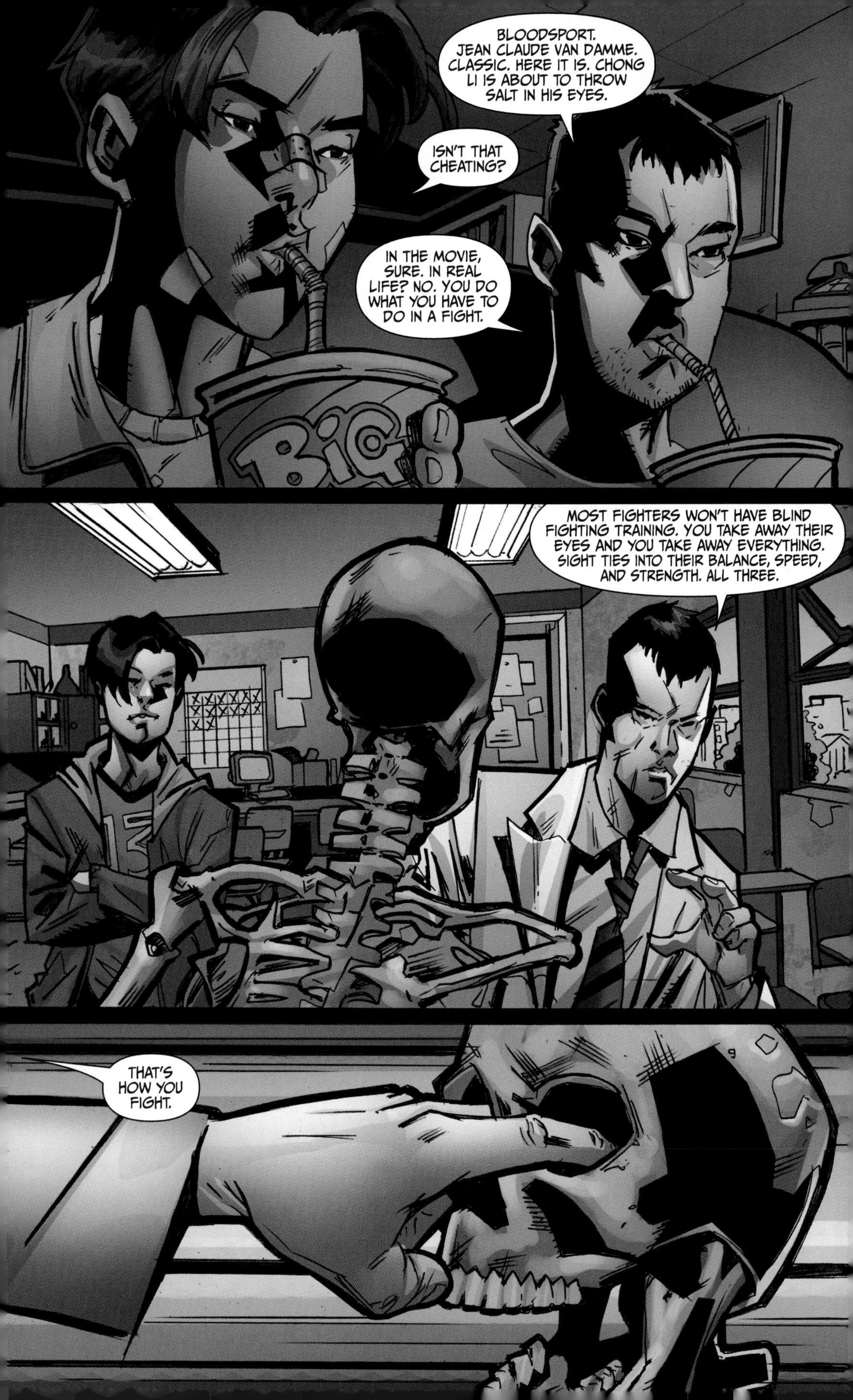
BLOODSPORT. JEAN CLAUDE VAN DAMME. CLASSIC. HERE IT IS. CHONG LI IS ABOUT TO THROW SALT IN HIS EYES.
ISN'T THAT CHEATING?
IN THE MOVIE, SURE. IN REAL LIFE? NO. YOU DO WHAT YOU HAVE TO DO IN A FIGHT.
BIG
MOST FIGHTERS WON'T HAVE BLIND FIGHTING TRAINING. YOU TAKE AWAY THEIR EYES AND YOU TAKE AWAY EVERYTHING. SIGHT TIES INTO THEIR BALANCE, SPEED, AND STRENGTH. ALL THREE.
THAT'S HOW YOU FIGHT.

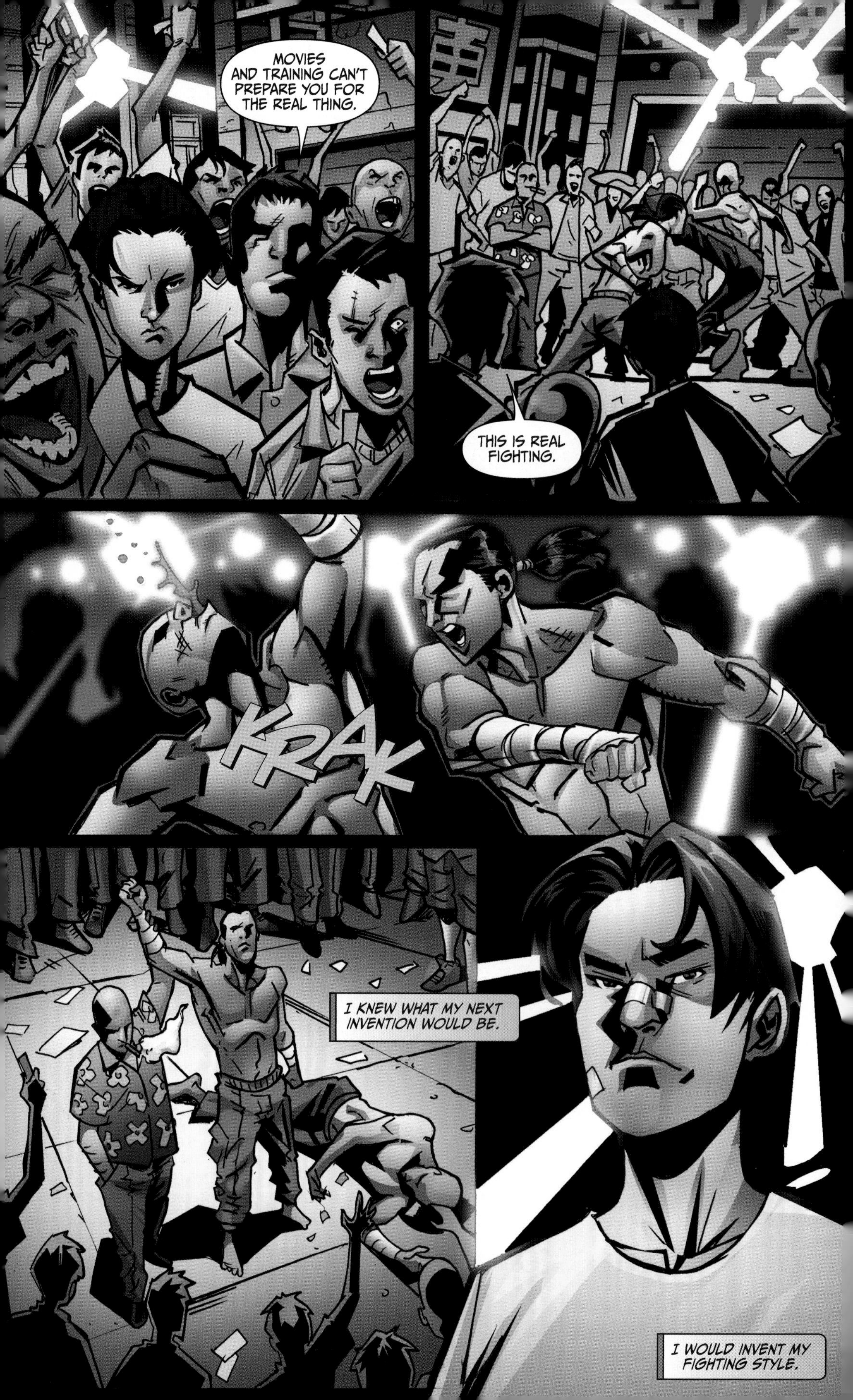
MOVIES AND TRAINING CAN'T PREPARE YOU FOR THE REAL THING.
THIS IS REAL FIGHTING.
KRAK
I KNEW WHAT MY NEXT INVENTION WOULD BE.
I WOULD INVENT MY FIGHTING STYLE.

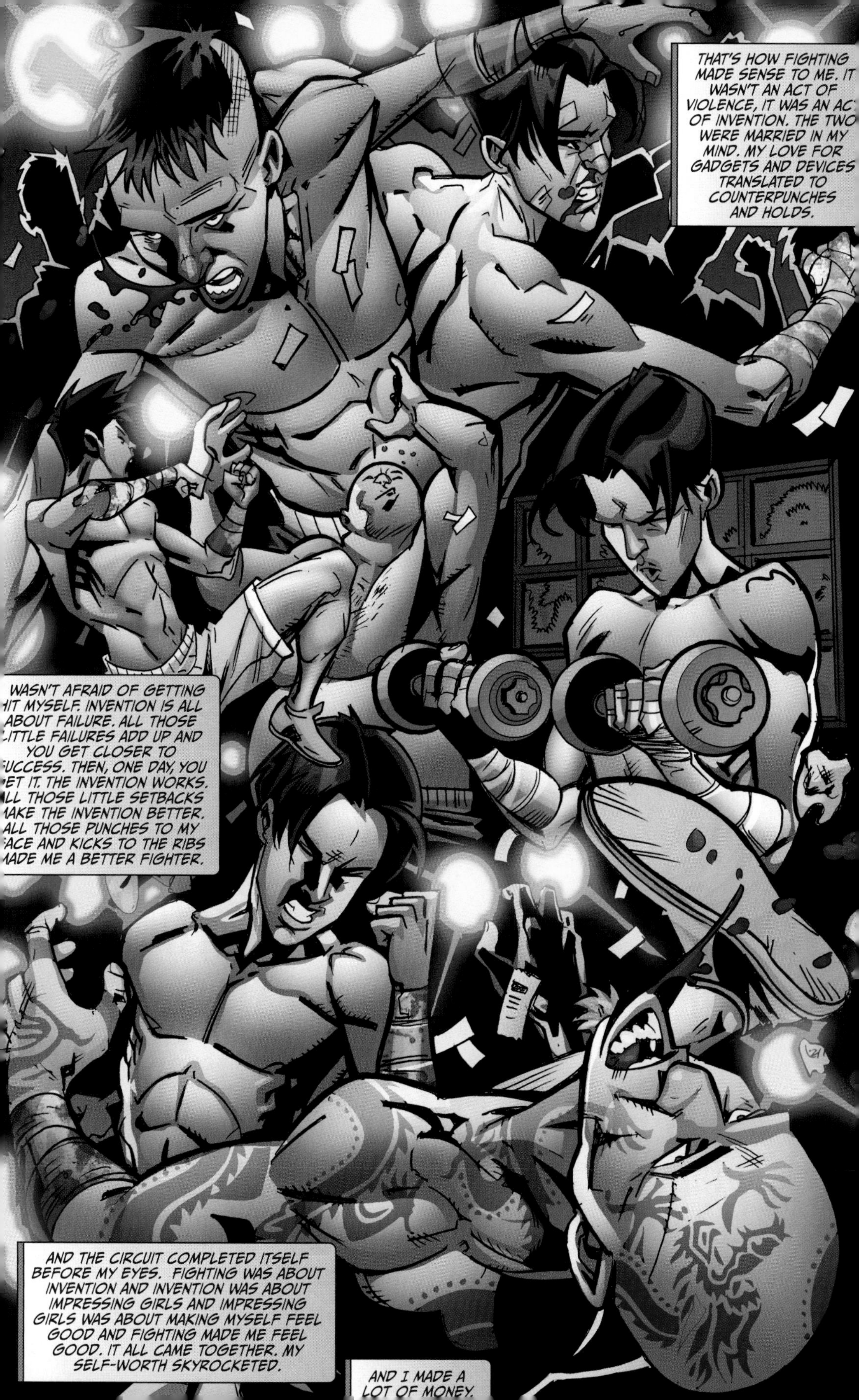
THAT'S HOW FIGHTING MADE SENSE TO ME. IT WASN'T AN ACT OF VIOLENCE, IT WAS AN ACT OF INVENTION. THE TWO WERE MARRIED IN MY MIND. MY LOVE FOR GADGETS AND DEVICES TRANSLATED TO COUNTERPUNCHES AND HOLDS.
WASN'T AFRAID OF GETTING HIT MYSELF. INVENTION IS ALL ABOUT FAILURE. ALL THOSE LITTLE FAILURES ADD UP AND YOU GET CLOSER TO SUCCESS. THEN, ONE DAY, YOU GET IT. THE INVENTION WORKS. ALL THOSE LITTLE SETBACKS MAKE THE INVENTION BETTER. ALL THOSE PUNCHES TO MY FACE AND KICKS TO THE RIBS MADE ME A BETTER FIGHTER.
AND THE CIRCUIT COMPLETED ITSELF BEFORE MY EYES. FIGHTING WAS ABOUT INVENTION AND INVENTION WAS ABOUT IMPRESSING GIRLS AND IMPRESSING GIRLS WAS ABOUT MAKING MYSELF FEEL GOOD AND FIGHTING MADE ME FEEL GOOD. IT ALL CAME TOGETHER. MY SELF-WORTH SKYROCKETED.
AND I MADE A LOT OF MONEY.

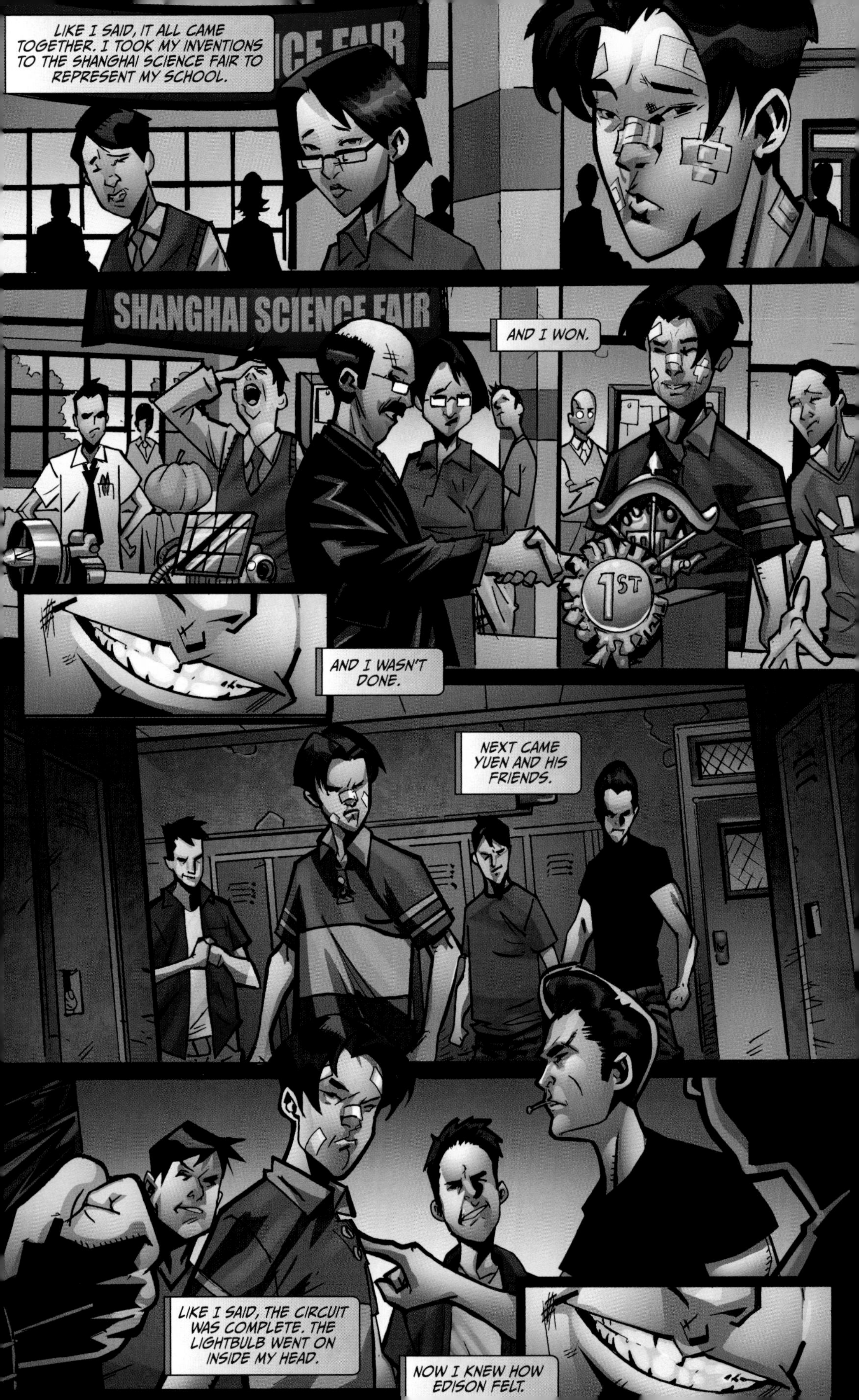
LIKE I SAID, IT ALL CAME TOGETHER. I TOOK MY INVENTIONS TO THE SHANGHAI SCIENCE FAIR TO REPRESENT MY SCHOOL.
SHANGHAI SCIENCE FAIR
AND I WON.
1ST
AND I WASN'T DONE.
NEXT CAME YUEN AND HIS FRIENDS.
LIKE I SAID, THE CIRCUIT WAS COMPLETE. THE LIGHTBULB WENT ON INSIDE MY HEAD.
NOW I KNEW HOW EDISON FELT.

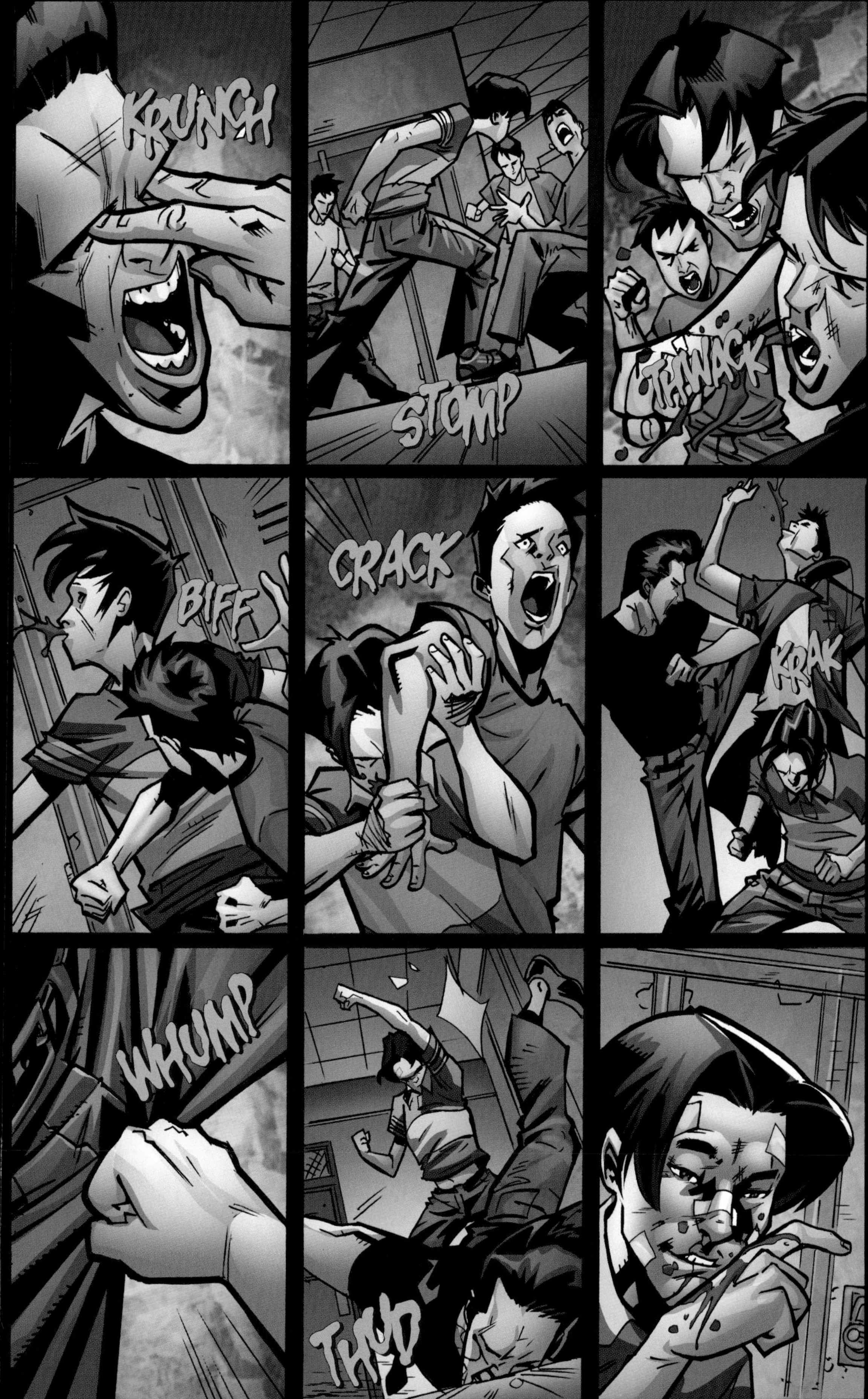
KRUNCH
STOMP
THWACK
BIFF
CRACK
KRAK
WHUMP
THUD

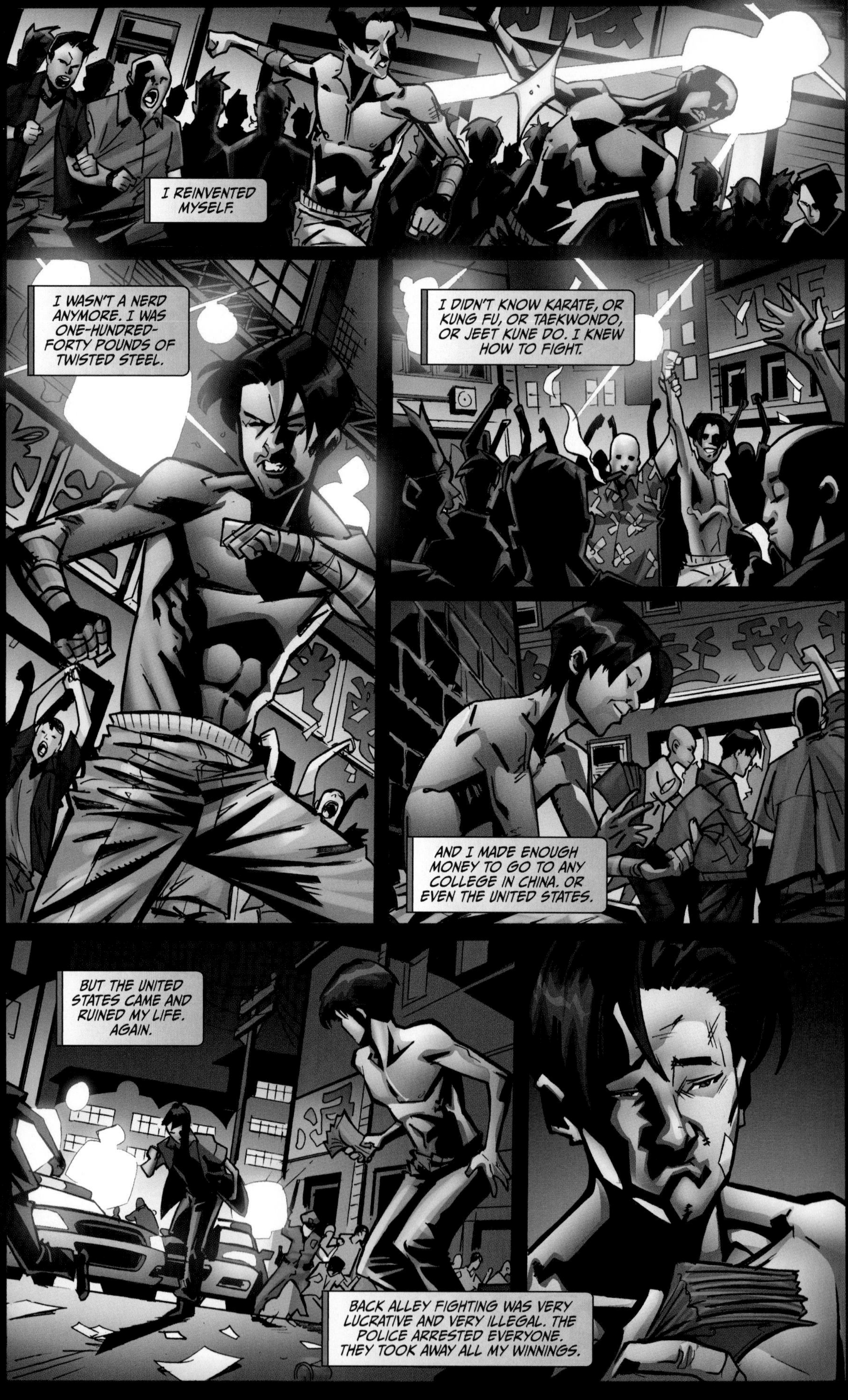
I REINVENTED MYSELF.
I WASN'T A NERD ANYMORE. I WAS ONE-HUNDRED-FORTY POUNDS OF TWISTED STEEL.
I DIDN'T KNOW KARATE, OR KUNG FU, OR TAEKWONDO, OR JEET KUNE DO. I KNEW HOW TO FIGHT.
AND I MADE ENOUGH MONEY TO GO TO ANY COLLEGE IN CHINA. OR EVEN THE UNITED STATES.
BUT THE UNITED STATES CAME AND RUINED MY LIFE. AGAIN.
BACK ALLEY FIGHTING WAS VERY LUCRATIVE AND VERY ILLEGAL. THE POLICE ARRESTED EVERYONE. THEY TOOK AWAY ALL MY WINNINGS.

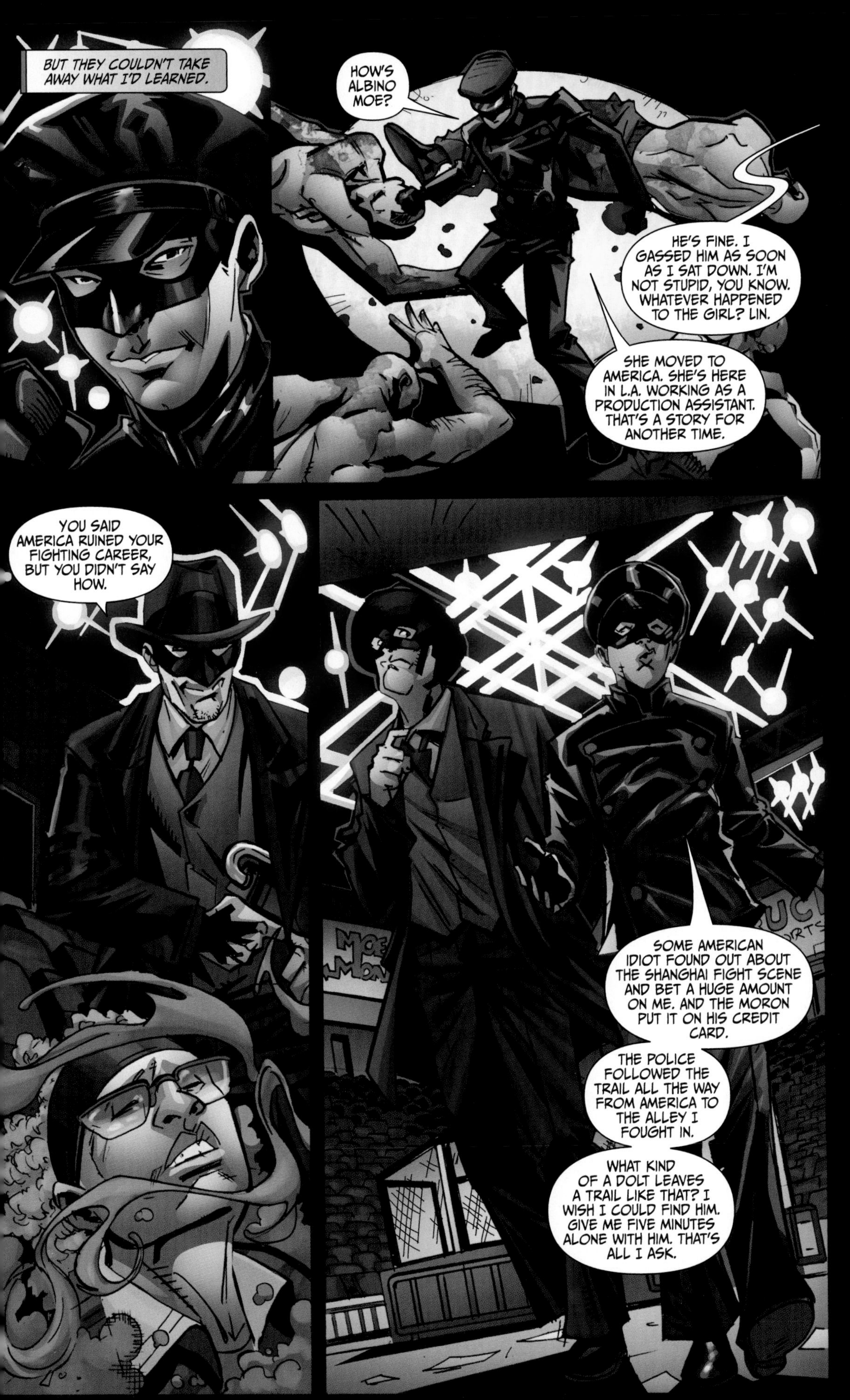

BUT THEY COULDN'T TAKE AWAY WHAT I'D LEARNED.
HOW'S ALBINO MOE?
HE'S FINE. I GASSED HIM AS SOON AS I SAT DOWN. I'M NOT STUPID, YOU KNOW. WHATEVER HAPPENED TO THE GIRL? LIN.
SHE MOVED TO AMERICA. SHE'S HERE IN L.A. WORKING AS A PRODUCTION ASSISTANT. THAT'S A STORY FOR ANOTHER TIME.
YOU SAID AMERICA RUINED YOUR FIGHTING CAREER, BUT YOU DIDN'T SAY HOW.
SOME AMERICAN IDIOT FOUND OUT ABOUT THE SHANGHAI FIGHT SCENE AND BET A HUGE AMOUNT ON ME. AND THE MORON PUT IT ON HIS CREDIT CARD.
THE POLICE FOLLOWED THE TRAIL ALL THE WAY FROM AMERICA TO THE ALLEY I FOUGHT IN.
WHAT KIND OF A DOLT LEAVES A TRAIL LIKE THAT? I WISH I COULD FIND HIM. GIVE ME FIVE MINUTES ALONE WITH HIM. THAT'S ALL I ASK.

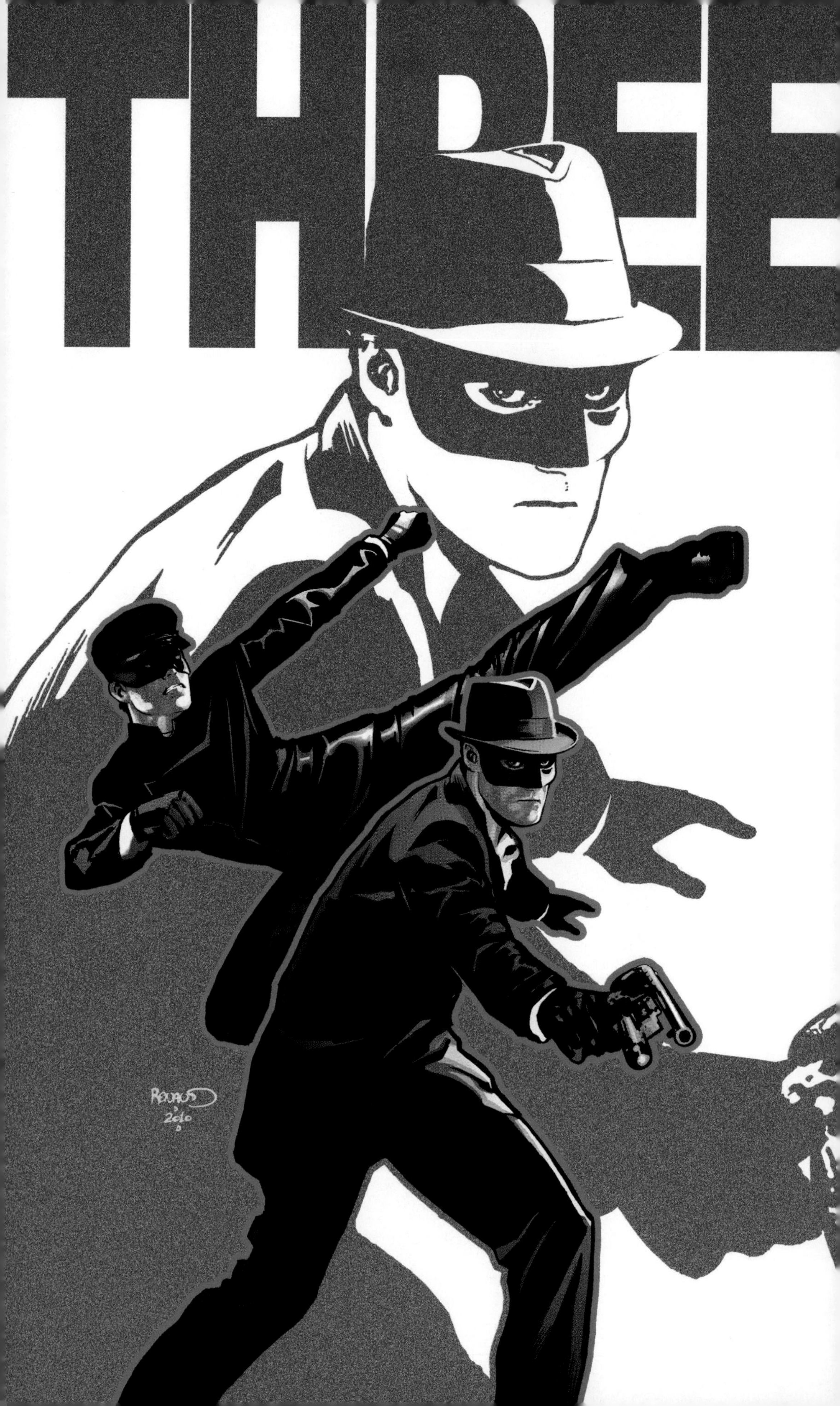
THREE

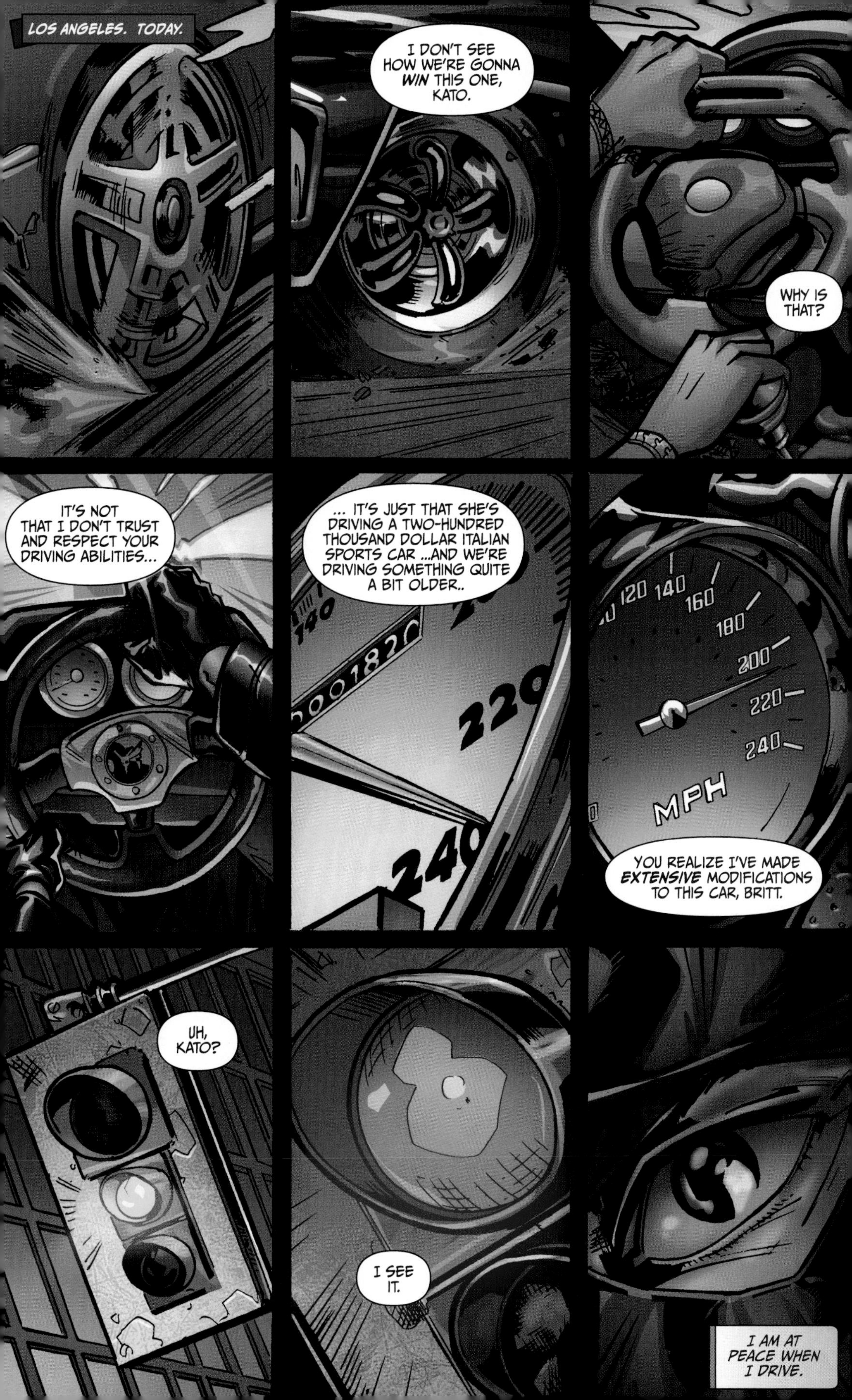
LOS ANGELES. TODAY.
I DON'T SEE HOW WE'RE GONNA WIN THIS ONE, KATO.
WHY IS THAT?
IT'S NOT THAT I DON'T TRUST AND RESPECT YOUR DRIVING ABILITIES...
... IT'S JUST THAT SHE'S DRIVING A TWO-HUNDRED THOUSAND DOLLAR ITALIAN SPORTS CAR ...AND WE'RE DRIVING SOMETHING QUITE A BIT OLDER..
YOU REALIZE I'VE MADE EXTENSIVE MODIFICATIONS TO THIS CAR, BRITT.
UH, KATO?
I SEE IT.
I AM AT PEACE WHEN I DRIVE.

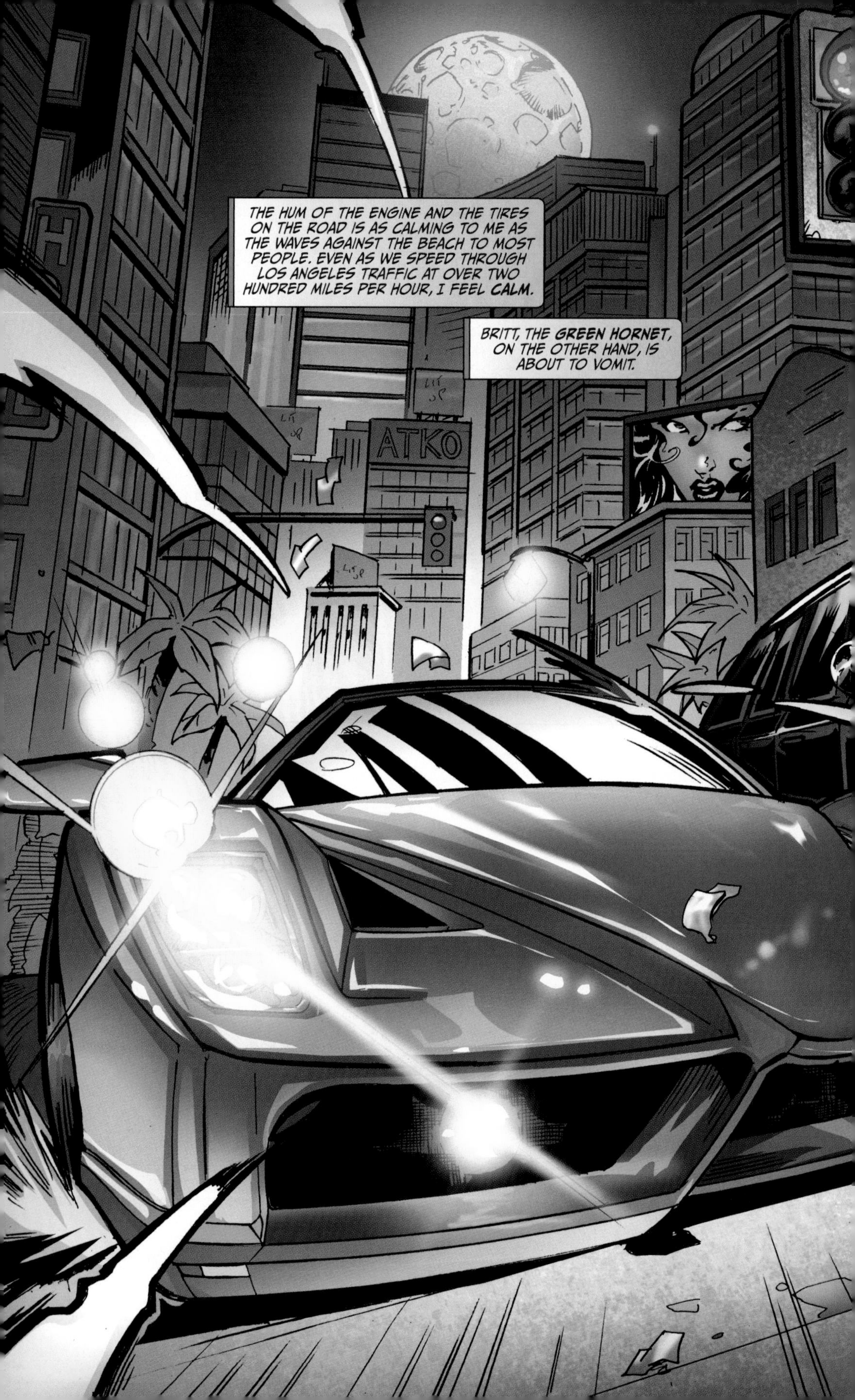

THE HUM OF THE ENGINE AND THE TIRES ON THE ROAD IS AS CALMING TO ME AS THE WAVES AGAINST THE BEACH TO MOST PEOPLE. EVEN AS WE SPEED THROUGH LOS ANGELES TRAFFIC AT OVER TWO HUNDRED MILES PER HOUR, I FEEL **CALM**.
BRITT, THE **GREEN HORNET**, ON THE OTHER HAND, IS ABOUT TO VOMIT.
ATKO

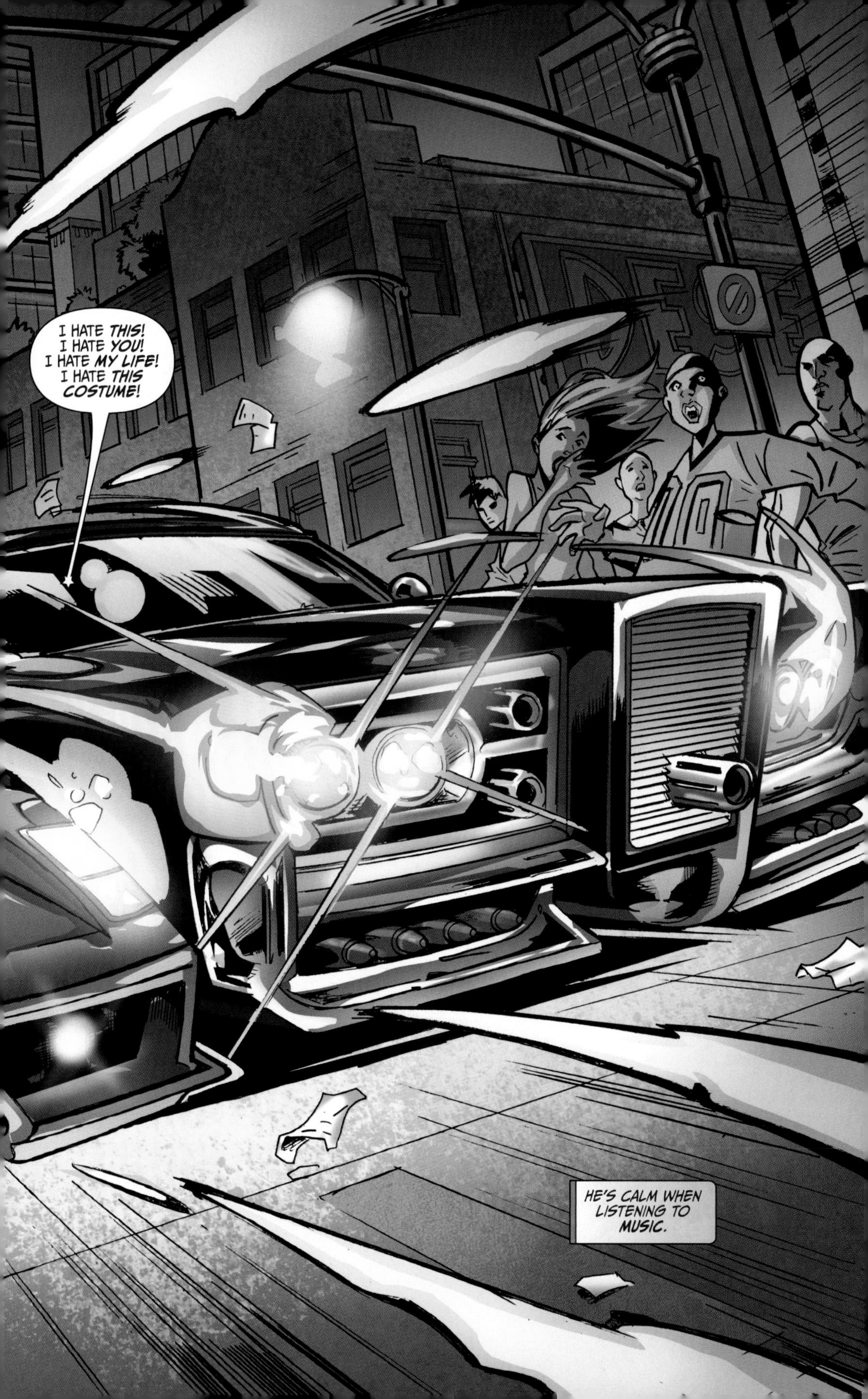
I HATE *THIS*! I HATE *YOU*! I HATE *MY LIFE*! I HATE *THIS COSTUME*!
HE'S CALM WHEN LISTENING TO MUSIC.

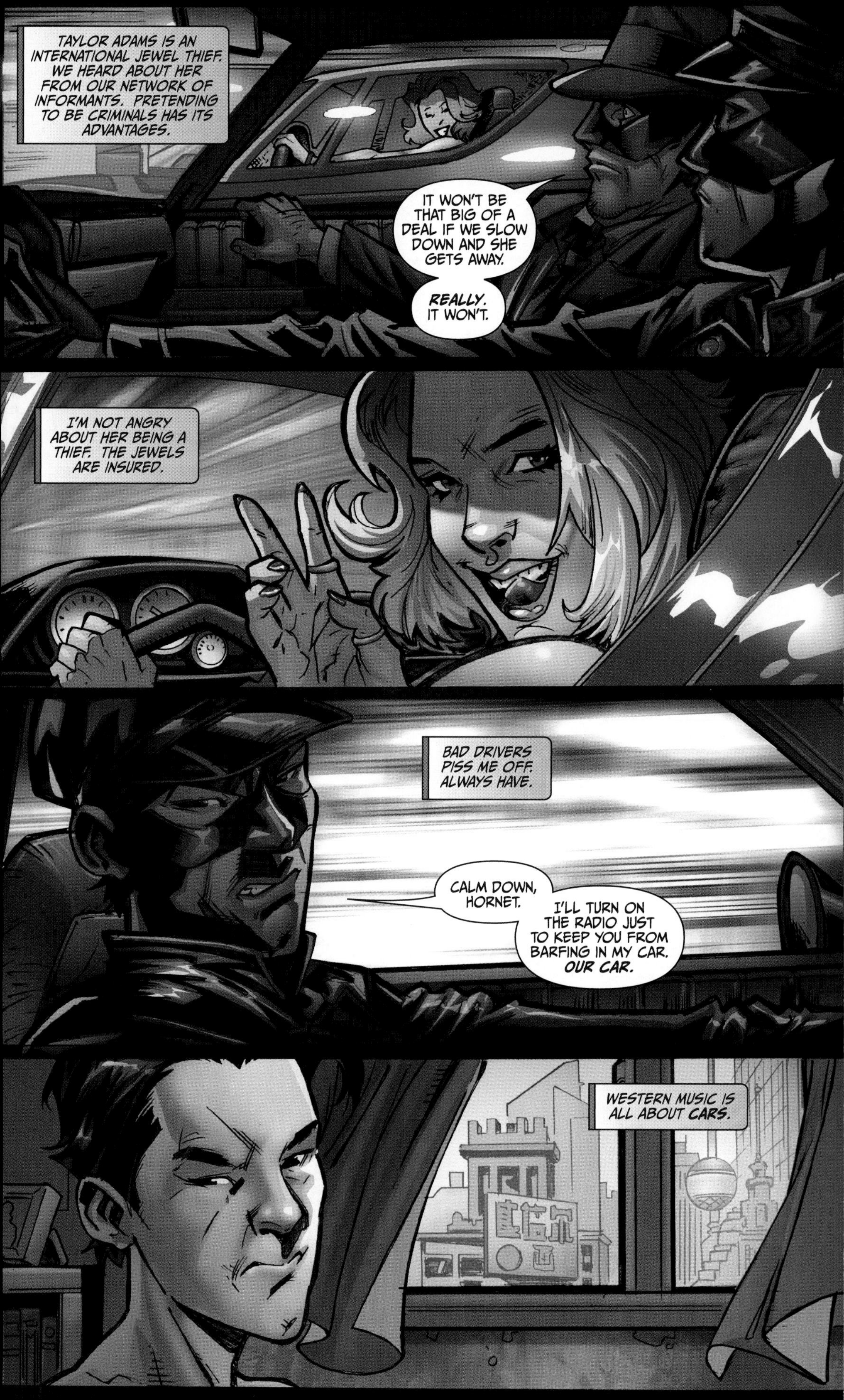
TAYLOR ADAMS IS AN INTERNATIONAL JEWEL THIEF. WE HEARD ABOUT HER FROM OUR NETWORK OF INFORMANTS. PRETENDING TO BE CRIMINALS HAS ITS ADVANTAGES.
IT WON'T BE THAT BIG OF A DEAL IF WE SLOW DOWN AND SHE GETS AWAY.
REALLY. IT WON'T.
I'M NOT ANGRY ABOUT HER BEING A THIEF. THE JEWELS ARE INSURED.
BAD DRIVERS PISS ME OFF. ALWAYS HAVE.
CALM DOWN, HORNET.
I'LL TURN ON THE RADIO JUST TO KEEP YOU FROM BARFING IN MY CAR. OUR CAR.
WESTERN MUSIC IS ALL ABOUT CARS.

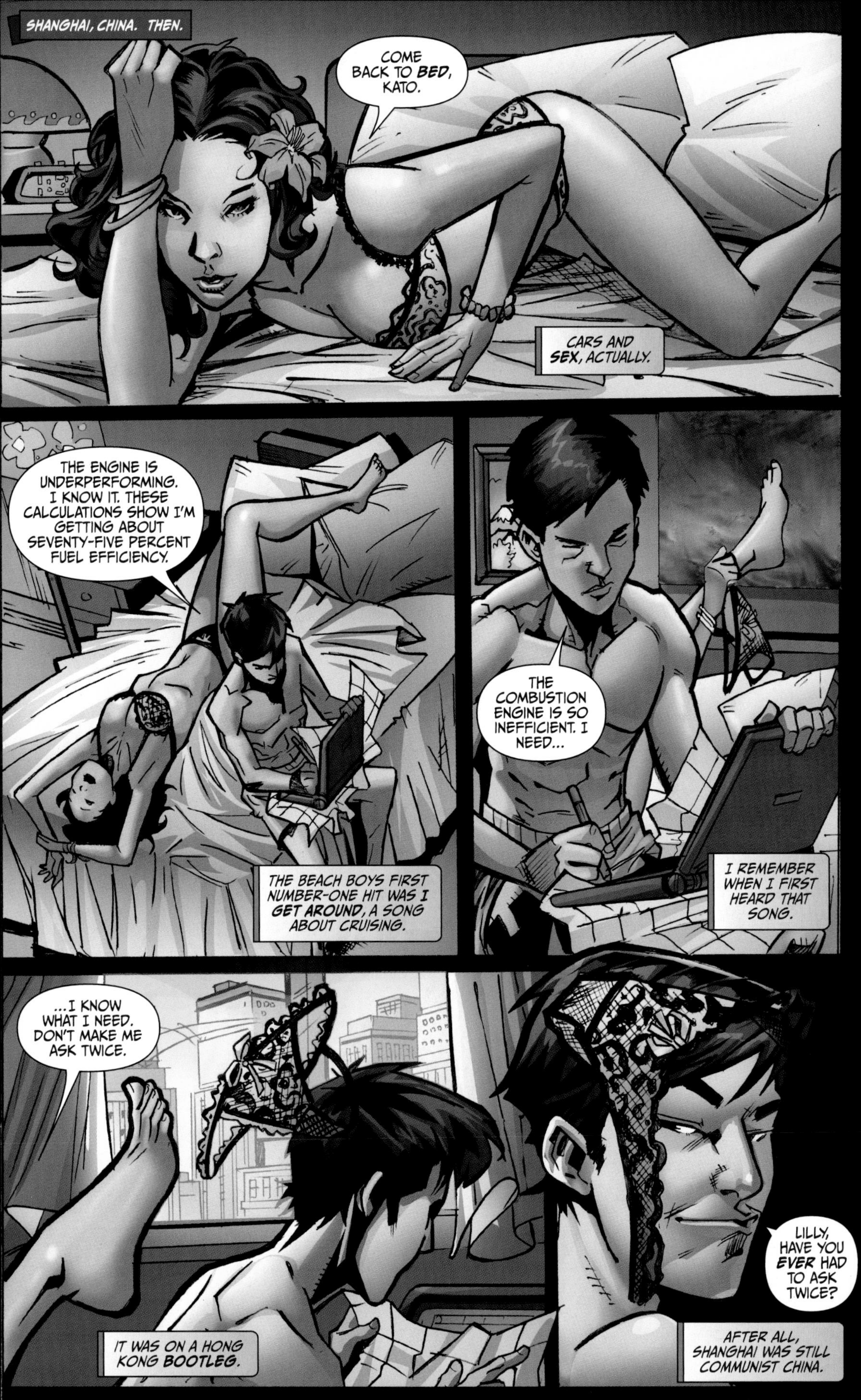
SHANGHAI, CHINA. THEN.
COME BACK TO BED, KATO.
CARS AND SEX, ACTUALLY.
THE ENGINE IS UNDERPERFORMING. I KNOW IT. THESE CALCULATIONS SHOW I'M GETTING ABOUT SEVENTY-FIVE PERCENT FUEL EFFICIENCY.
THE BEACH BOYS FIRST NUMBER-ONE HIT WAS I GET AROUND, A SONG ABOUT CRUISING.
THE COMBUSTION ENGINE IS SO INEFFICIENT. I NEED...
I REMEMBER WHEN I FIRST HEARD THAT SONG.
...I KNOW WHAT I NEED. DON'T MAKE ME ASK TWICE.
IT WAS ON A HONG KONG BOOTLEG.
LILLY, HAVE YOU EVER HAD TO ASK TWICE?
AFTER ALL, SHANGHAI WAS STILL COMMUNIST CHINA.

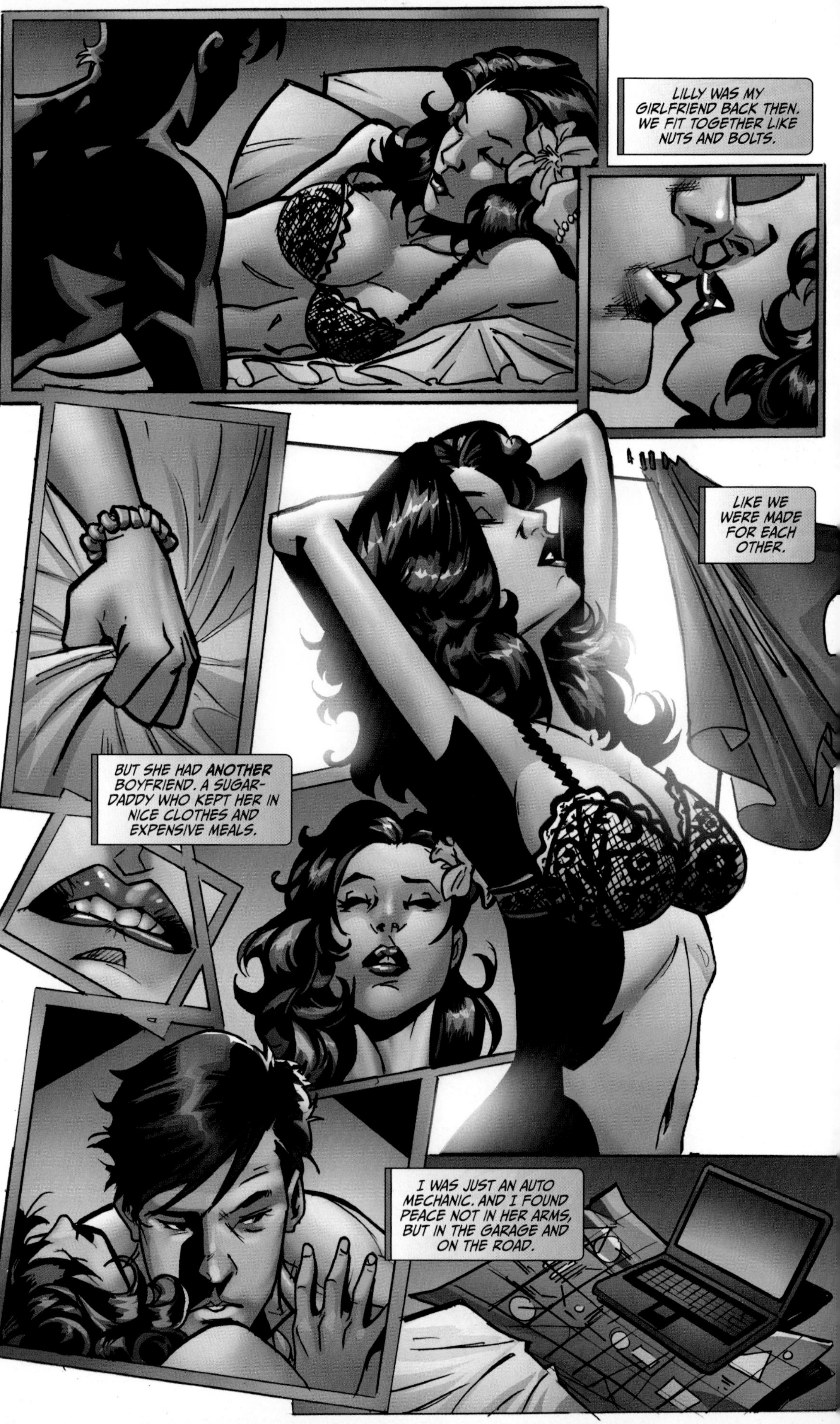
LILLY WAS MY GIRLFRIEND BACK THEN. WE FIT TOGETHER LIKE NUTS AND BOLTS.
LIKE WE WERE MADE FOR EACH OTHER.
BUT SHE HAD ANOTHER BOYFRIEND. A SUGAR-DADDY WHO KEPT HER IN NICE CLOTHES AND EXPENSIVE MEALS.
I WAS JUST AN AUTO MECHANIC. AND I FOUND PEACE NOT IN HER ARMS, BUT IN THE GARAGE AND ON THE ROAD.

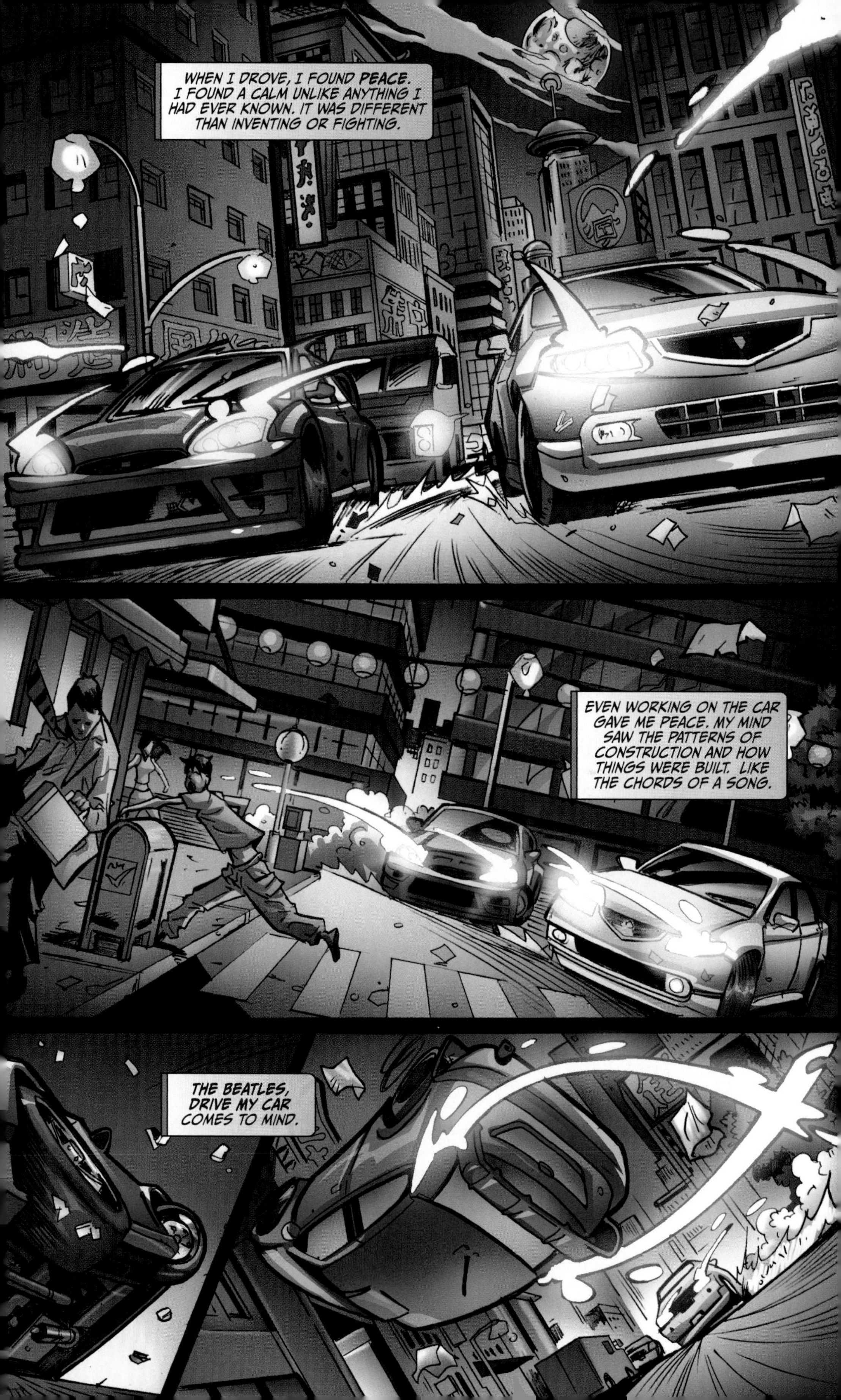
WHEN I DROVE, I FOUND PEACE. I FOUND A CALM UNLIKE ANYTHING I HAD EVER KNOWN. IT WAS DIFFERENT THAN INVENTING OR FIGHTING.
EVEN WORKING ON THE CAR GAVE ME PEACE. MY MIND SAW THE PATTERNS OF CONSTRUCTION AND HOW THINGS WERE BUILT. LIKE THE CHORDS OF A SONG.
THE BEATLES, DRIVE MY CAR COMES TO MIND.

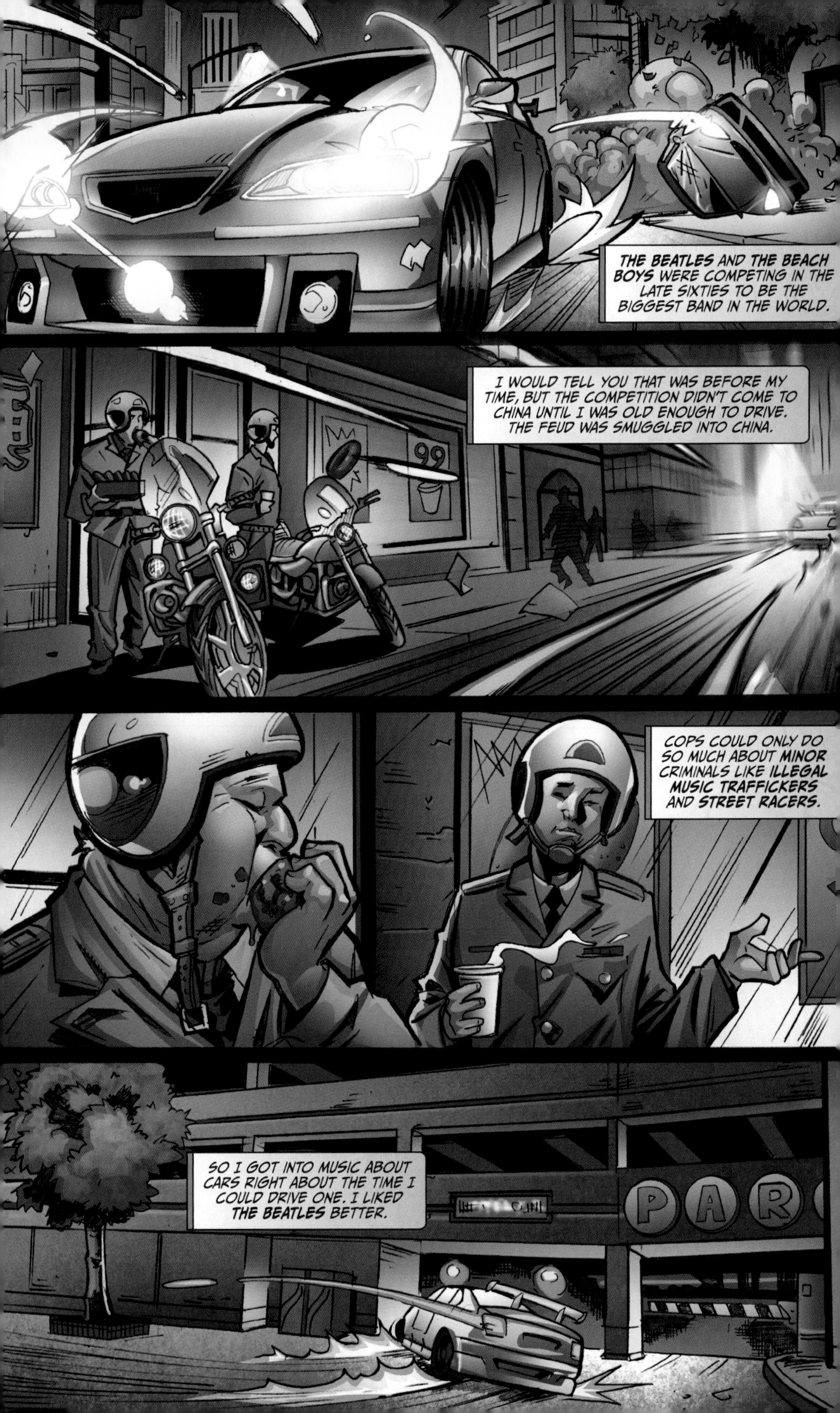
THE BEATLES AND THE BEACH BOYS WERE COMPETING IN THE LATE SIXTIES TO BE THE BIGGEST BAND IN THE WORLD.
I WOULD TELL YOU THAT WAS BEFORE MY TIME, BUT THE COMPETITION DIDN'T COME TO CHINA UNTIL I WAS OLD ENOUGH TO DRIVE. THE FEUD WAS SMUGGLED INTO CHINA.
99
COPS COULD ONLY DO SO MUCH ABOUT MINOR CRIMINALS LIKE ILLEGAL MUSIC TRAFFICKERS AND STREET RACERS.
SO I GOT INTO MUSIC ABOUT CARS RIGHT ABOUT THE TIME I COULD DRIVE ONE. I LIKED THE BEATLES BETTER.
PAR

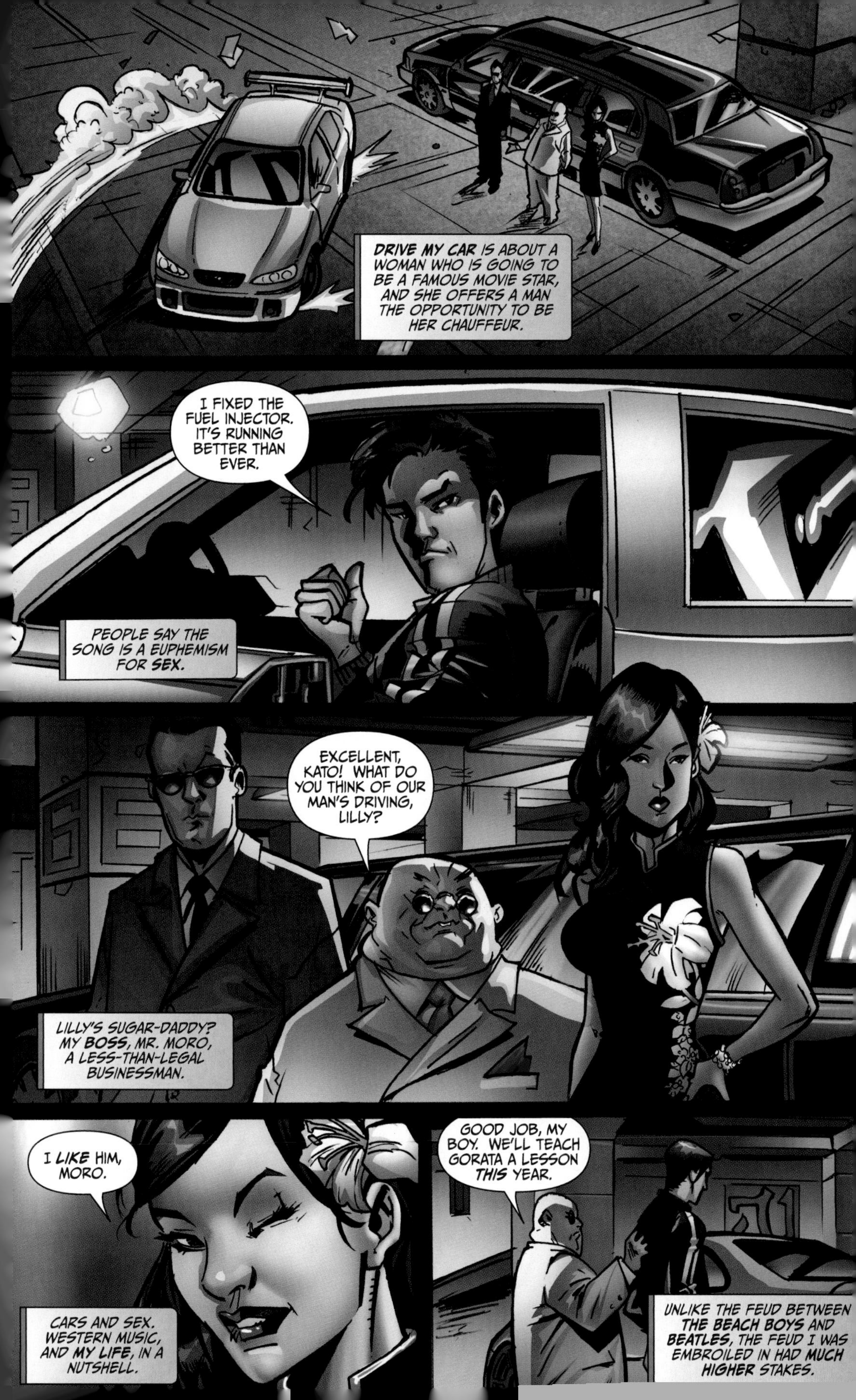
DRIVE MY CAR IS ABOUT A WOMAN WHO IS GOING TO BE A FAMOUS MOVIE STAR, AND SHE OFFERS A MAN THE OPPORTUNITY TO BE HER CHAUFFEUR.
I FIXED THE FUEL INJECTOR. IT'S RUNNING BETTER THAN EVER.
PEOPLE SAY THE SONG IS A EUPHEMISM FOR SEX.
EXCELLENT, KATO! WHAT DO YOU THINK OF OUR MAN'S DRIVING, LILLY?
LILLY'S SUGAR-DADDY? MY BOSS, MR. MORO, A LESS-THAN-LEGAL BUSINESSMAN.
I LIKE HIM, MORO.
CARS AND SEX. WESTERN MUSIC, AND MY LIFE, IN A NUTSHELL.
GOOD JOB, MY BOY. WE'LL TEACH GORATA A LESSON THIS YEAR.
UNLIKE THE FEUD BETWEEN THE BEACH BOYS AND BEATLES, THE FEUD I WAS EMBROILED IN HAD MUCH HIGHER STAKES.

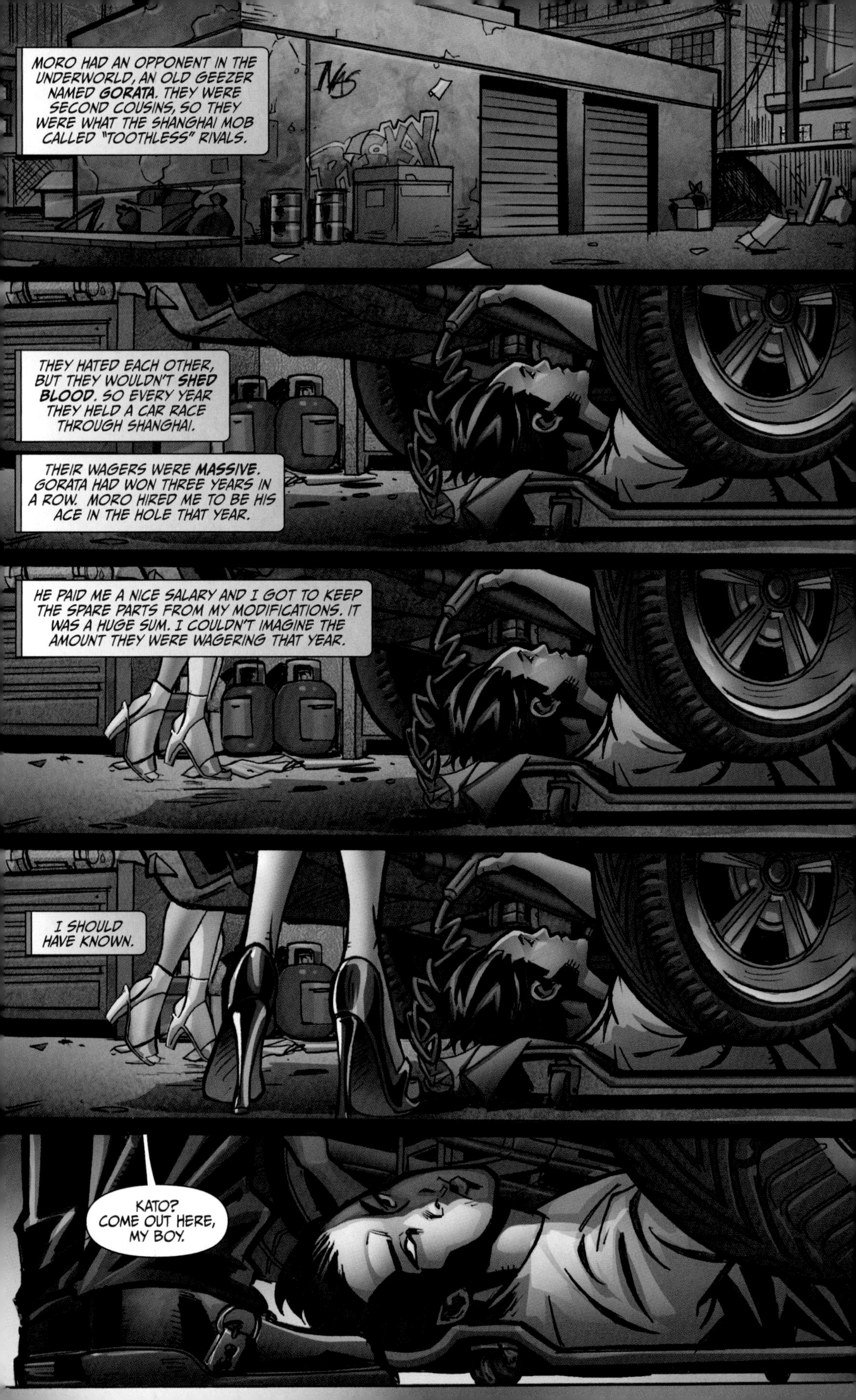
MORO HAD AN OPPONENT IN THE UNDERWORLD, AN OLD GEEZER NAMED GORATA. THEY WERE SECOND COUSINS, SO THEY WERE WHAT THE SHANGHAI MOB CALLED "TOOTHLESS" RIVALS.
THEY HATED EACH OTHER, BUT THEY WOULDN'T SHED BLOOD. SO EVERY YEAR THEY HELD A CAR RACE THROUGH SHANGHAI.
THEIR WAGERS WERE MASSIVE. GORATA HAD WON THREE YEARS IN A ROW. MORO HIRED ME TO BE HIS ACE IN THE HOLE THAT YEAR.
HE PAID ME A NICE SALARY AND I GOT TO KEEP THE SPARE PARTS FROM MY MODIFICATIONS. IT WAS A HUGE SUM. I COULDN'T IMAGINE THE AMOUNT THEY WERE WAGERING THAT YEAR.
I SHOULD HAVE KNOWN.
KATO? COME OUT HERE, MY BOY.

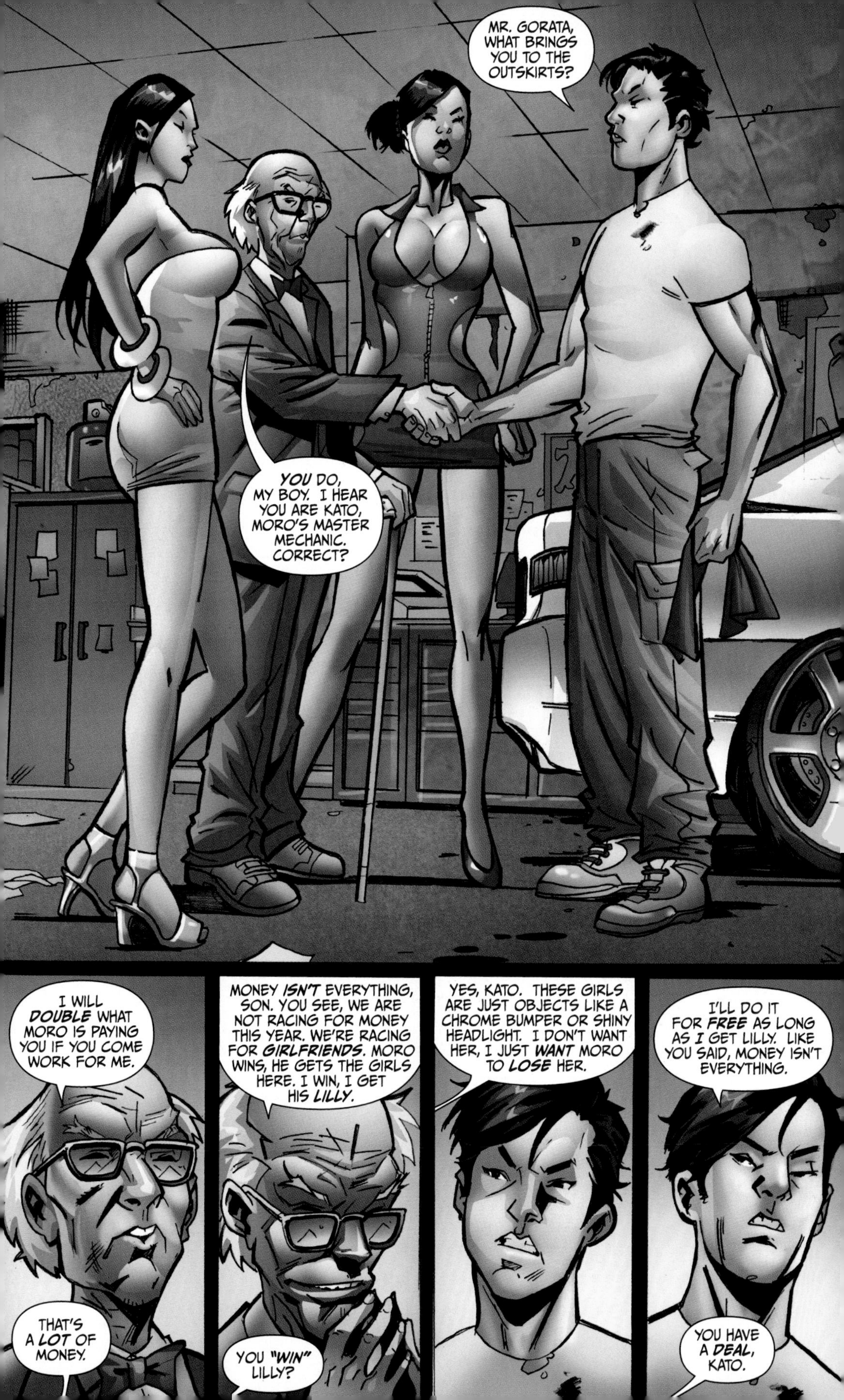
MR. GORATA, WHAT BRINGS YOU TO THE OUTSKIRTS?
YOU DO, MY BOY. I HEAR YOU ARE KATO, MORO'S MASTER MECHANIC. CORRECT?
I WILL DOUBLE WHAT MORO IS PAYING YOU IF YOU COME WORK FOR ME.
THAT'S A LOT OF MONEY.
MONEY ISN'T EVERYTHING, SON. YOU SEE, WE ARE NOT RACING FOR MONEY THIS YEAR. WE'RE RACING FOR GIRLFRIENDS. MORO WINS, HE GETS THE GIRLS HERE. I WIN, I GET HIS LILLY.
YOU "WIN" LILLY?
YES, KATO. THESE GIRLS ARE JUST OBJECTS LIKE A CHROME BUMPER OR SHINY HEADLIGHT. I DON'T WANT HER, I JUST WANT MORO TO LOSE HER.
I'LL DO IT FOR FREE AS LONG AS I GET LILLY. LIKE YOU SAID, MONEY ISN'T EVERYTHING.
YOU HAVE A DEAL, KATO.

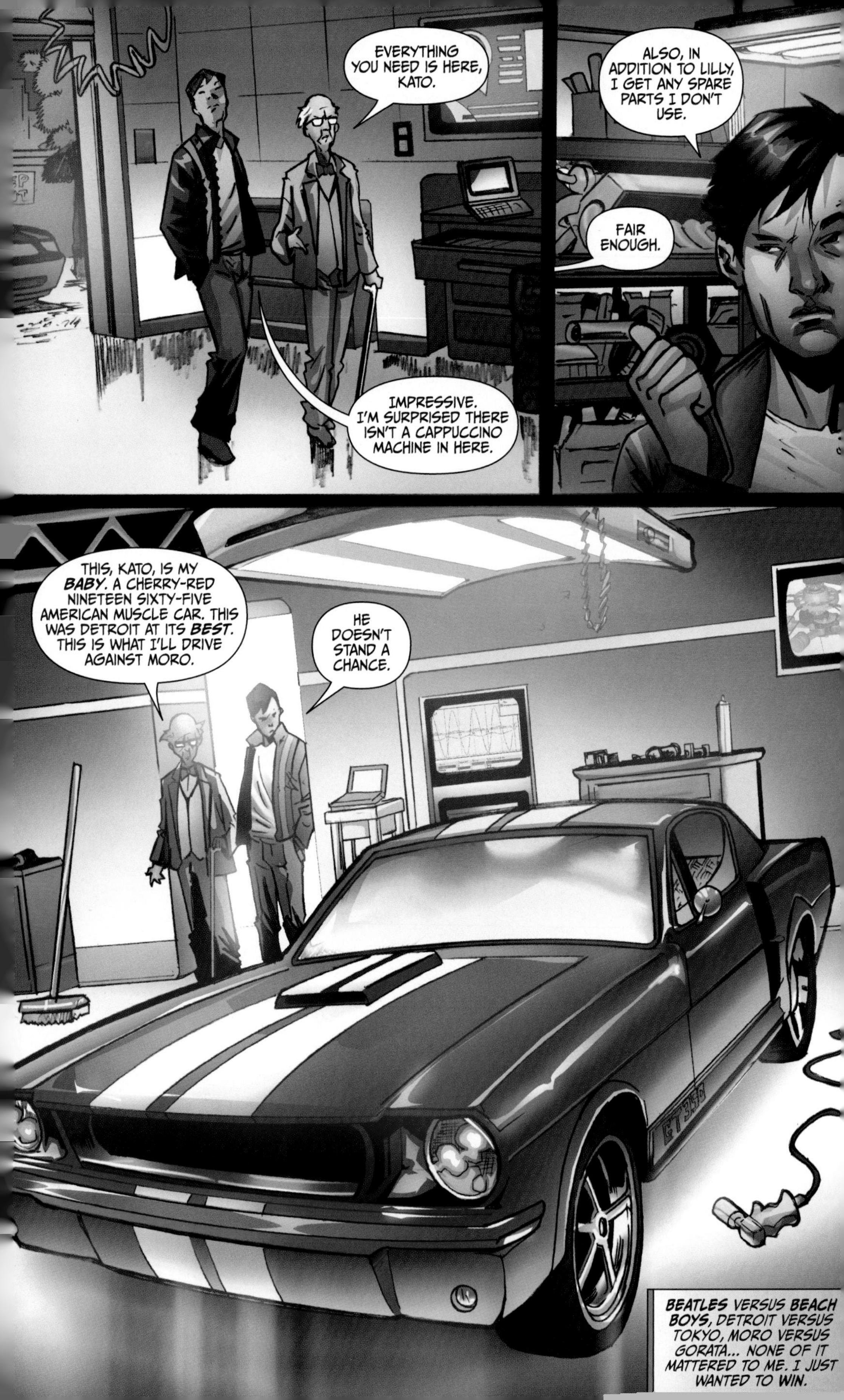
EVERYTHING YOU NEED IS HERE, KATO.
IMPRESSIVE. I'M SURPRISED THERE ISN'T A CAPPUCCINO MACHINE IN HERE.
ALSO, IN ADDITION TO LILLY, I GET ANY SPARE PARTS I DON'T USE.
FAIR ENOUGH.
THIS, KATO, IS MY **BABY**. A CHERRY-RED NINETEEN SIXTY-FIVE AMERICAN MUSCLE CAR. THIS WAS DETROIT AT ITS **BEST**. THIS IS WHAT I'LL DRIVE AGAINST MORO.
HE DOESN'T STAND A CHANCE.
GT350
BEATLES VERSUS BEACH BOYS, DETROIT VERSUS TOKYO, MORO VERSUS GORATA... NONE OF IT MATTERED TO ME. I JUST WANTED TO WIN.

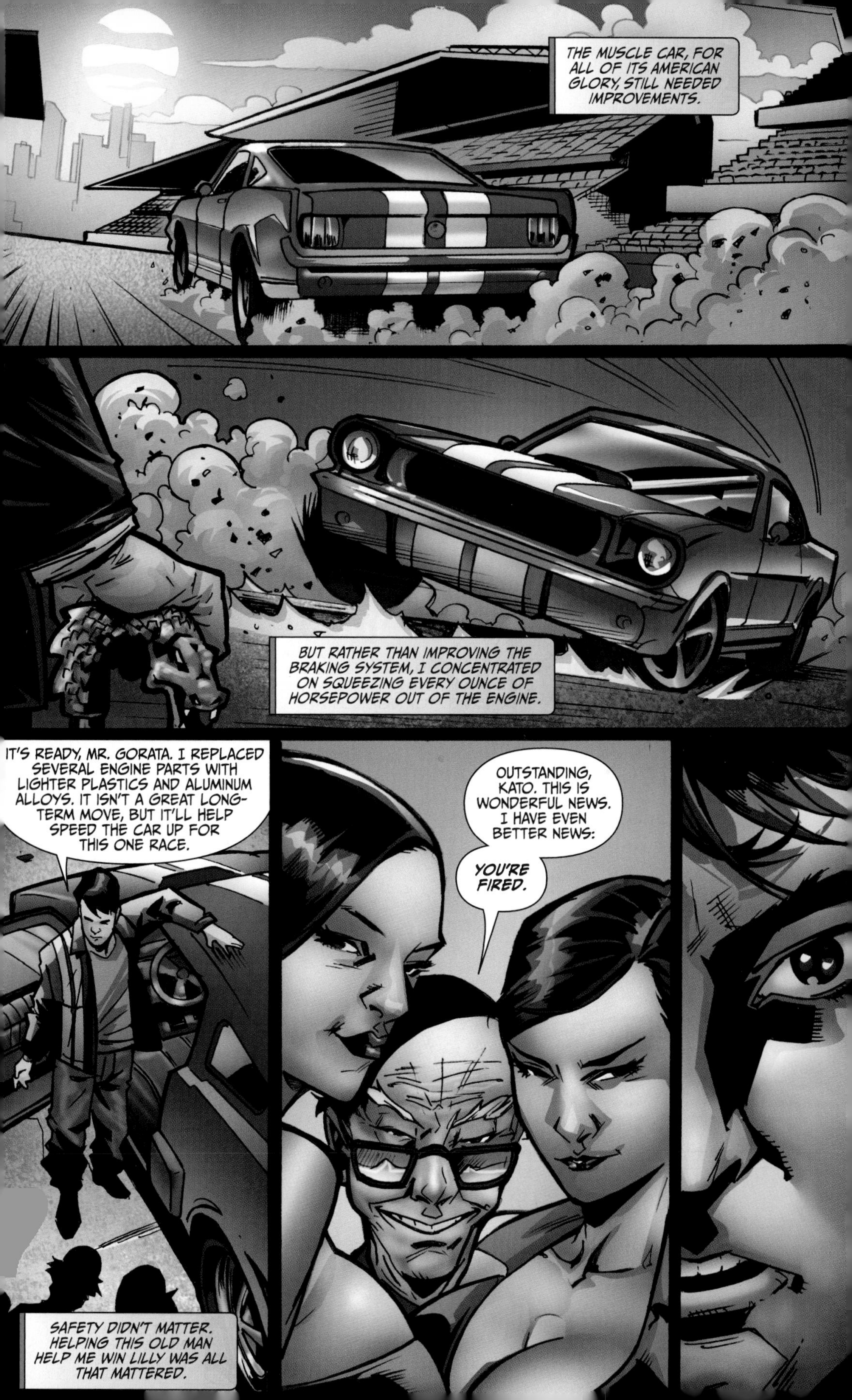
THE MUSCLE CAR, FOR ALL OF ITS AMERICAN GLORY, STILL NEEDED IMPROVEMENTS.
BUT RATHER THAN IMPROVING THE BRAKING SYSTEM, I CONCENTRATED ON SQUEEZING EVERY OUNCE OF HORSEPOWER OUT OF THE ENGINE.
IT'S READY, MR. GORATA. I REPLACED SEVERAL ENGINE PARTS WITH LIGHTER PLASTICS AND ALUMINUM ALLOYS. IT ISN'T A GREAT LONG-TERM MOVE, BUT IT'LL HELP SPEED THE CAR UP FOR THIS ONE RACE.
OUTSTANDING, KATO. THIS IS WONDERFUL NEWS. I HAVE EVEN BETTER NEWS:
YOU'RE FIRED.
SAFETY DIDN'T MATTER. HELPING THIS OLD MAN HELP ME WIN LILLY WAS ALL THAT MATTERED.

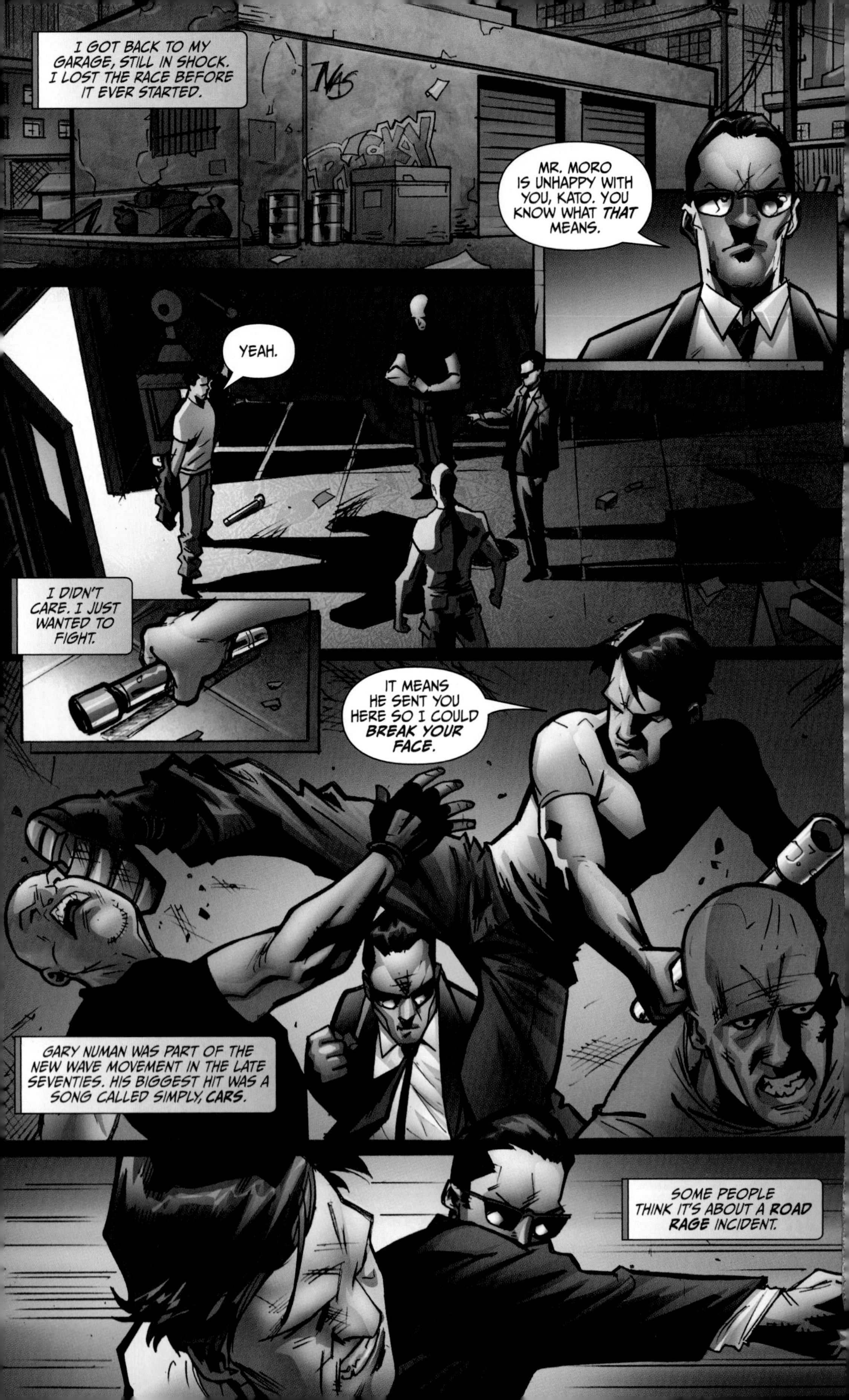

I GOT BACK TO MY GARAGE, STILL IN SHOCK. I LOST THE RACE BEFORE IT EVER STARTED.
MR. MORO IS UNHAPPY WITH YOU, KATO. YOU KNOW WHAT THAT MEANS.
YEAH.
I DIDN'T CARE. I JUST WANTED TO FIGHT.
IT MEANS HE SENT YOU HERE SO I COULD BREAK YOUR FACE.
GARY NUMAN WAS PART OF THE NEW WAVE MOVEMENT IN THE LATE SEVENTIES. HIS BIGGEST HIT WAS A SONG CALLED SIMPLY, CARS.
SOME PEOPLE THINK IT'S ABOUT A ROAD RAGE INCIDENT.

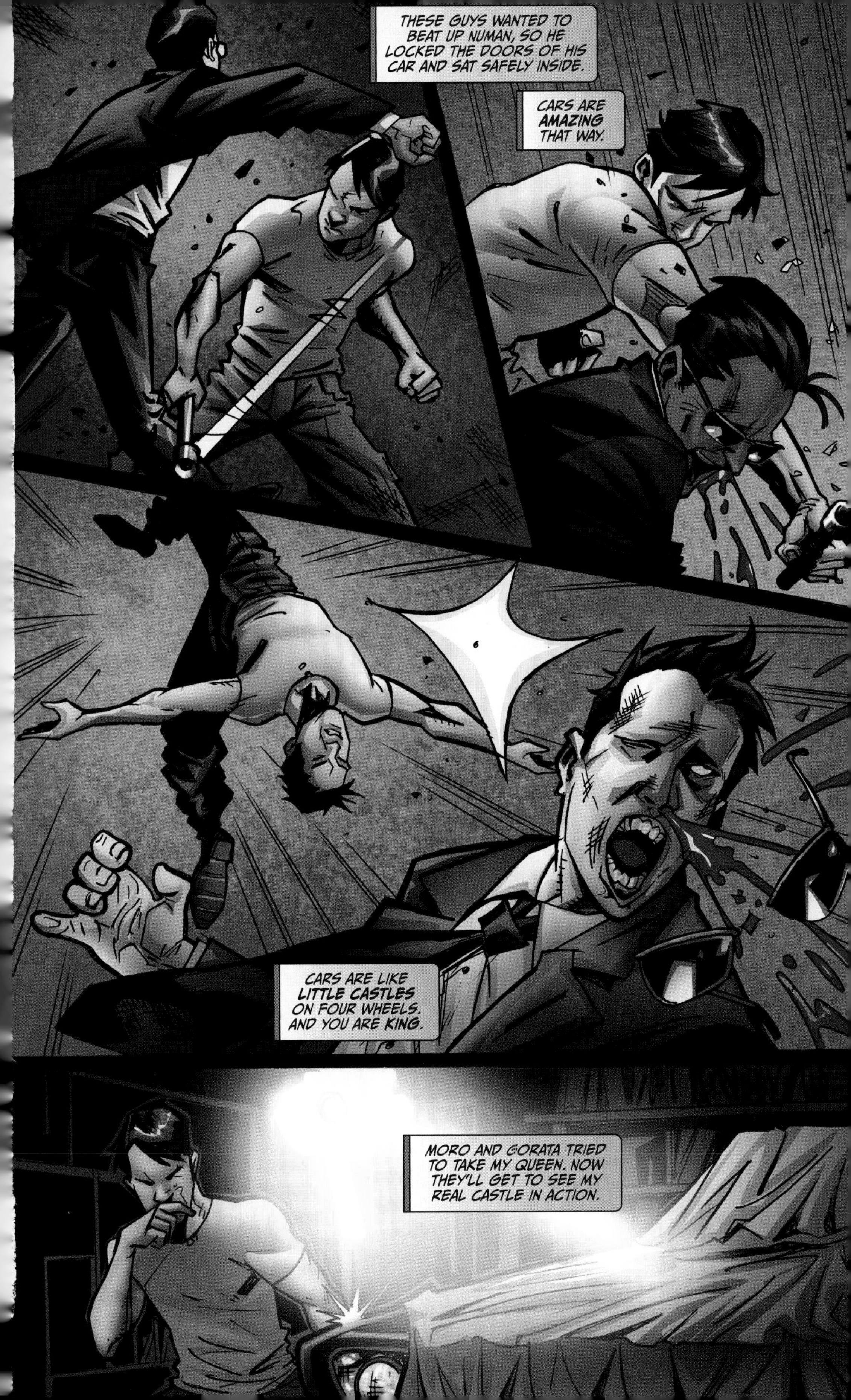
THESE GUYS WANTED TO BEAT UP NUMAN, SO HE LOCKED THE DOORS OF HIS CAR AND SAT SAFELY INSIDE.
CARS ARE AMAZING THAT WAY.
CARS ARE LIKE LITTLE CASTLES ON FOUR WHEELS. AND YOU ARE KING.
MORO AND GORATA TRIED TO TAKE MY QUEEN. NOW THEY'LL GET TO SEE MY REAL CASTLE IN ACTION.

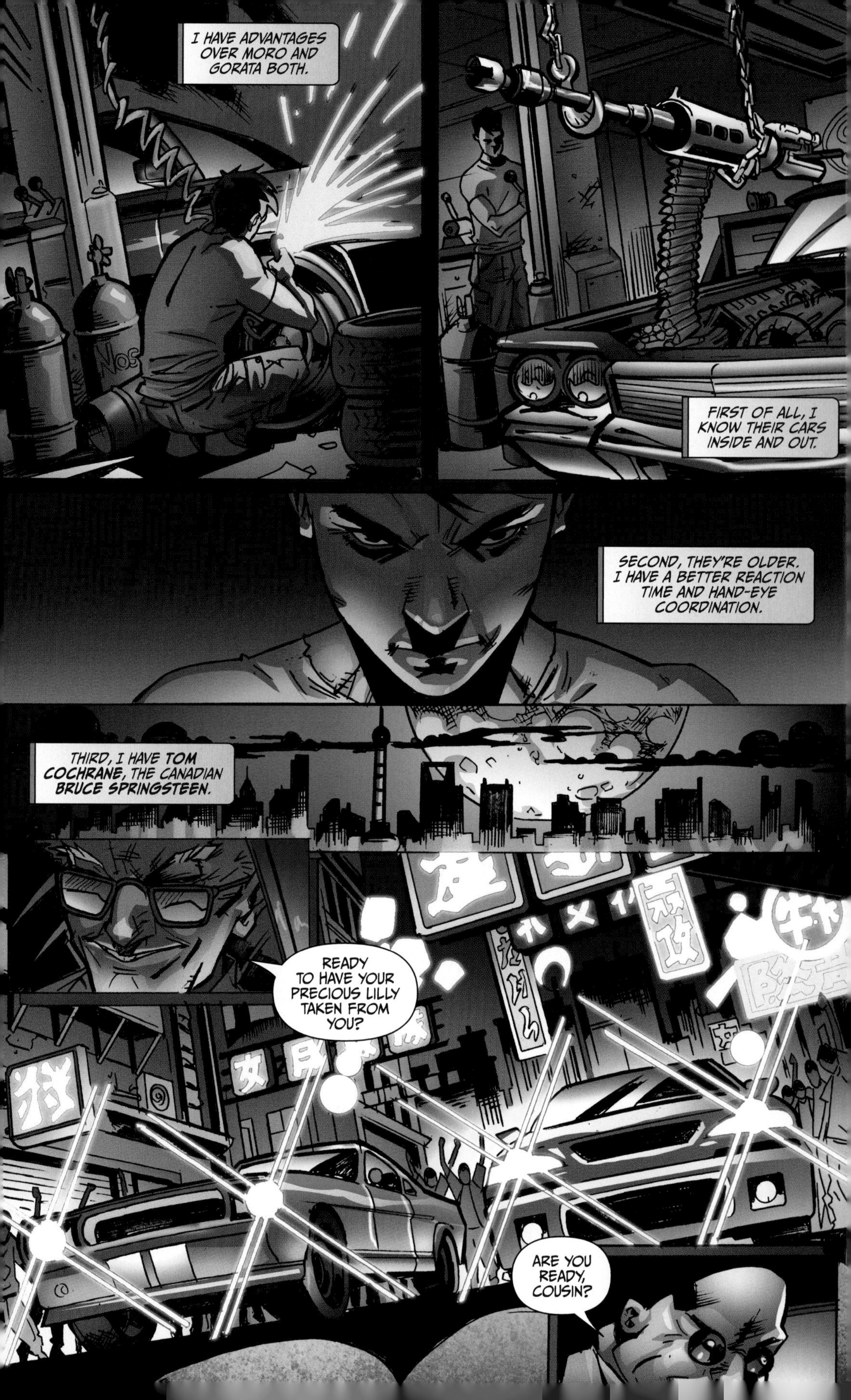
I HAVE ADVANTAGES OVER MORO AND GORATA BOTH.
FIRST OF ALL, I KNOW THEIR CARS INSIDE AND OUT.
SECOND, THEY'RE OLDER. I HAVE A BETTER REACTION TIME AND HAND-EYE COORDINATION.
THIRD, I HAVE TOM COCHRANE, THE CANADIAN BRUCE SPRINGSTEEN.
READY TO HAVE YOUR PRECIOUS LILLY TAKEN FROM YOU?
ARE YOU READY, COUSIN?

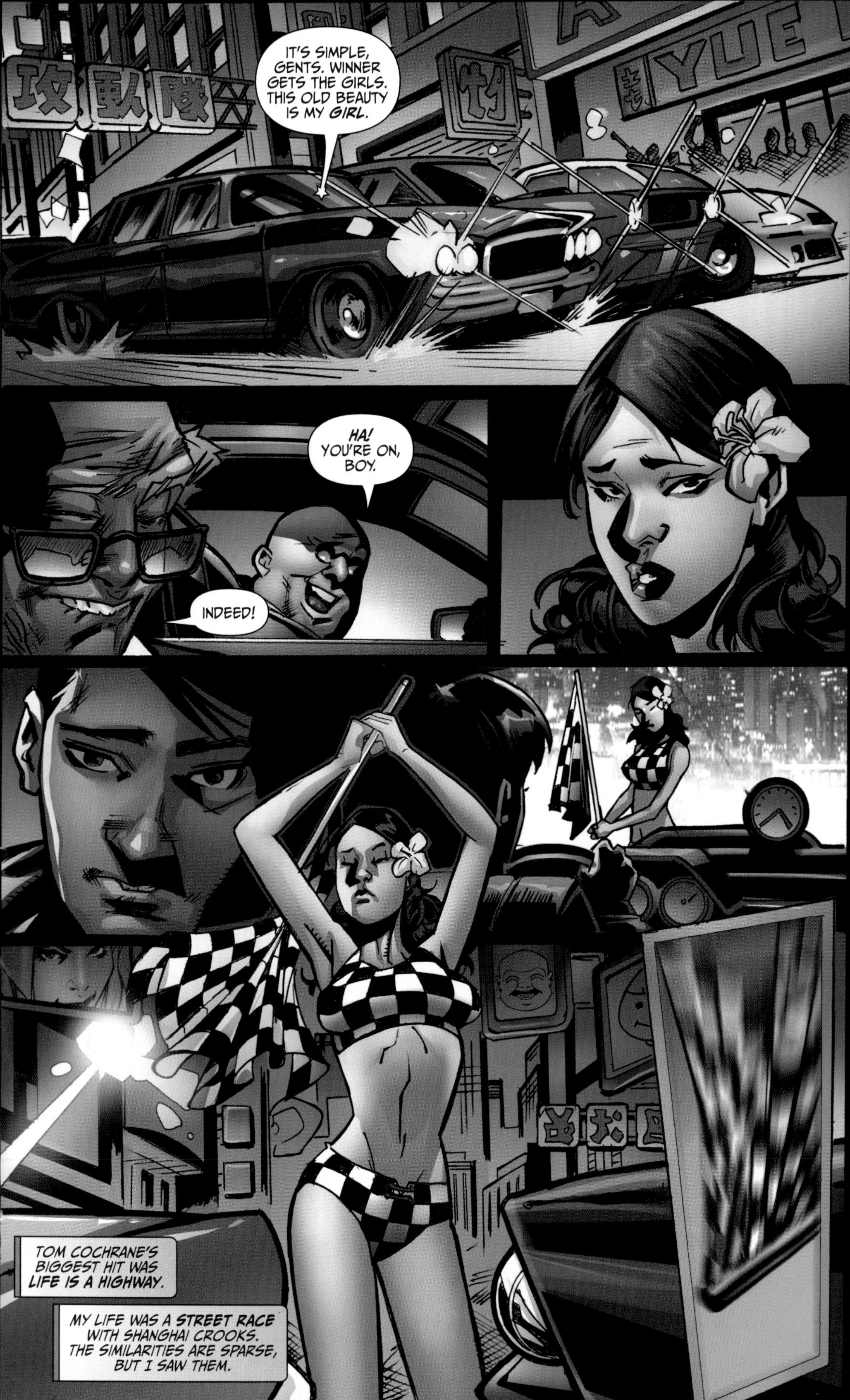
IT'S SIMPLE, GENTS. WINNER GETS THE GIRLS. THIS OLD BEAUTY IS MY GIRL.
HA! YOU'RE ON, BOY.
INDEED!
TOM COCHRANE'S BIGGEST HIT WAS LIFE IS A HIGHWAY.
MY LIFE WAS A STREET RACE WITH SHANGHAI CROOKS. THE SIMILARITIES ARE SPARSE, BUT I SAW THEM.

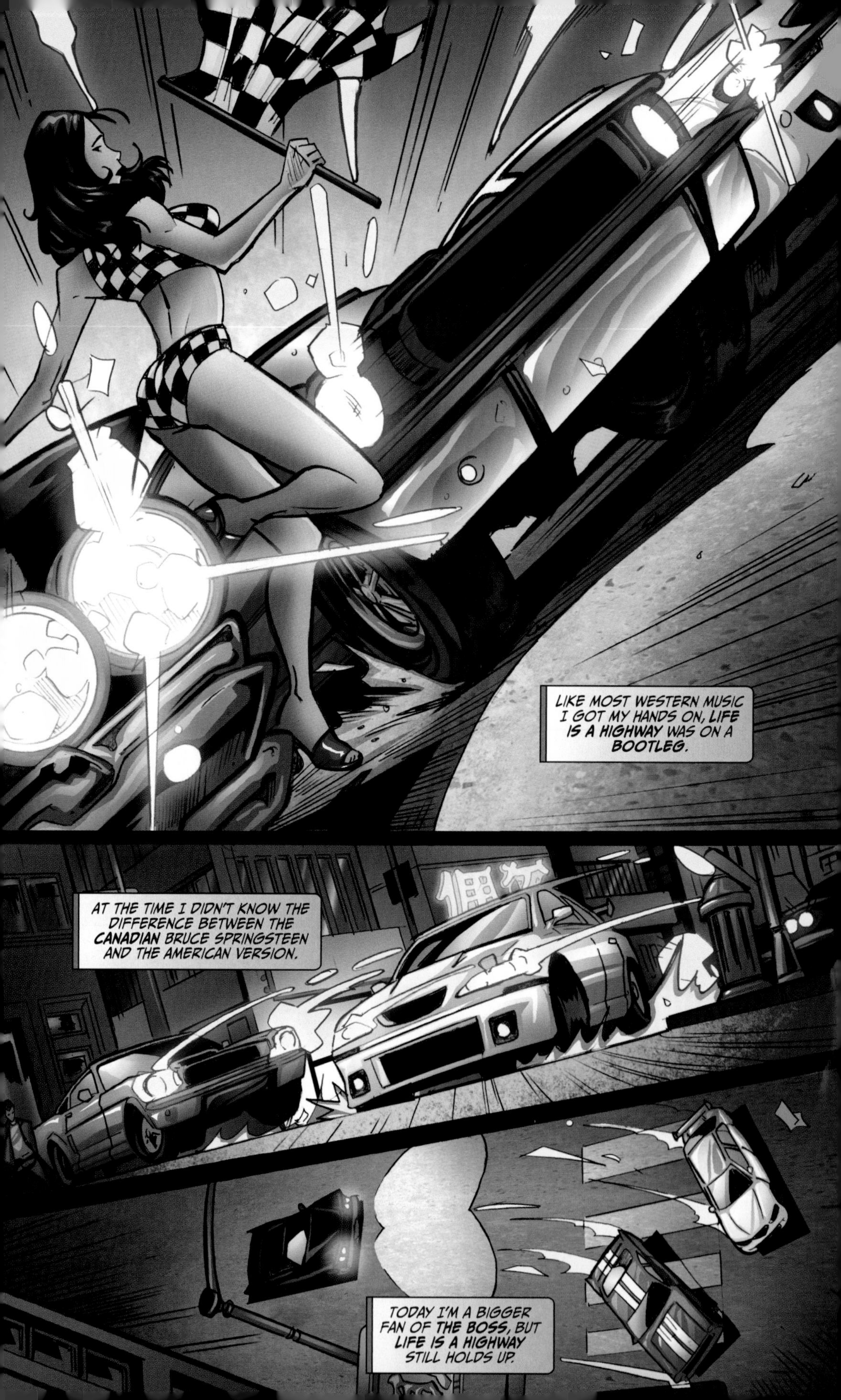
LIKE MOST WESTERN MUSIC I GOT MY HANDS ON, LIFE IS A HIGHWAY WAS ON A BOOTLEG.
AT THE TIME I DIDN'T KNOW THE DIFFERENCE BETWEEN THE CANADIAN BRUCE SPRINGSTEEN AND THE AMERICAN VERSION.
TODAY I'M A BIGGER FAN OF THE BOSS, BUT LIFE IS A HIGHWAY STILL HOLDS UP.

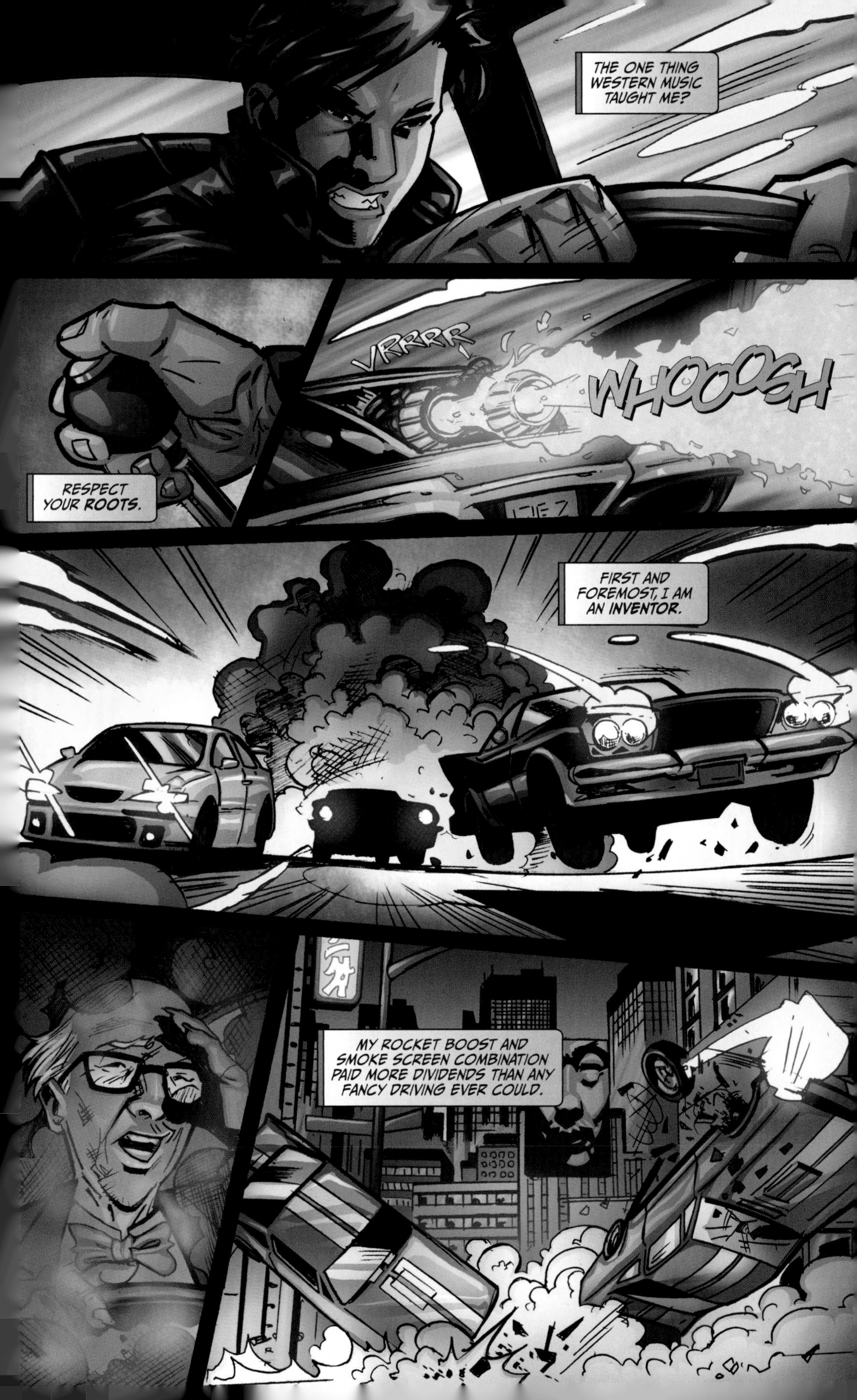
THE ONE THING WESTERN MUSIC TAUGHT ME?
RESPECT YOUR ROOTS.
VRRRR
WHOOOOSH
FIRST AND FOREMOST, I AM AN INVENTOR.
MY ROCKET BOOST AND SMOKE SCREEN COMBINATION PAID MORE DIVIDENDS THAN ANY FANCY DRIVING EVER COULD.

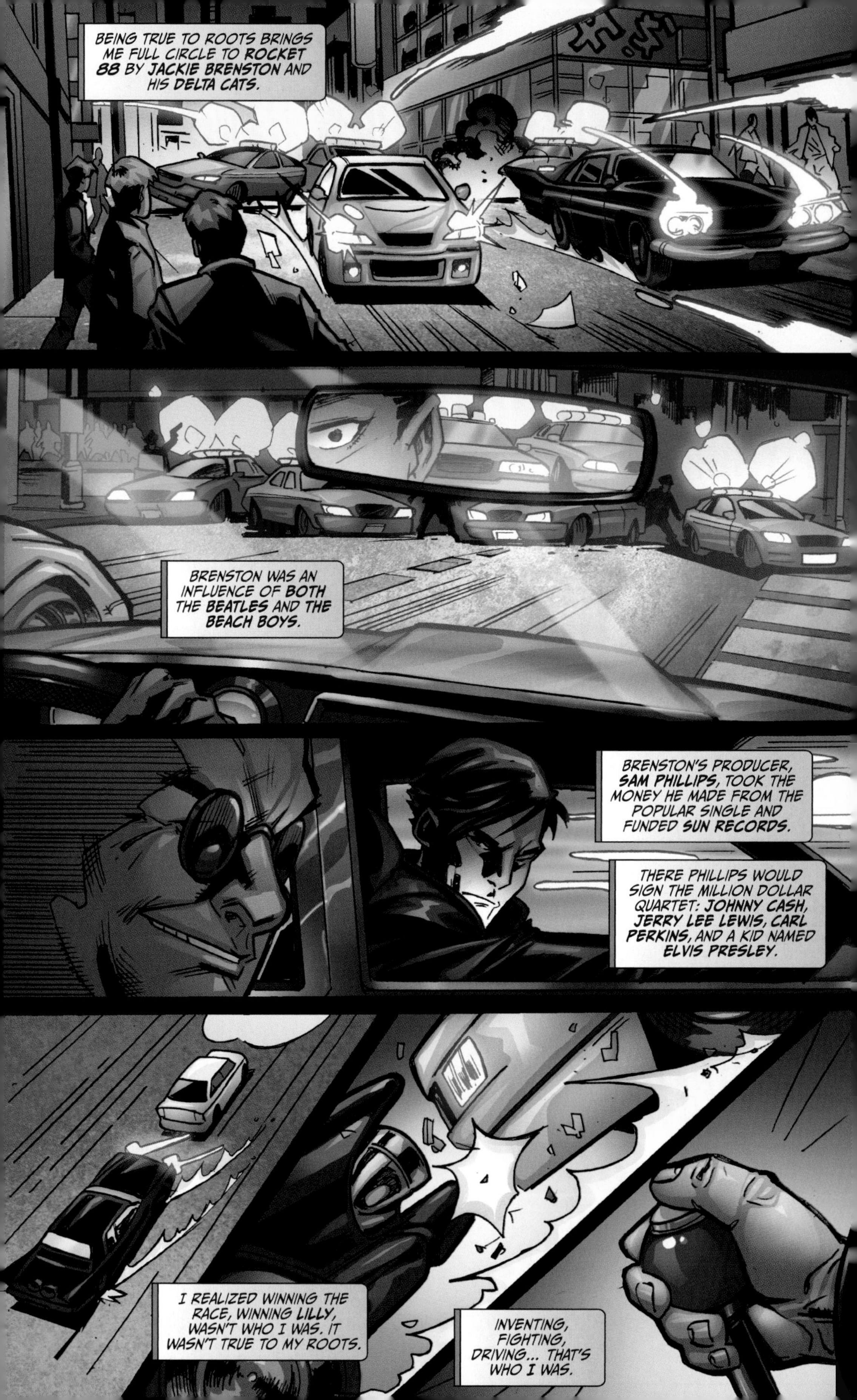
BEING TRUE TO ROOTS BRINGS ME FULL CIRCLE TO ROCKET 88 BY JACKIE BRENSTON AND HIS DELTA CATS.
BRENSTON WAS AN INFLUENCE OF BOTH THE BEATLES AND THE BEACH BOYS.
BRENSTON'S PRODUCER, SAM PHILLIPS, TOOK THE MONEY HE MADE FROM THE POPULAR SINGLE AND FUNDED SUN RECORDS.
THERE PHILLIPS WOULD SIGN THE MILLION DOLLAR QUARTET: JOHNNY CASH, JERRY LEE LEWIS, CARL PERKINS, AND A KID NAMED ELVIS PRESLEY.
I REALIZED WINNING THE RACE, WINNING LILLY, WASN'T WHO I WAS. IT WASN'T TRUE TO MY ROOTS.
INVENTING, FIGHTING, DRIVING... THAT'S WHO I WAS.

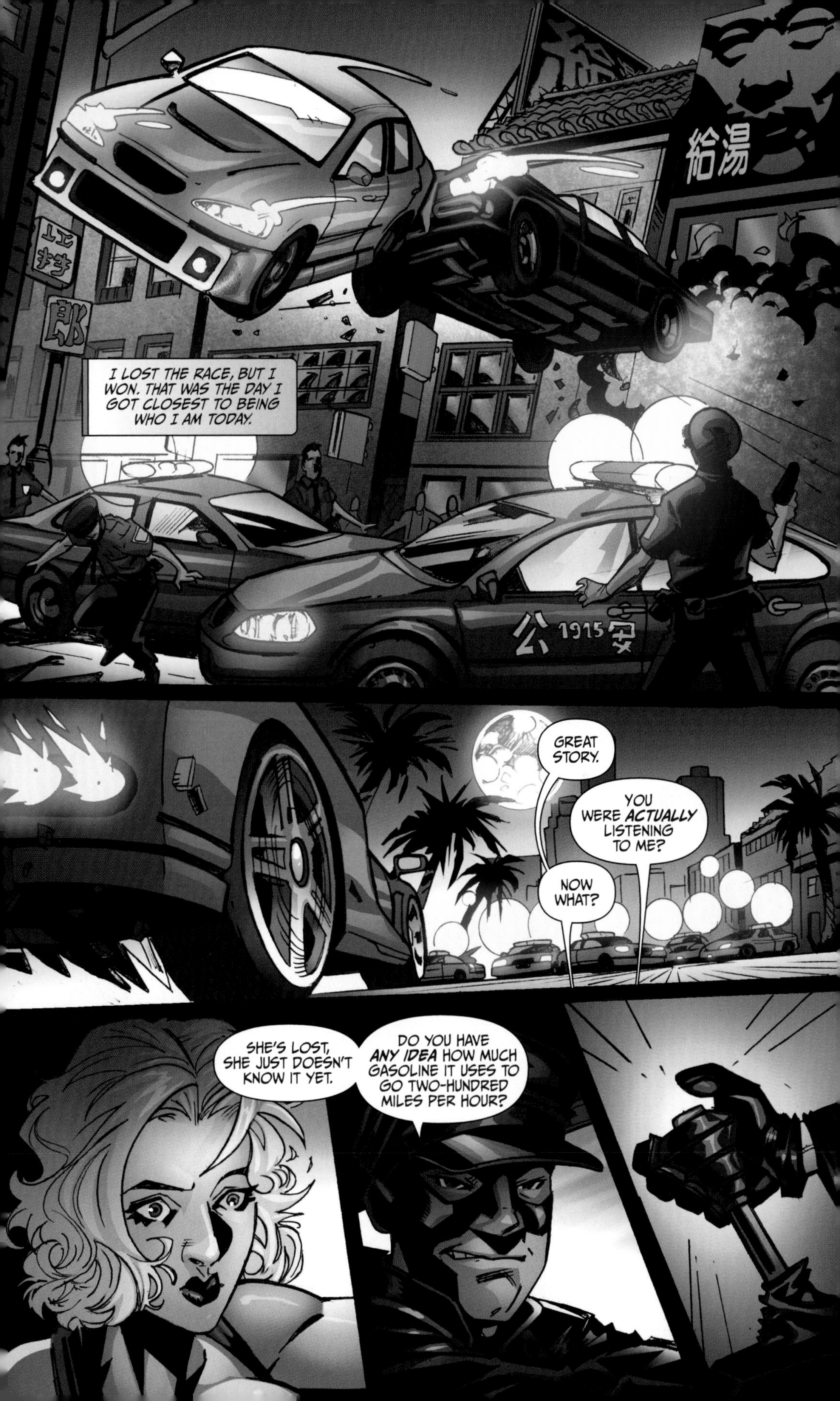

給湯
I LOST THE RACE, BUT I WON. THAT WAS THE DAY I GOT CLOSEST TO BEING WHO I AM TODAY.
公 1915 安
GREAT STORY.
YOU WERE ACTUALLY LISTENING TO ME?
NOW WHAT?
SHE'S LOST, SHE JUST DOESN'T KNOW IT YET.
DO YOU HAVE ANY IDEA HOW MUCH GASOLINE IT USES TO GO TWO-HUNDRED MILES PER HOUR?

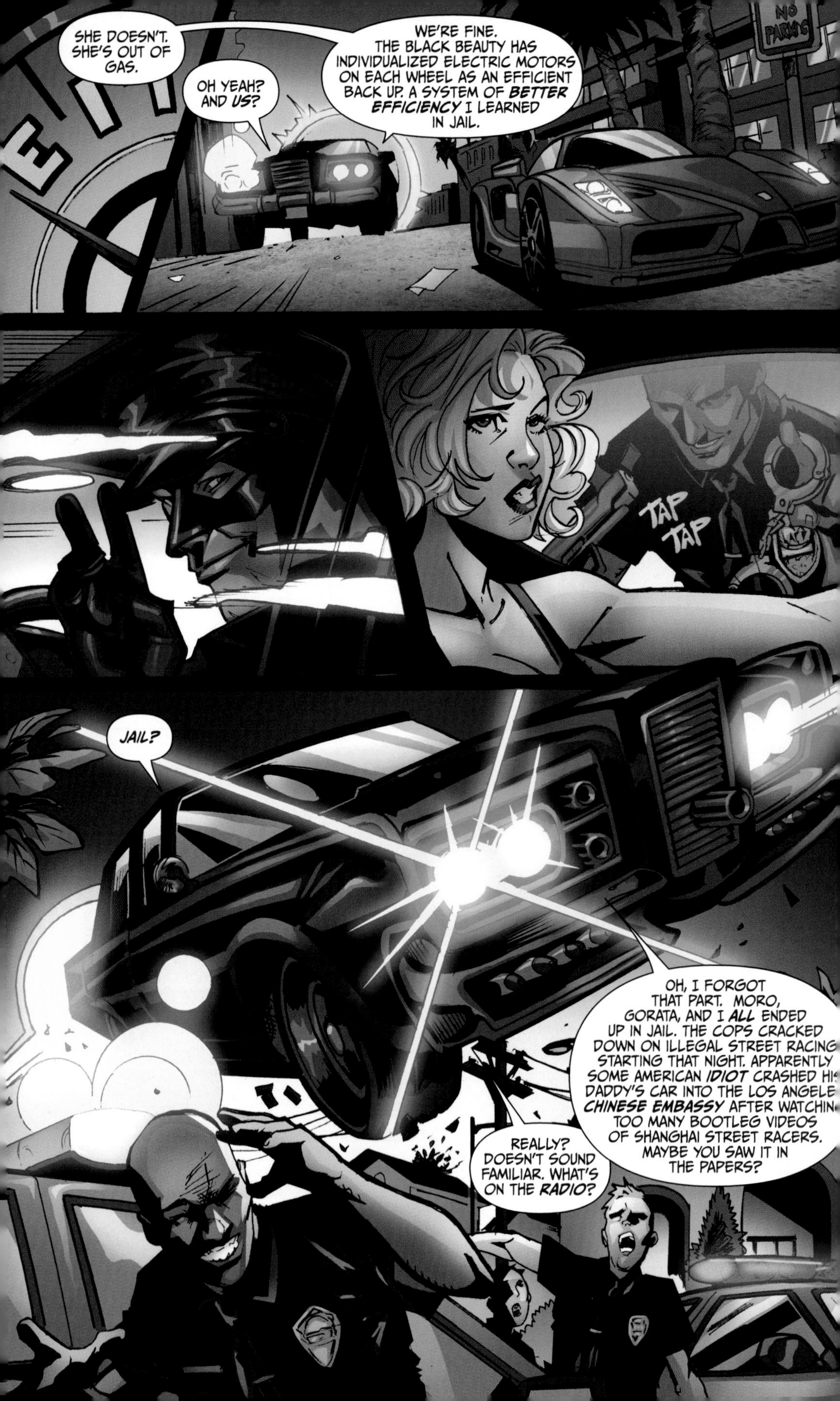
SHE DOESN'T. SHE'S OUT OF GAS.
OH YEAH? AND US?
WE'RE FINE. THE BLACK BEAUTY HAS INDIVIDUALIZED ELECTRIC MOTORS ON EACH WHEEL AS AN EFFICIENT BACK UP. A SYSTEM OF BETTER EFFICIENCY I LEARNED IN JAIL.
NO PARKING
TAP TAP
JAIL?
OH, I FORGOT THAT PART. MORO, GORATA, AND I ALL ENDED UP IN JAIL. THE COPS CRACKED DOWN ON ILLEGAL STREET RACING STARTING THAT NIGHT. APPARENTLY SOME AMERICAN IDIOT CRASHED HI DADDY'S CAR INTO THE LOS ANGELE CHINESE EMBASSY AFTER WATCHIN TOO MANY BOOTLEG VIDEOS OF SHANGHAI STREET RACERS. MAYBE YOU SAW IT IN THE PAPERS?
REALLY? DOESN'T SOUND FAMILIAR. WHAT'S ON THE RADIO?

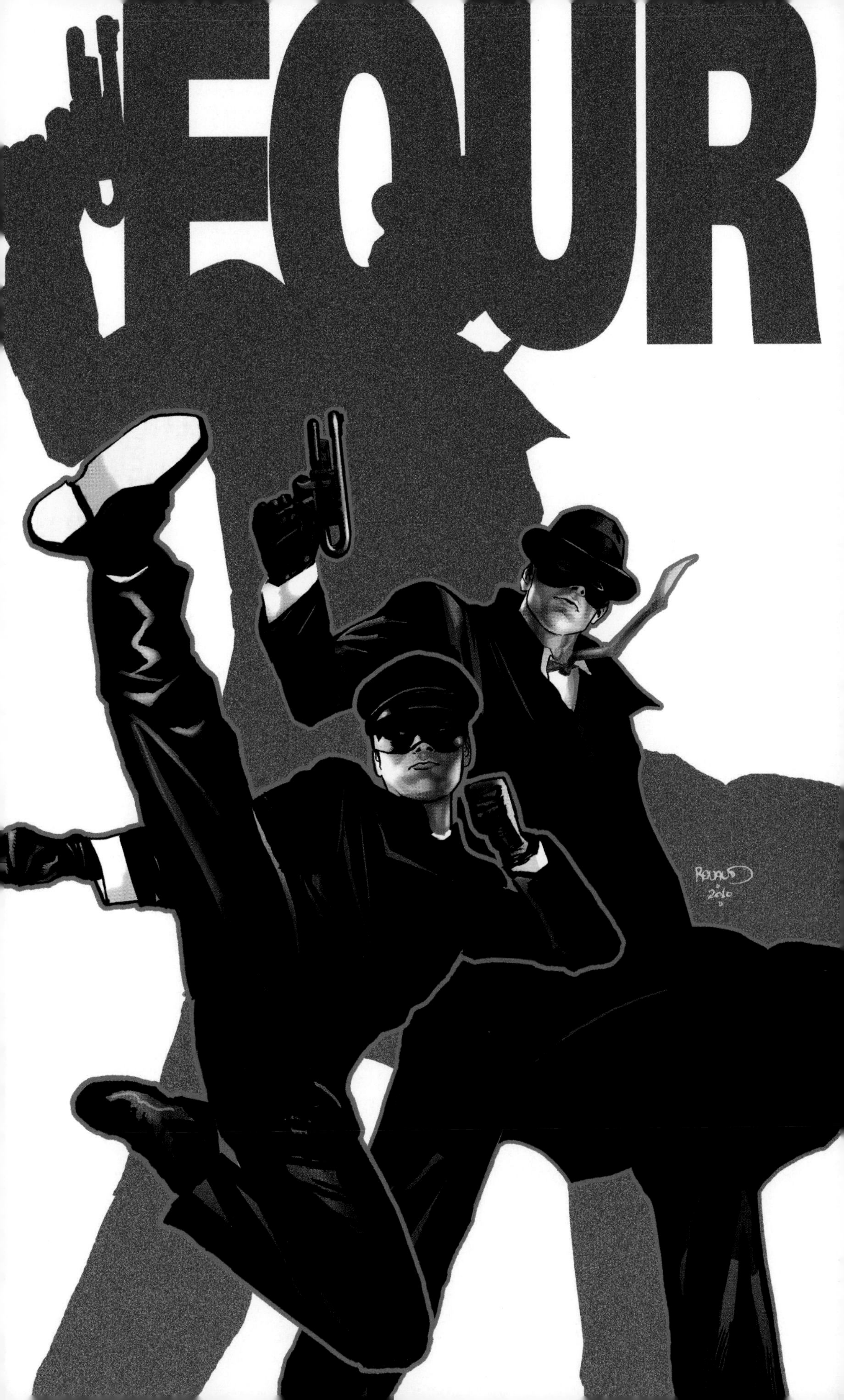
FOUR

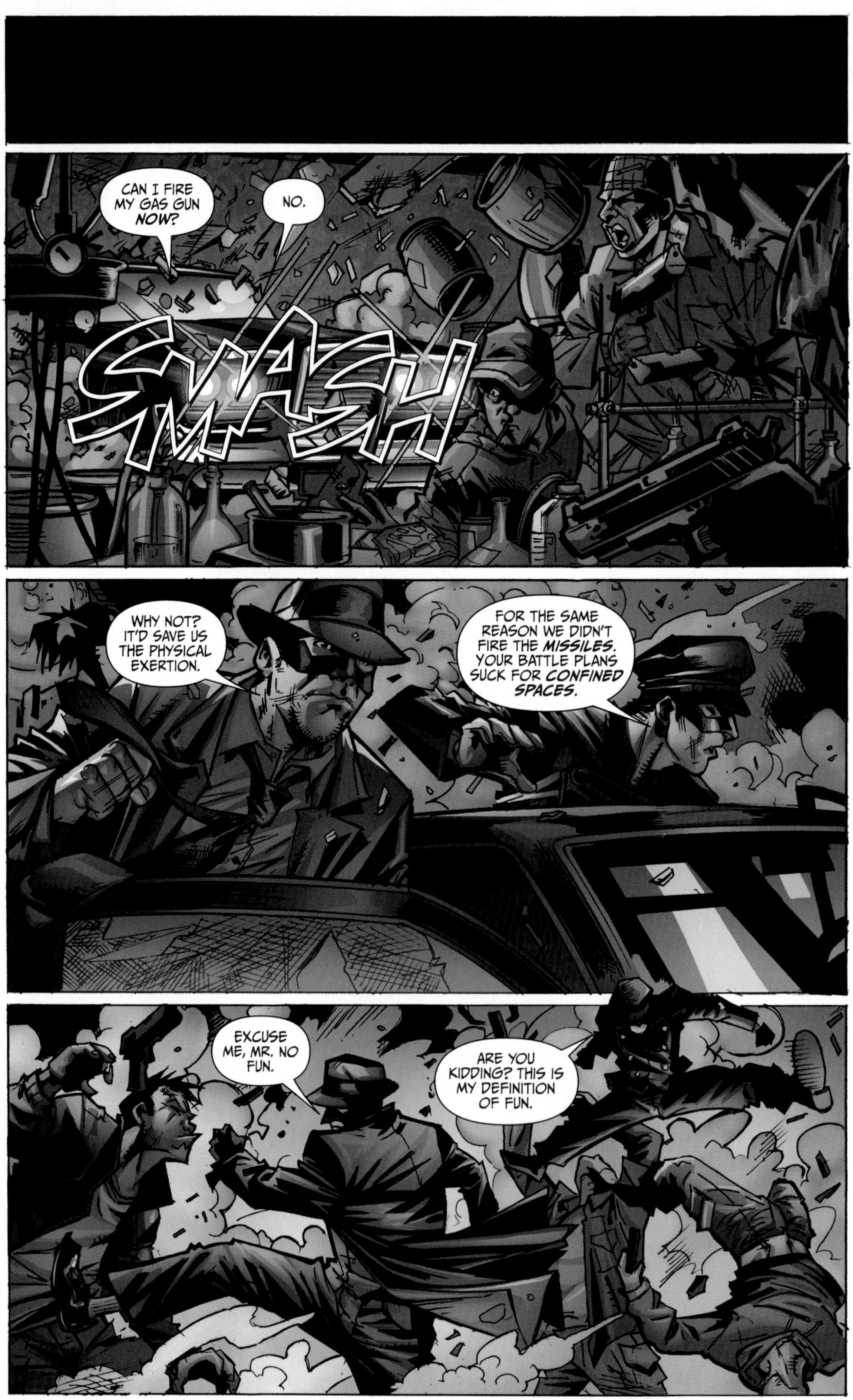
CAN I FIRE MY GAS GUN NOW?
NO.
SMASH
WHY NOT? IT'D SAVE US THE PHYSICAL EXERTION.
FOR THE SAME REASON WE DIDN'T FIRE THE MISSILES. YOUR BATTLE PLANS SUCK FOR CONFINED SPACES.
EXCUSE ME, MR. NO FUN.
ARE YOU KIDDING? THIS IS MY DEFINITION OF FUN.

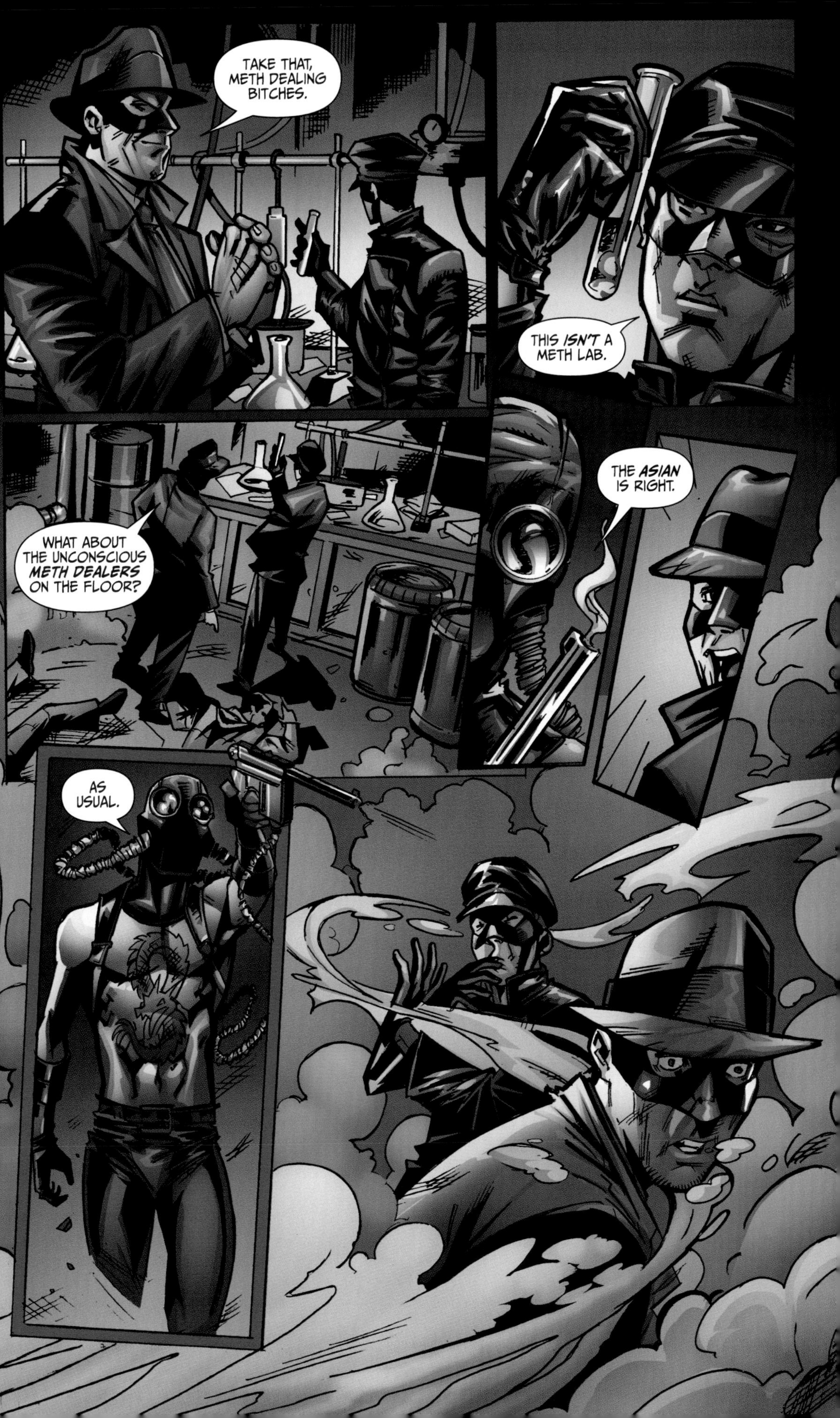
TAKE THAT, METH DEALING BITCHES.
THIS *ISN'T* A METH LAB.
WHAT ABOUT THE UNCONSCIOUS *METH DEALERS* ON THE FLOOR?
THE *ASIAN* IS RIGHT.
AS USUAL.

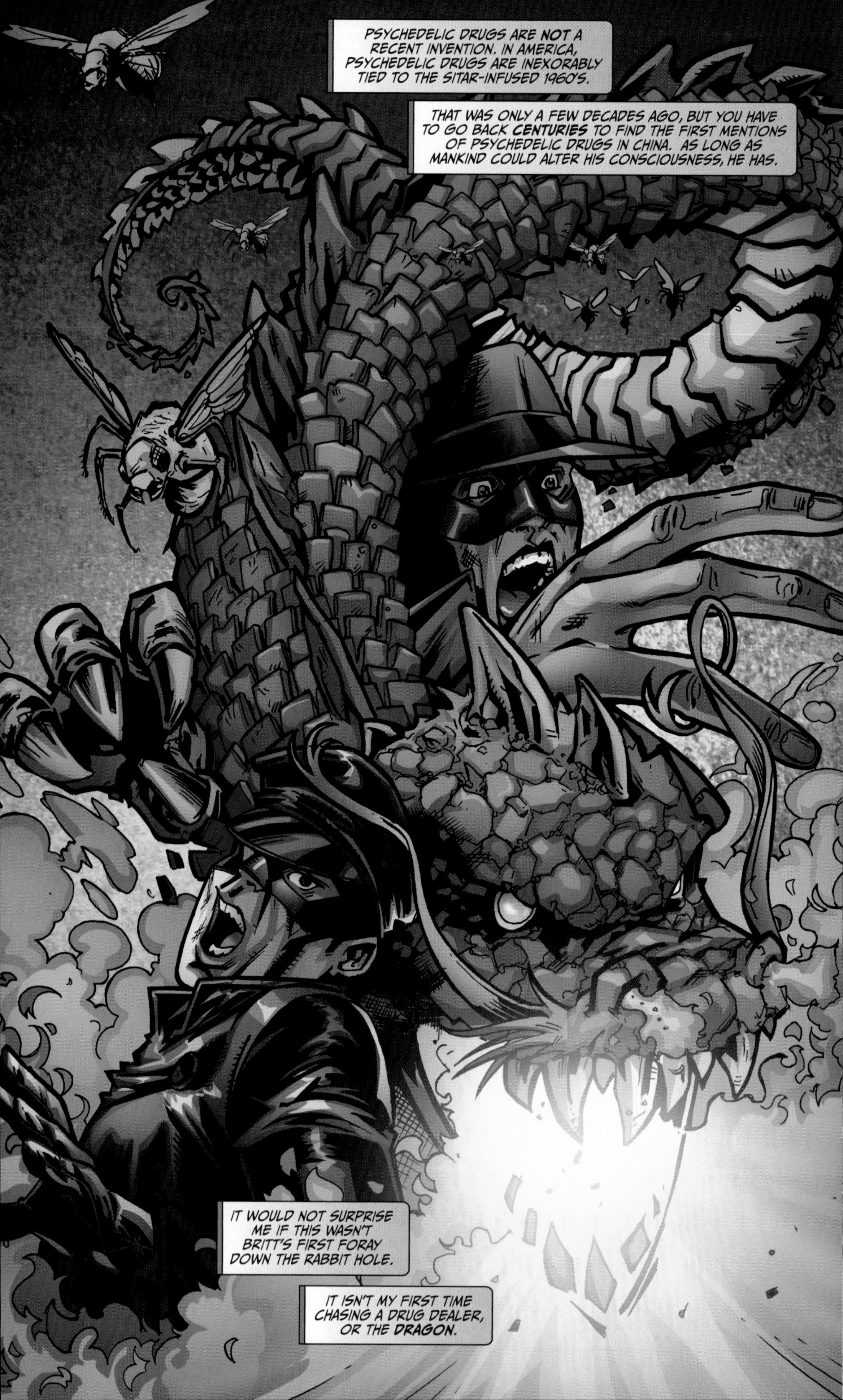
PSYCHEDELIC DRUGS ARE NOT A RECENT INVENTION. IN AMERICA, PSYCHEDELIC DRUGS ARE INEXORABLY TIED TO THE SITAR-INFUSED 1960'S.
THAT WAS ONLY A FEW DECADES AGO, BUT YOU HAVE TO GO BACK CENTURIES TO FIND THE FIRST MENTIONS OF PSYCHEDELIC DRUGS IN CHINA. AS LONG AS MANKIND COULD ALTER HIS CONSCIOUSNESS, HE HAS.
IT WOULD NOT SURPRISE ME IF THIS WASN'T BRITT'S FIRST FORAY DOWN THE RABBIT HOLE.
IT ISN'T MY FIRST TIME CHASING A DRUG DEALER, OR THE DRAGON.

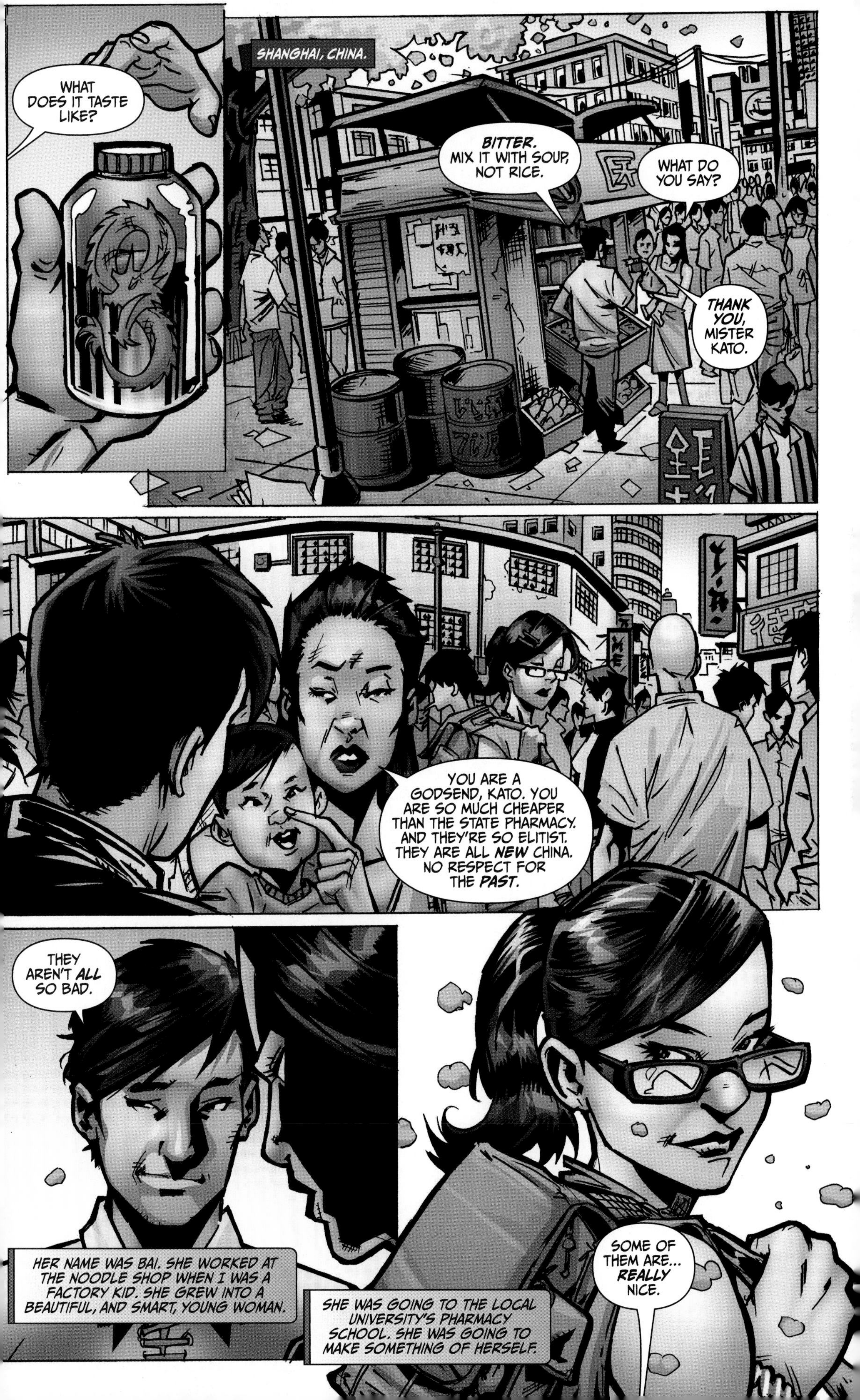

WHAT DOES IT TASTE LIKE?
SHANGHAI, CHINA.
BITTER. MIX IT WITH SOUP, NOT RICE.
WHAT DO YOU SAY?
THANK YOU, MISTER KATO.
YOU ARE A GODSEND, KATO. YOU ARE SO MUCH CHEAPER THAN THE STATE PHARMACY. AND THEY'RE SO ELITIST. THEY ARE ALL NEW CHINA. NO RESPECT FOR THE PAST.
THEY AREN'T ALL SO BAD.
HER NAME WAS BAI. SHE WORKED AT THE NOODLE SHOP WHEN I WAS A FACTORY KID. SHE GREW INTO A BEAUTIFUL, AND SMART, YOUNG WOMAN.
SHE WAS GOING TO THE LOCAL UNIVERSITY'S PHARMACY SCHOOL. SHE WAS GOING TO MAKE SOMETHING OF HERSELF.
SOME OF THEM ARE... REALLY NICE.

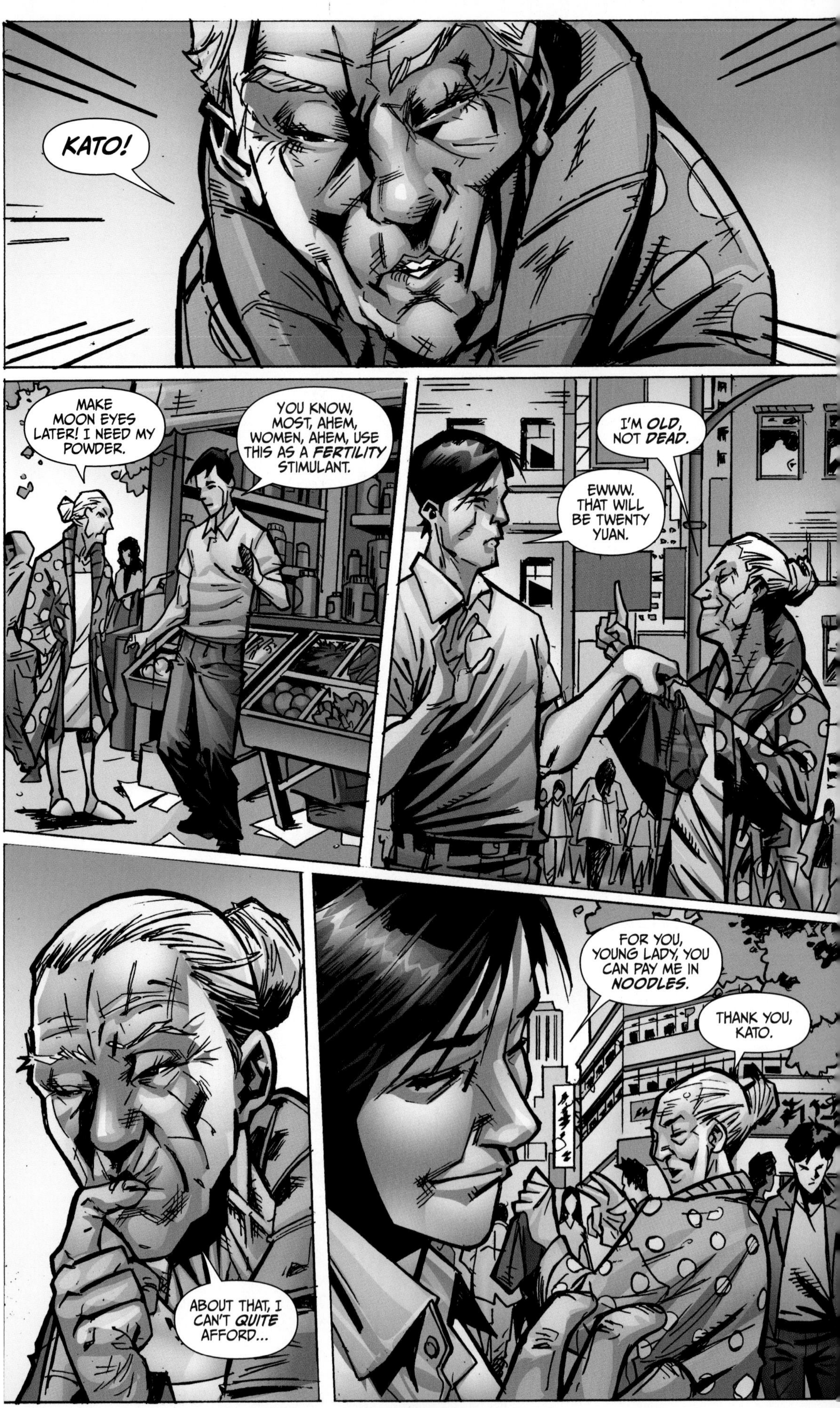
KATO!
MAKE MOON EYES LATER! I NEED MY POWDER.
YOU KNOW, MOST, AHEM, WOMEN, AHEM, USE THIS AS A *FERTILITY* STIMULANT.
I'M *OLD*, NOT *DEAD*.
EWWW. THAT WILL BE TWENTY YUAN.
ABOUT THAT, I CAN'T *QUITE* AFFORD...
FOR YOU, YOUNG LADY, YOU CAN PAY ME IN *NOODLES*.
THANK YOU, KATO.

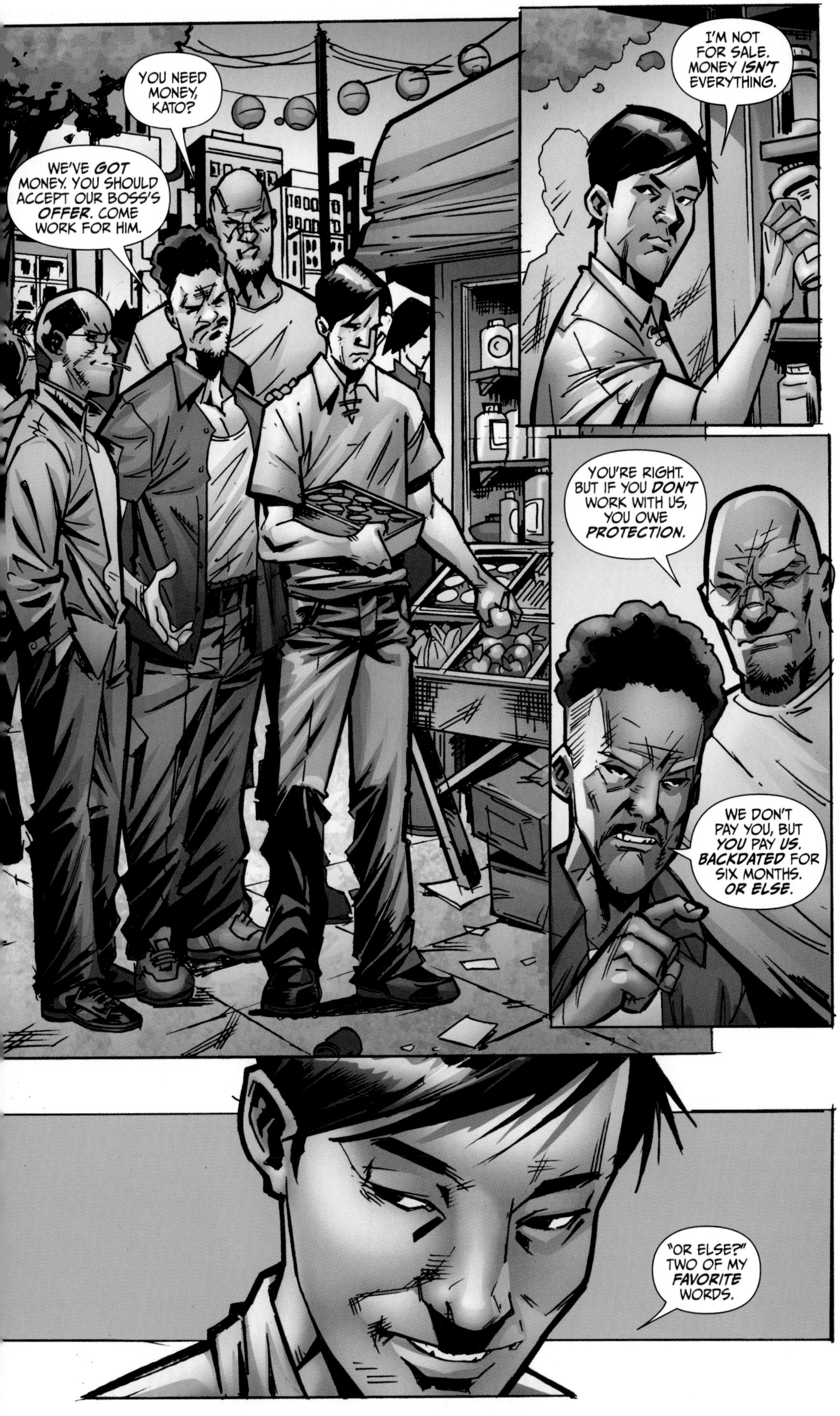
YOU NEED MONEY, KATO?
WE'VE GOT MONEY. YOU SHOULD ACCEPT OUR BOSS'S OFFER. COME WORK FOR HIM.
I'M NOT FOR SALE. MONEY ISN'T EVERYTHING.
YOU'RE RIGHT. BUT IF YOU DON'T WORK WITH US, YOU OWE PROTECTION.
WE DON'T PAY YOU, BUT YOU PAY US. BACKDATED FOR SIX MONTHS. OR ELSE.
"OR ELSE?" TWO OF MY FAVORITE WORDS.

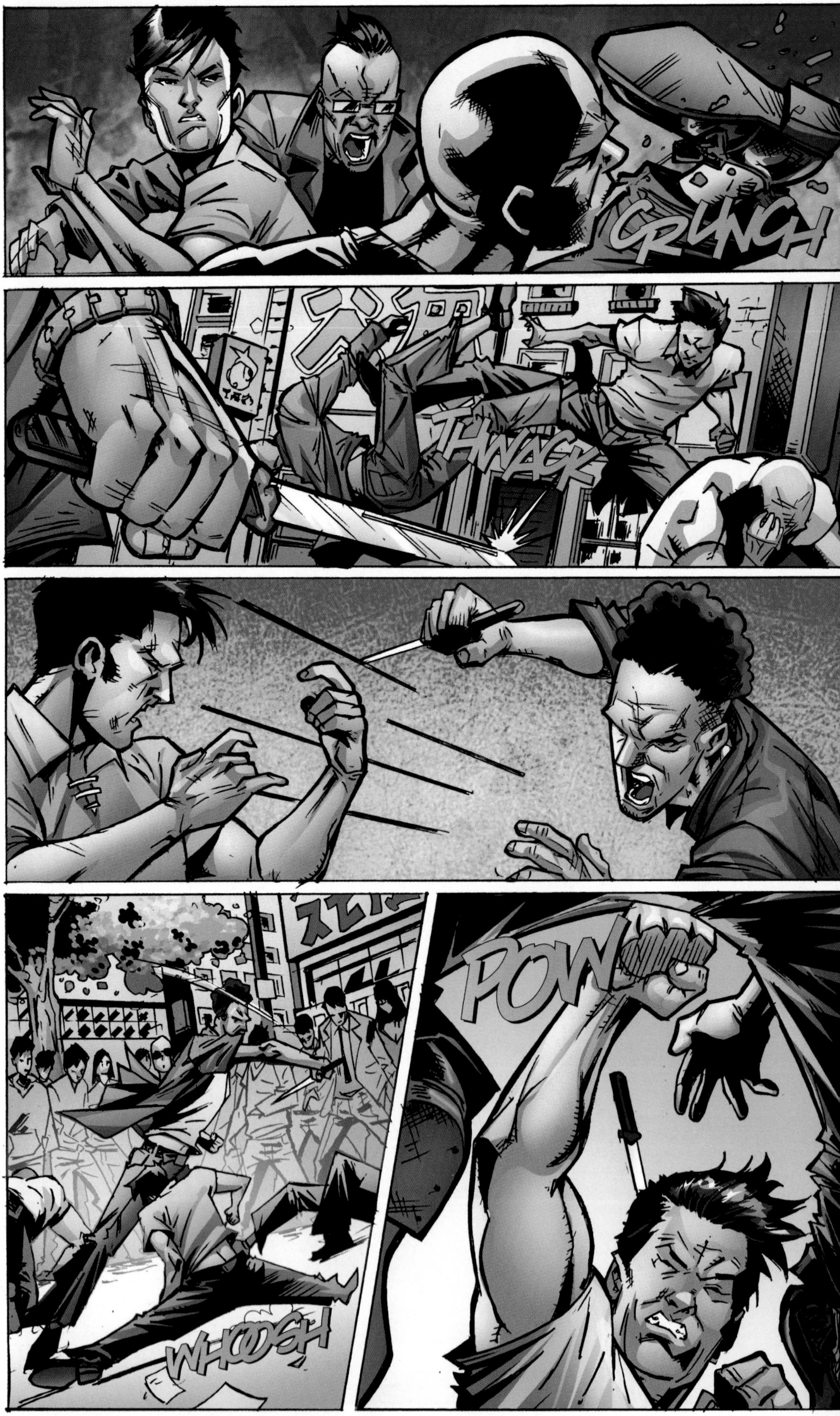
CRUNCH
THWACK
POW
WHOOSH

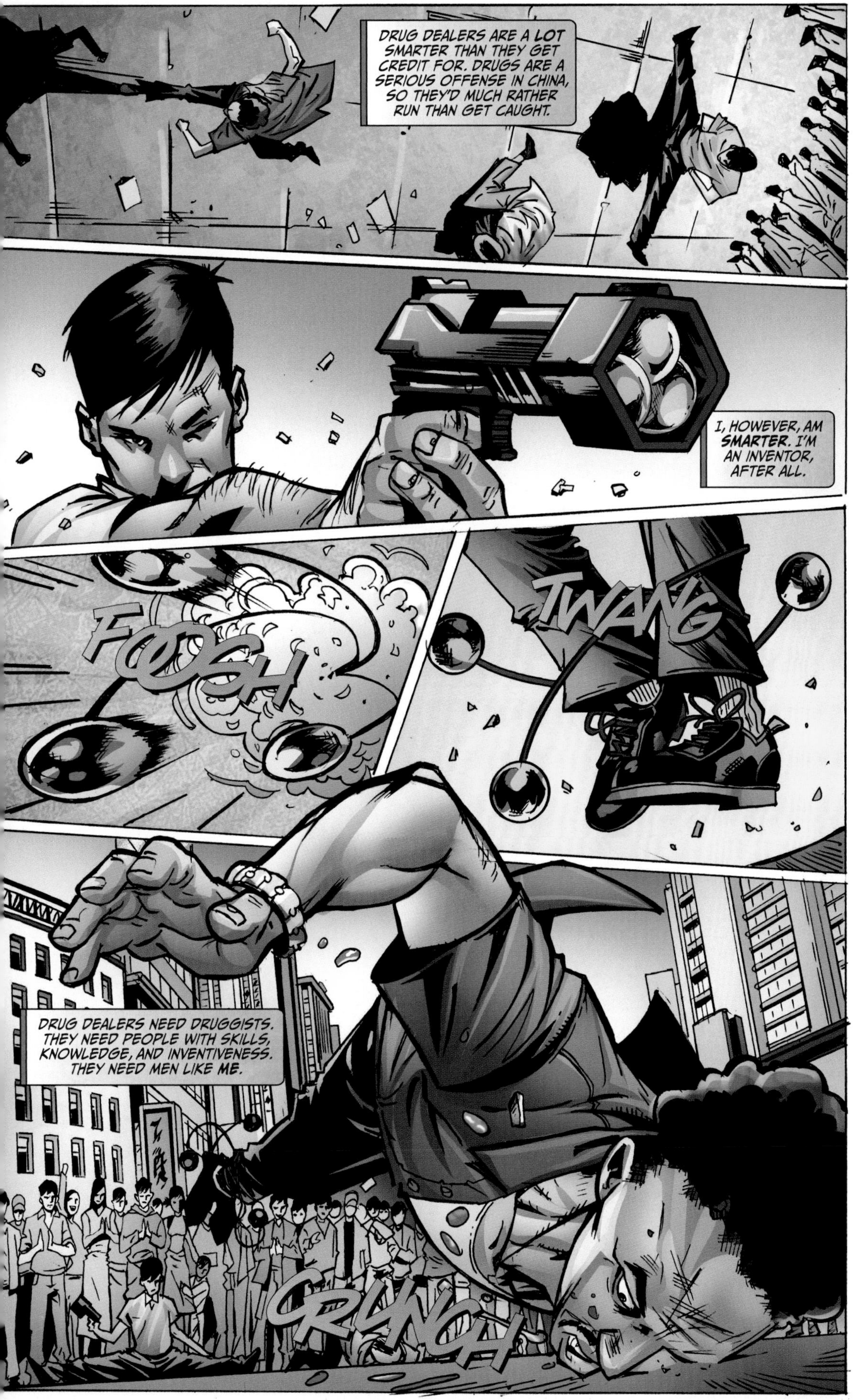
DRUG DEALERS ARE A LOT SMARTER THAN THEY GET CREDIT FOR. DRUGS ARE A SERIOUS OFFENSE IN CHINA, SO THEY'D MUCH RATHER RUN THAN GET CAUGHT.
I, HOWEVER, AM SMARTER. I'M AN INVENTOR, AFTER ALL.
FOOSH
TWANG
DRUG DEALERS NEED DRUGGISTS. THEY NEED PEOPLE WITH SKILLS, KNOWLEDGE, AND INVENTIVENESS. THEY NEED MEN LIKE ME.
CRUNCH

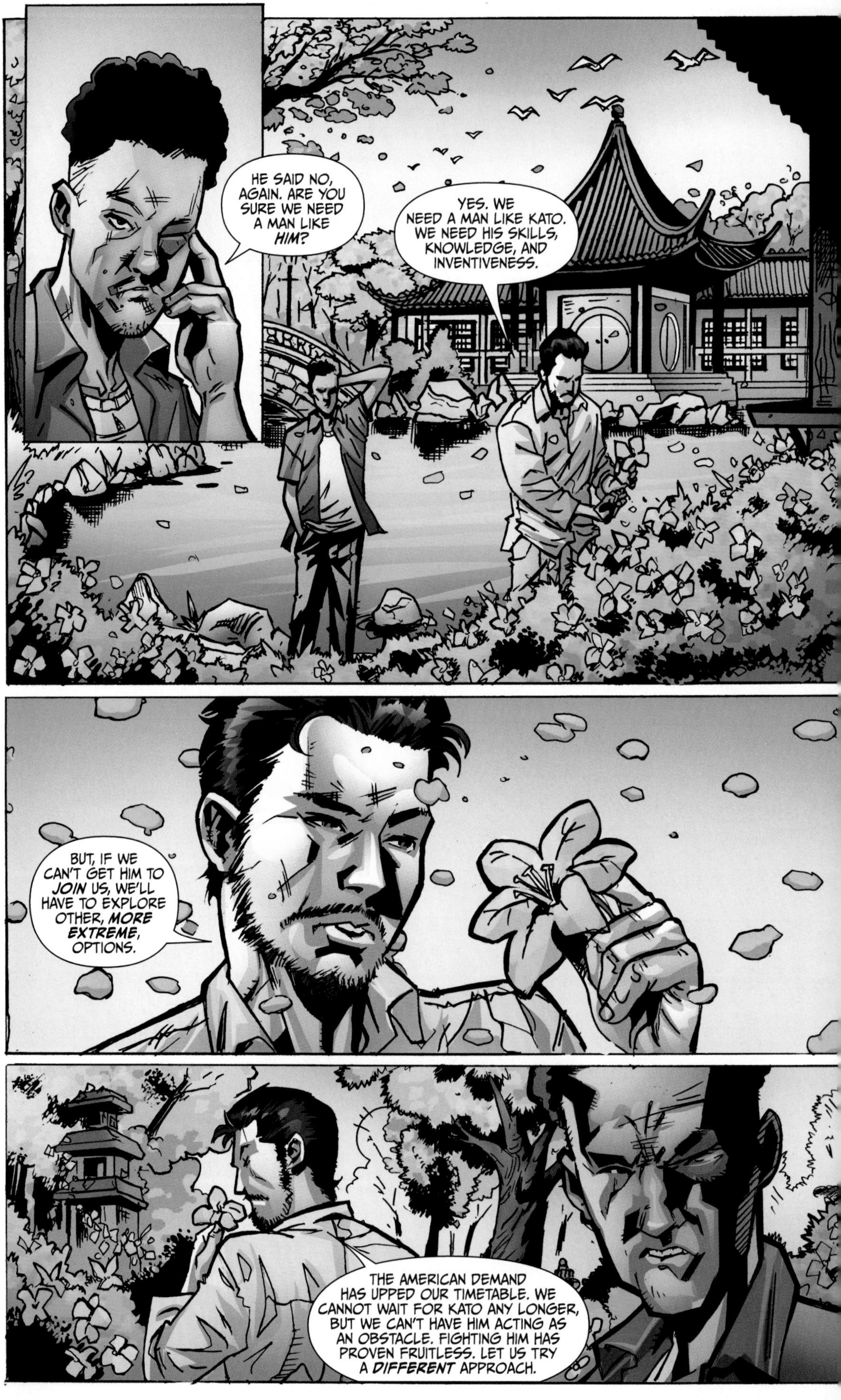
HE SAID NO, AGAIN. ARE YOU SURE WE NEED A MAN LIKE *HIM*?
YES. WE NEED A MAN LIKE KATO. WE NEED HIS SKILLS, KNOWLEDGE, AND INVENTIVENESS.
BUT, IF WE CAN'T GET HIM TO *JOIN* US, WE'LL HAVE TO EXPLORE OTHER, *MORE EXTREME*, OPTIONS.
THE AMERICAN DEMAND HAS UPPED OUR TIMETABLE. WE CANNOT WAIT FOR KATO ANY LONGER, BUT WE CAN'T HAVE HIM ACTING AS AN OBSTACLE. FIGHTING HIM HAS PROVEN FRUITLESS. LET US TRY A *DIFFERENT* APPROACH.

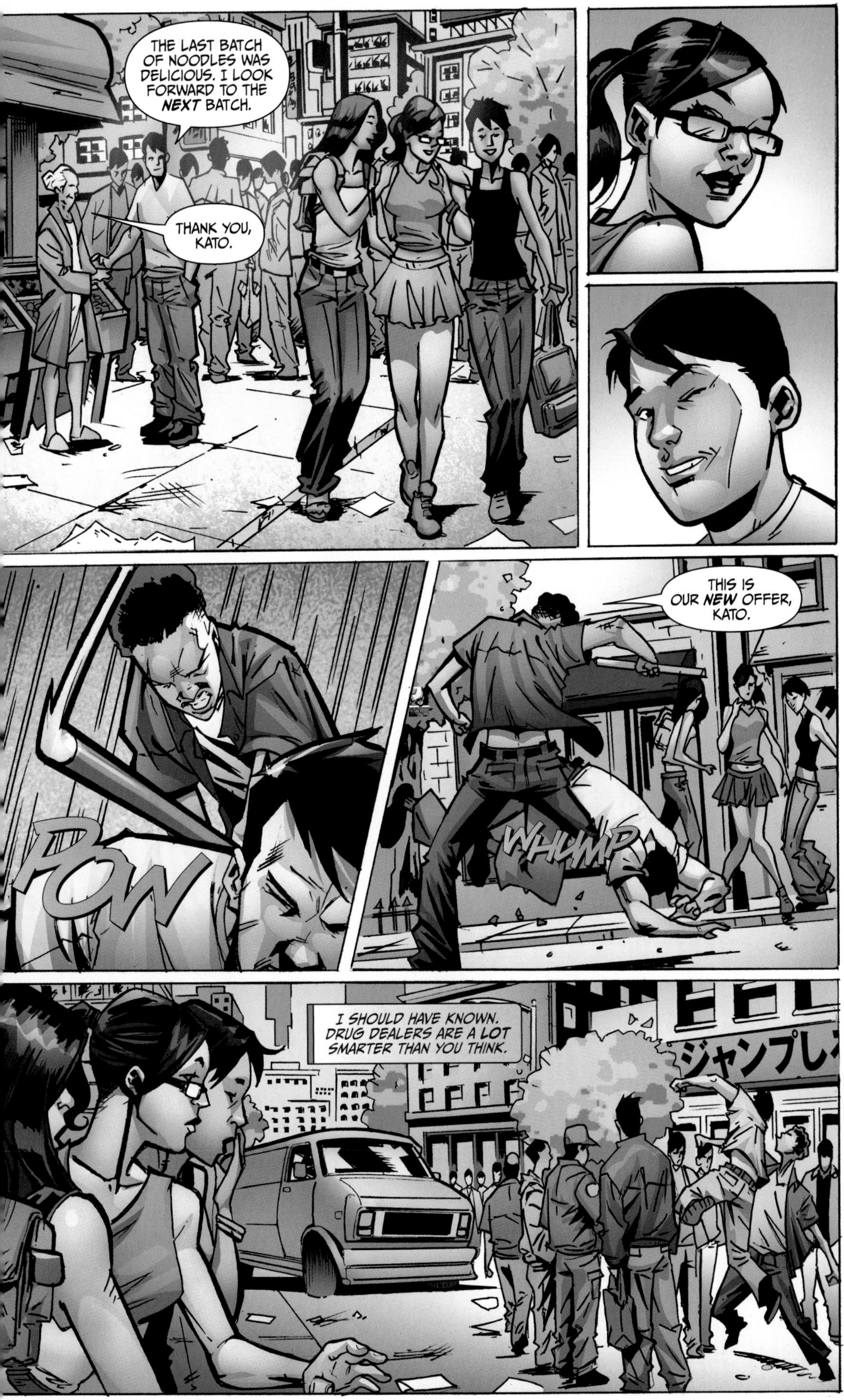
THE LAST BATCH OF NOODLES WAS DELICIOUS. I LOOK FORWARD TO THE NEXT BATCH.
THANK YOU, KATO.
POW
THIS IS OUR NEW OFFER, KATO.
WHUMP
I SHOULD HAVE KNOWN. DRUG DEALERS ARE A LOT SMARTER THAN YOU THINK.

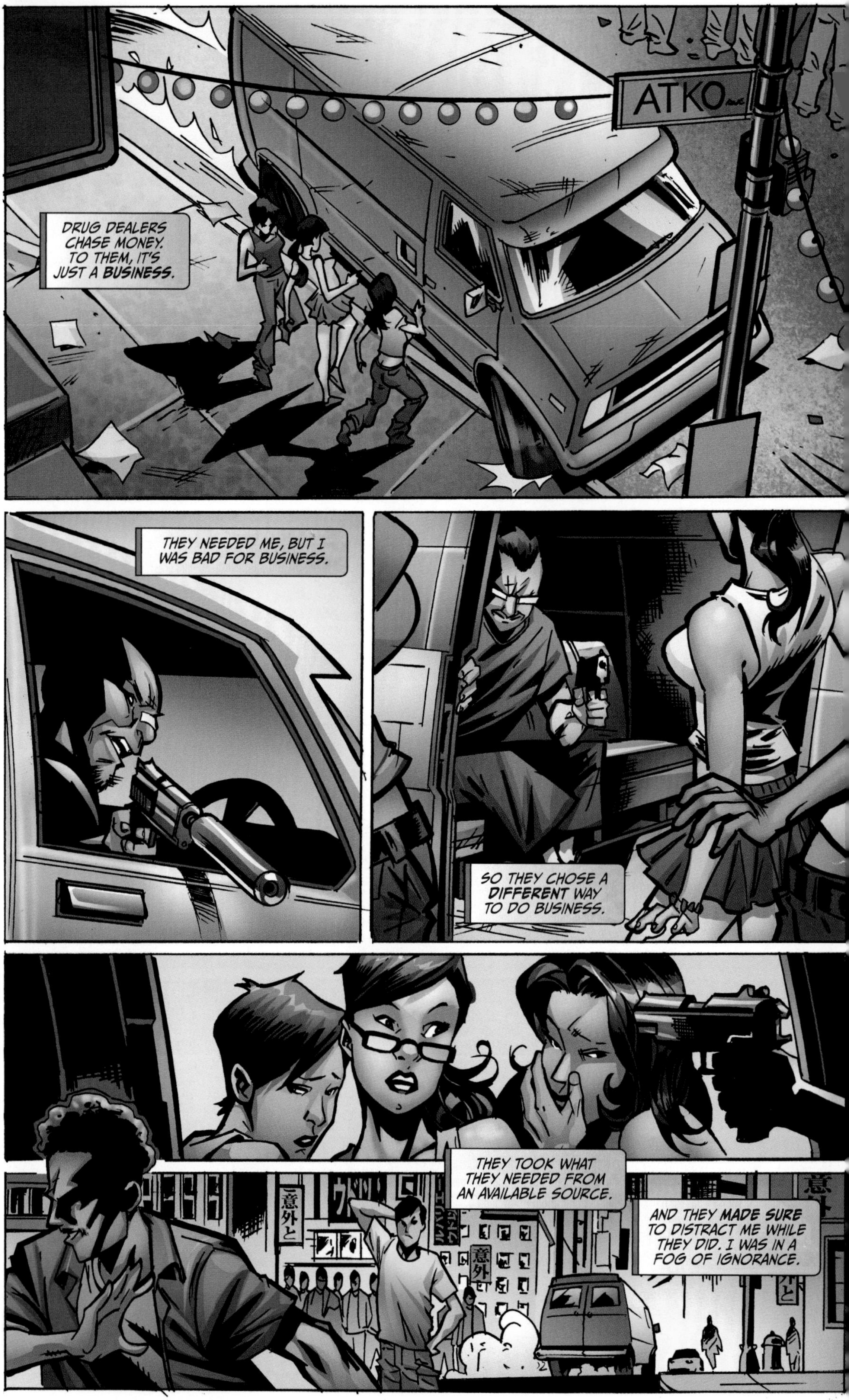
ATKO
DRUG DEALERS CHASE MONEY. TO THEM, IT'S JUST A BUSINESS.
THEY NEEDED ME, BUT I WAS BAD FOR BUSINESS.
SO THEY CHOSE A DIFFERENT WAY TO DO BUSINESS.
THEY TOOK WHAT THEY NEEDED FROM AN AVAILABLE SOURCE.
AND THEY MADE SURE TO DISTRACT ME WHILE THEY DID. I WAS IN A FOG OF IGNORANCE.

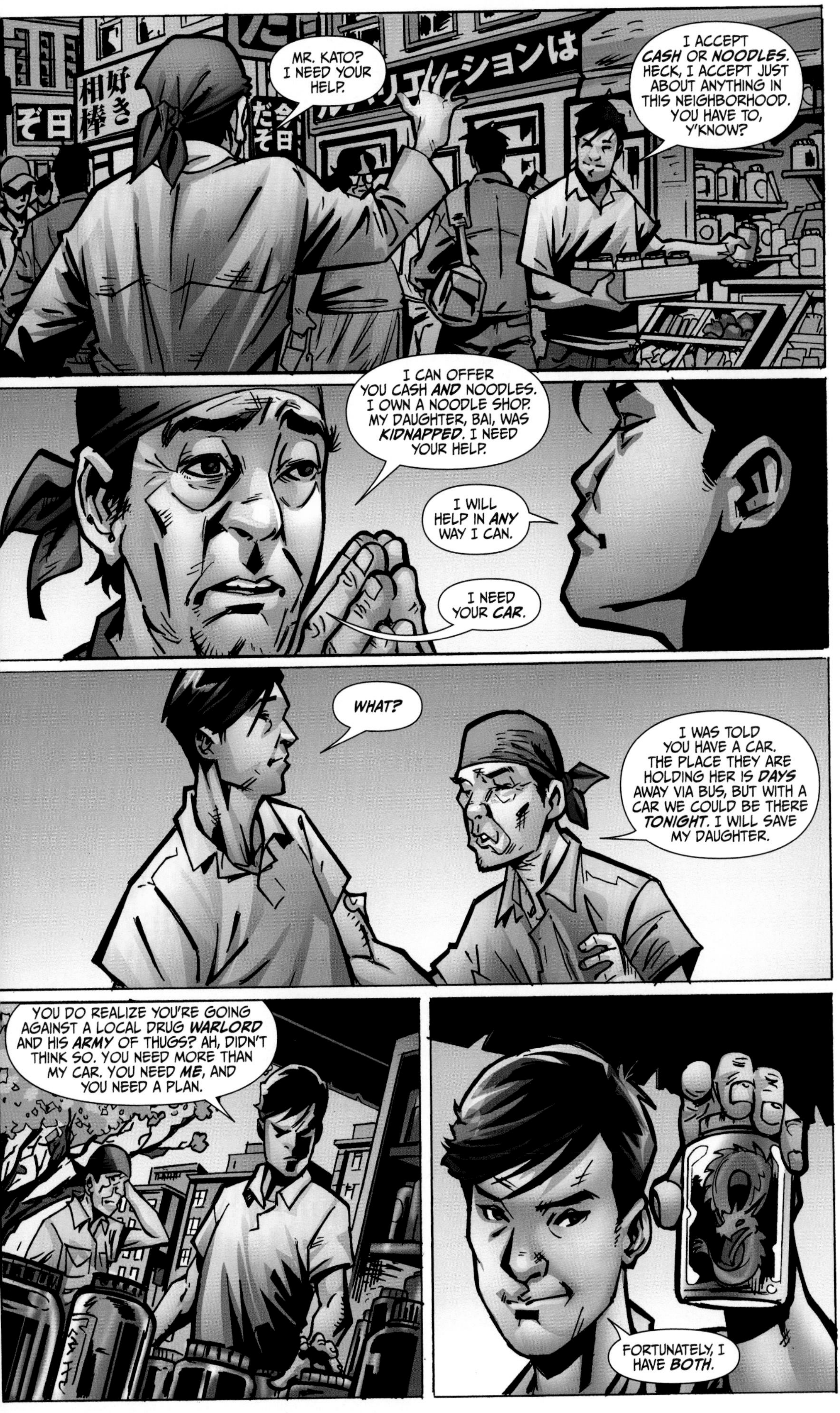
MR. KATO? I NEED YOUR HELP.
I ACCEPT CASH OR NOODLES. HECK, I ACCEPT JUST ABOUT ANYTHING IN THIS NEIGHBORHOOD. YOU HAVE TO, Y'KNOW?
I CAN OFFER YOU CASH AND NOODLES. I OWN A NOODLE SHOP. MY DAUGHTER, BAI, WAS KIDNAPPED. I NEED YOUR HELP.
I WILL HELP IN ANY WAY I CAN.
I NEED YOUR CAR.
WHAT?
I WAS TOLD YOU HAVE A CAR. THE PLACE THEY ARE HOLDING HER IS DAYS AWAY VIA BUS, BUT WITH A CAR WE COULD BE THERE TONIGHT. I WILL SAVE MY DAUGHTER.
YOU DO REALIZE YOU'RE GOING AGAINST A LOCAL DRUG WARLORD AND HIS ARMY OF THUGS? AH, DIDN'T THINK SO. YOU NEED MORE THAN MY CAR. YOU NEED ME, AND YOU NEED A PLAN.
FORTUNATELY, I HAVE BOTH.

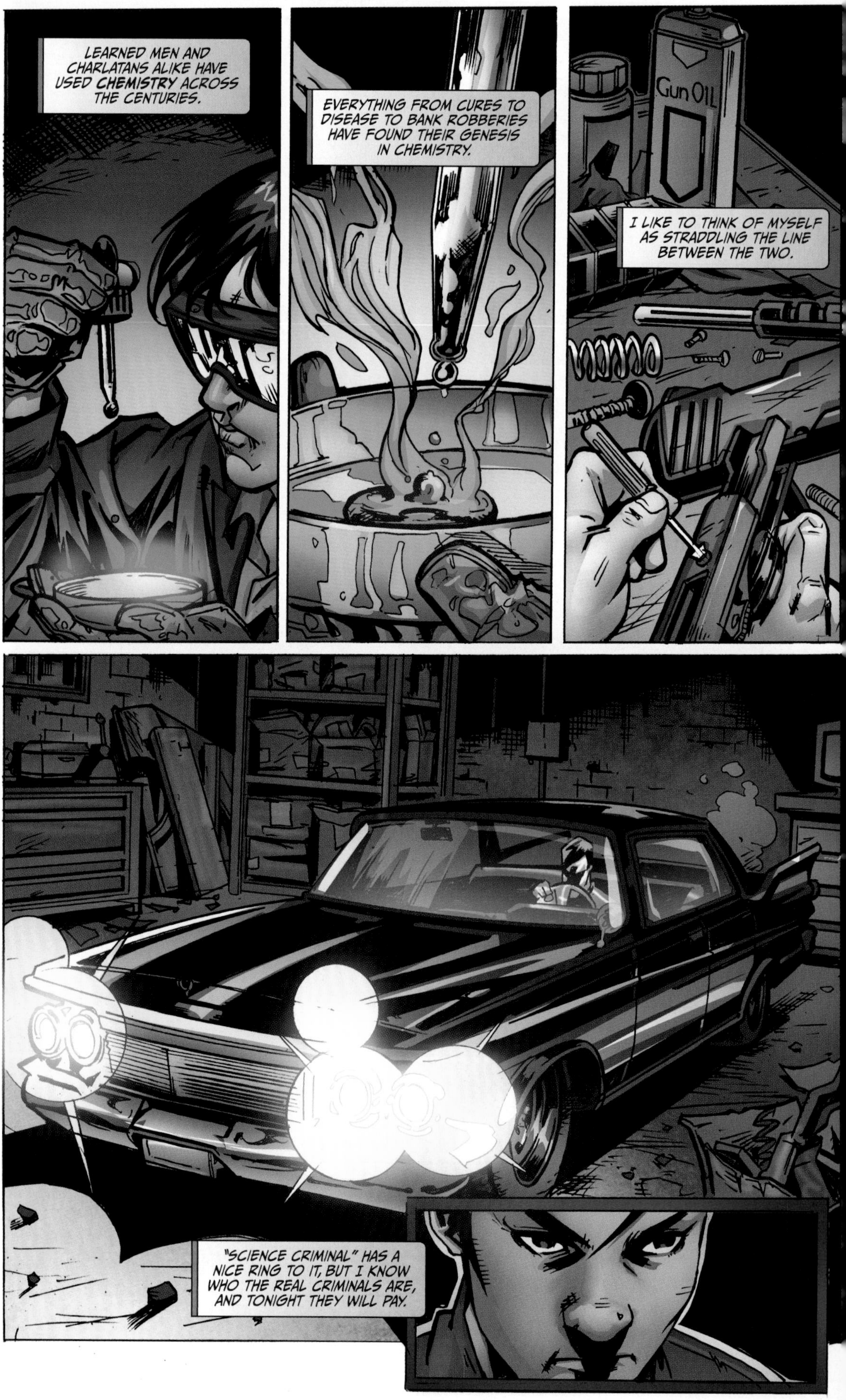
LEARNED MEN AND CHARLATANS ALIKE HAVE USED CHEMISTRY ACROSS THE CENTURIES.
EVERYTHING FROM CURES TO DISEASE TO BANK ROBBERIES HAVE FOUND THEIR GENESIS IN CHEMISTRY.
Gun OIL
I LIKE TO THINK OF MYSELF AS STRADDLING THE LINE BETWEEN THE TWO.
"SCIENCE CRIMINAL" HAS A NICE RING TO IT, BUT I KNOW WHO THE REAL CRIMINALS ARE, AND TONIGHT THEY WILL PAY.

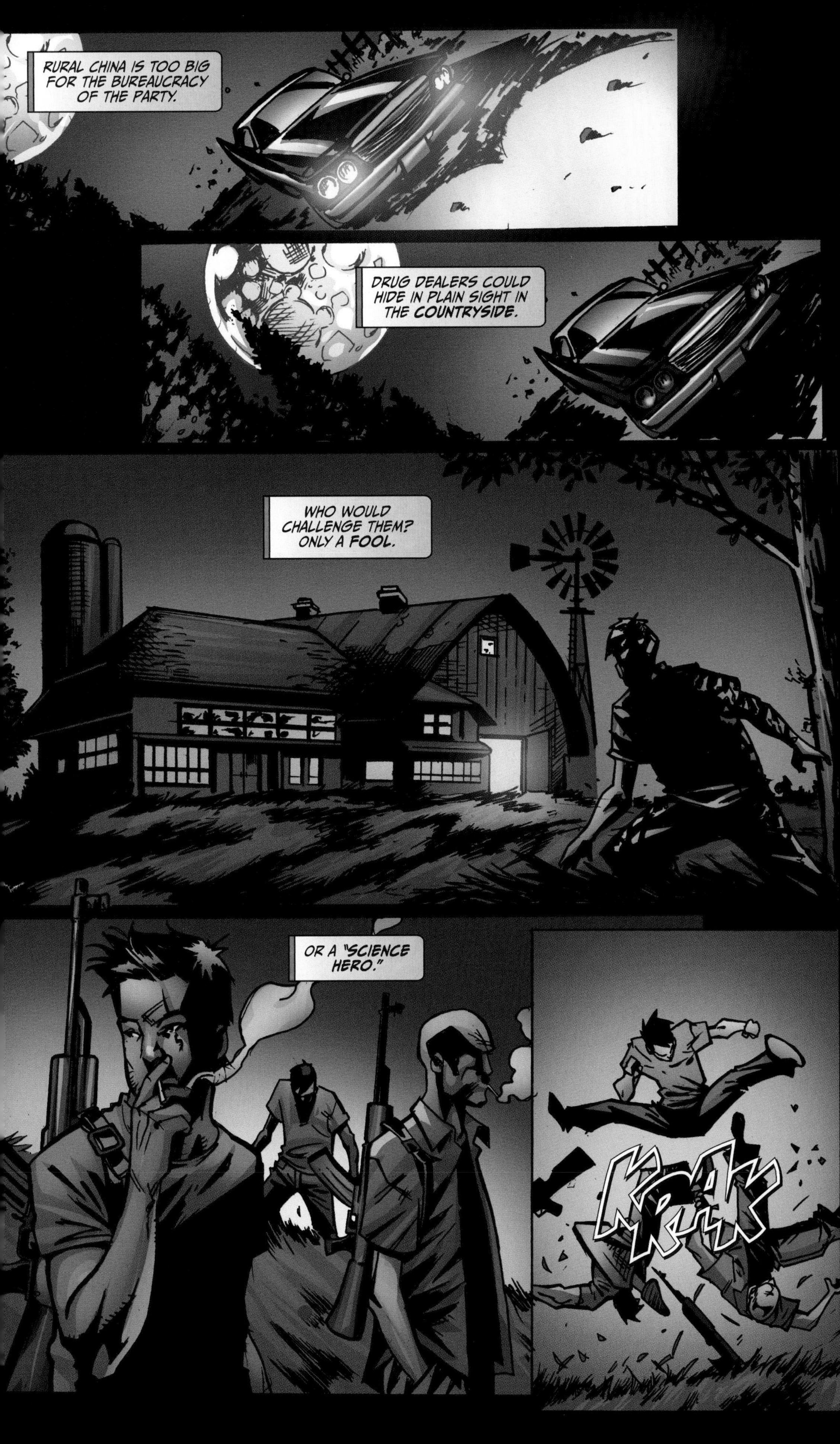
RURAL CHINA IS TOO BIG FOR THE BUREAUCRACY OF THE PARTY.
DRUG DEALERS COULD HIDE IN PLAIN SIGHT IN THE COUNTRYSIDE.
WHO WOULD CHALLENGE THEM? ONLY A FOOL.
OR A "SCIENCE HERO."
KRAK

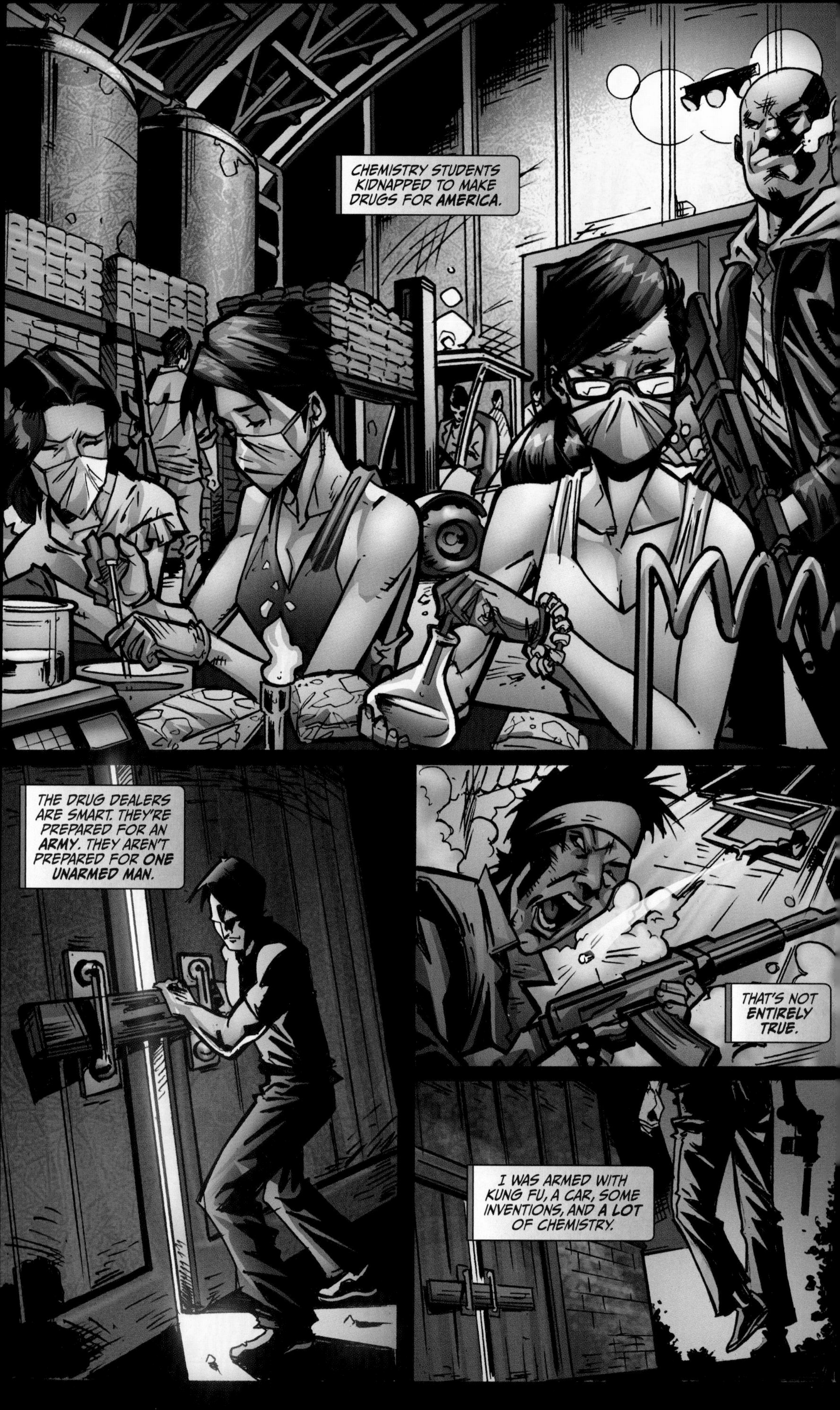
CHEMISTRY STUDENTS KIDNAPPED TO MAKE DRUGS FOR AMERICA.
THE DRUG DEALERS ARE SMART. THEY'RE PREPARED FOR AN ARMY. THEY AREN'T PREPARED FOR ONE UNARMED MAN.
THAT'S NOT ENTIRELY TRUE.
I WAS ARMED WITH KUNG FU, A CAR, SOME INVENTIONS, AND A LOT OF CHEMISTRY.

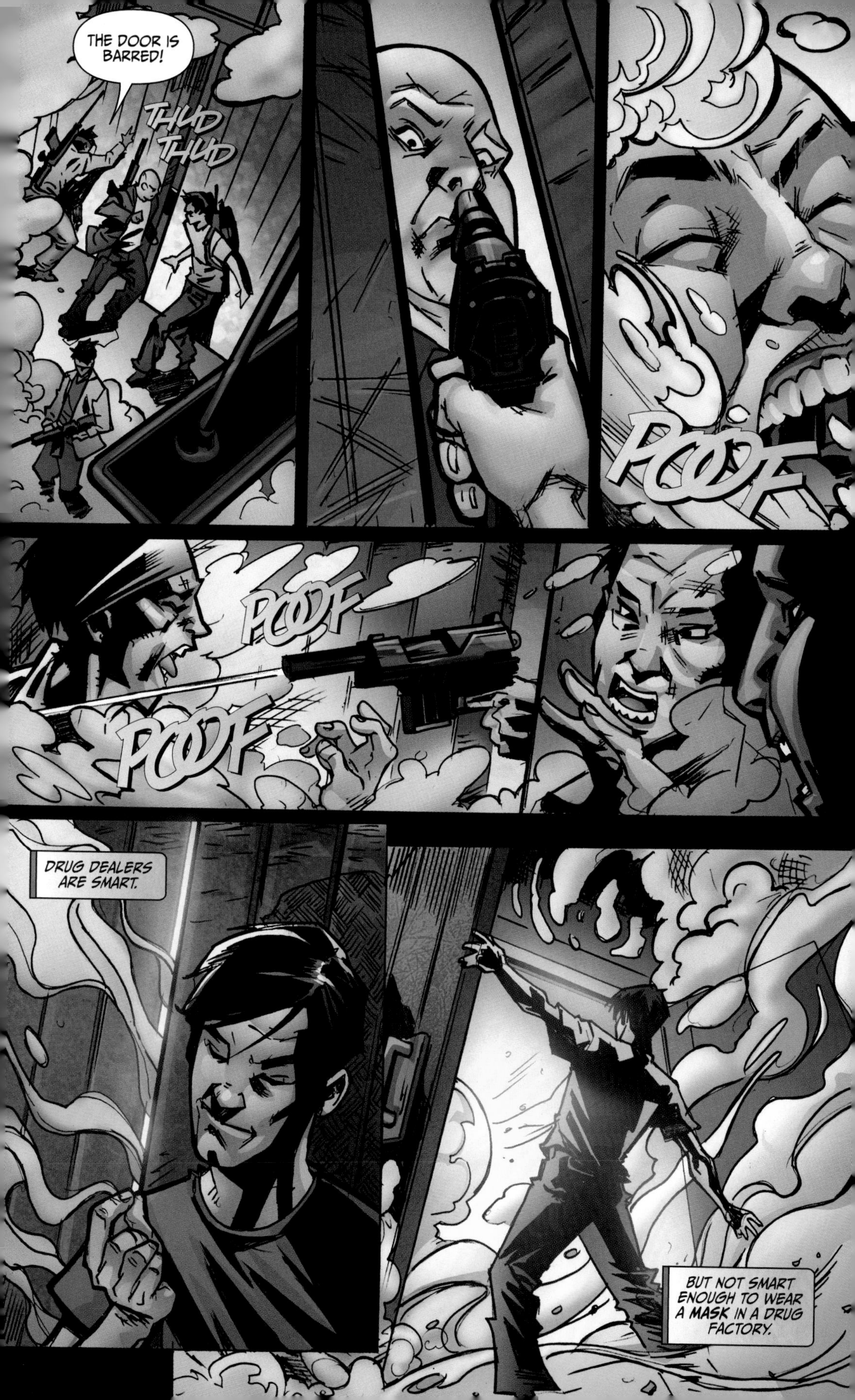
THE DOOR IS BARRED!
THUD THUD
POOF
POOF
POOF
DRUG DEALERS ARE SMART.
BUT NOT SMART ENOUGH TO WEAR A **MASK** IN A DRUG FACTORY.

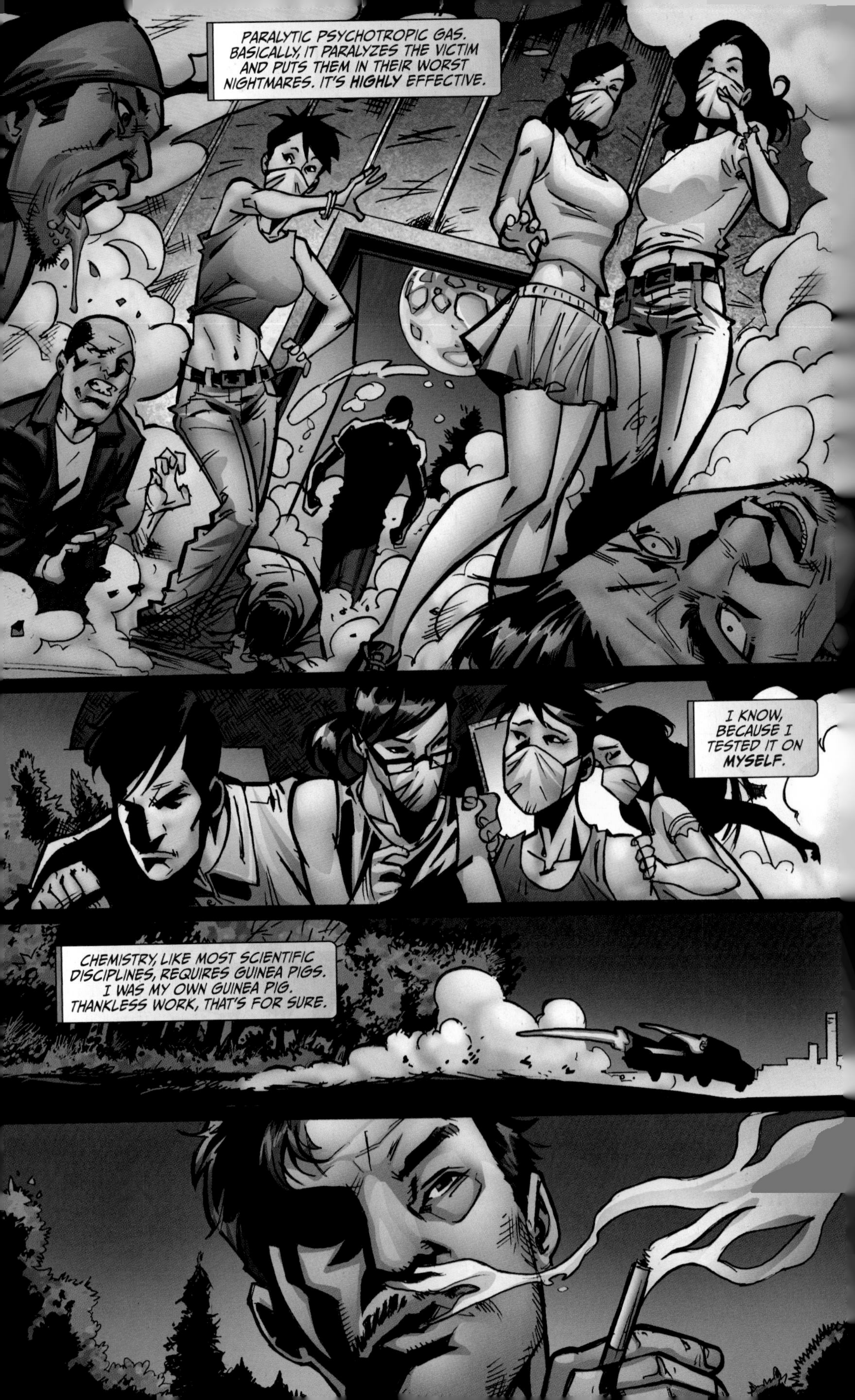
PARALYTIC PSYCHOTROPIC GAS. BASICALLY, IT PARALYZES THE VICTIM AND PUTS THEM IN THEIR WORST NIGHTMARES. IT'S HIGHLY EFFECTIVE.
I KNOW, BECAUSE I TESTED IT ON MYSELF.
CHEMISTRY, LIKE MOST SCIENTIFIC DISCIPLINES, REQUIRES GUINEA PIGS. I WAS MY OWN GUINEA PIG. THANKLESS WORK, THAT'S FOR SURE.

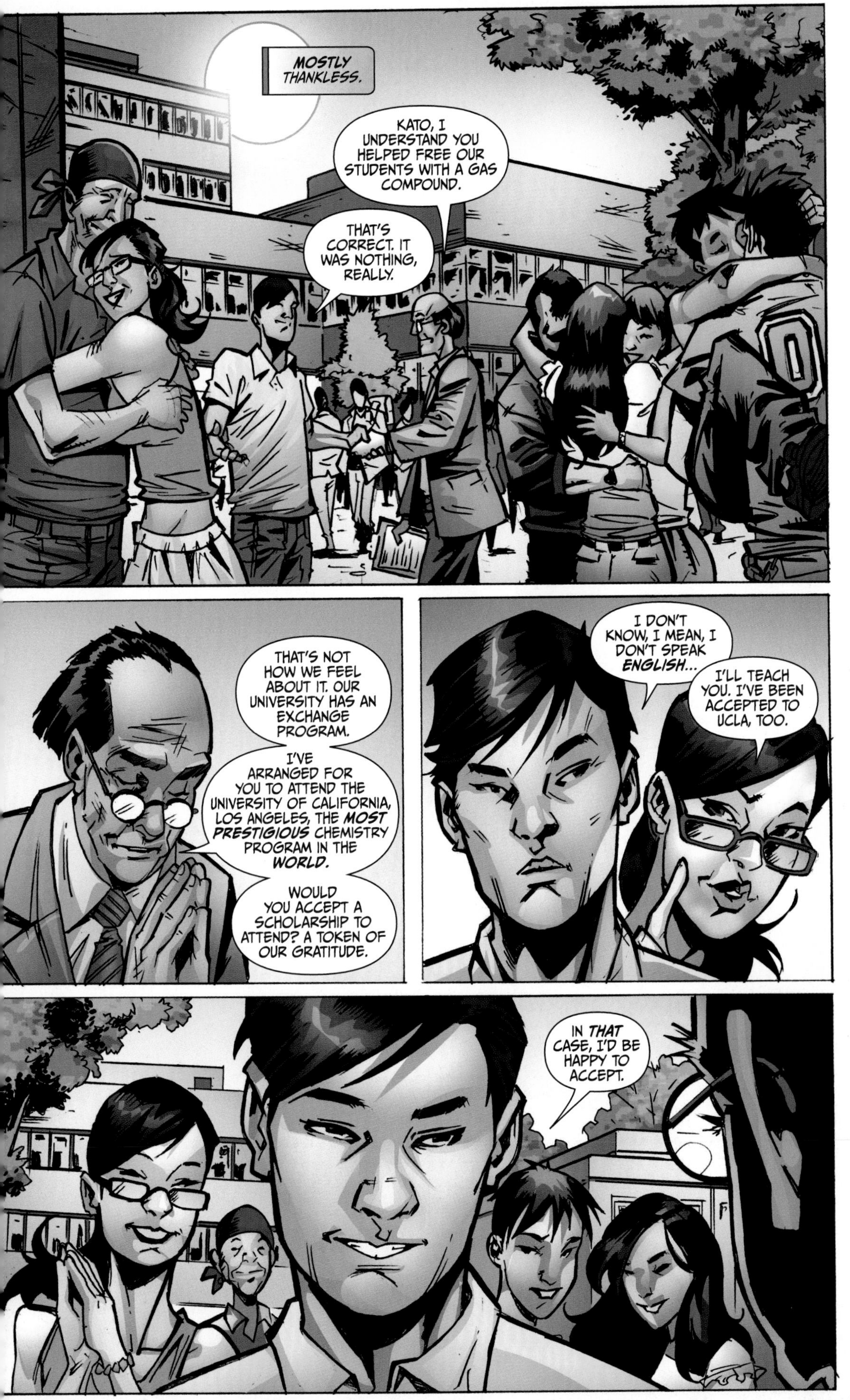
MOSTLY THANKLESS.
KATO, I UNDERSTAND YOU HELPED FREE OUR STUDENTS WITH A GAS COMPOUND.
THAT'S CORRECT. IT WAS NOTHING, REALLY.
THAT'S NOT HOW WE FEEL ABOUT IT. OUR UNIVERSITY HAS AN EXCHANGE PROGRAM.
I'VE ARRANGED FOR YOU TO ATTEND THE UNIVERSITY OF CALIFORNIA, LOS ANGELES, THE MOST PRESTIGIOUS CHEMISTRY PROGRAM IN THE WORLD.
WOULD YOU ACCEPT A SCHOLARSHIP TO ATTEND? A TOKEN OF OUR GRATITUDE.
I DON'T KNOW, I MEAN, I DON'T SPEAK ENGLISH...
I'LL TEACH YOU. I'VE BEEN ACCEPTED TO UCLA, TOO.
IN THAT CASE, I'D BE HAPPY TO ACCEPT.

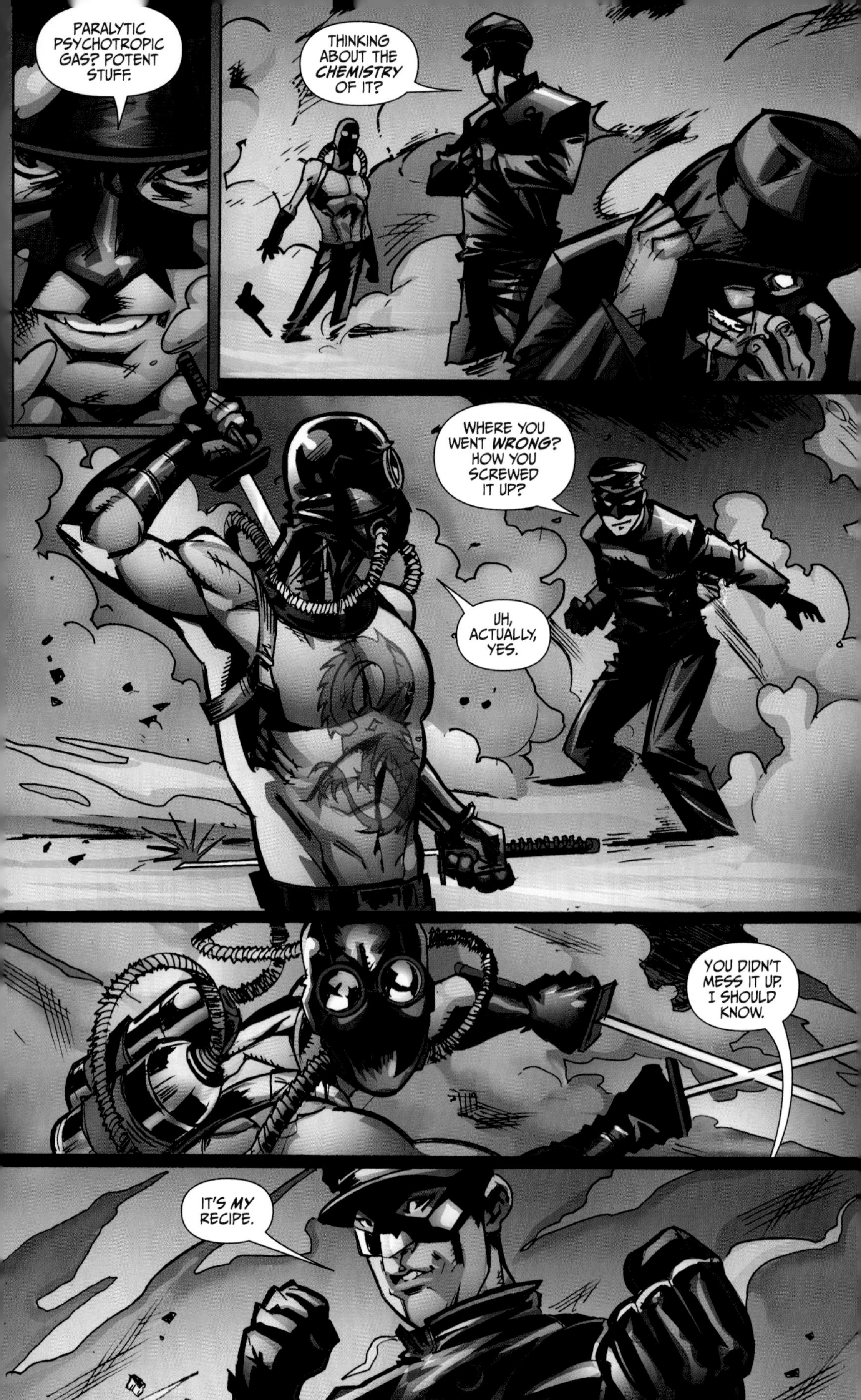

PARALYTIC PSYCHOTROPIC GAS? POTENT STUFF.
THINKING ABOUT THE CHEMISTRY OF IT?
WHERE YOU WENT WRONG? HOW YOU SCREWED IT UP?
UH, ACTUALLY, YES.
YOU DIDN'T MESS IT UP. I SHOULD KNOW.
IT'S MY RECIPE.

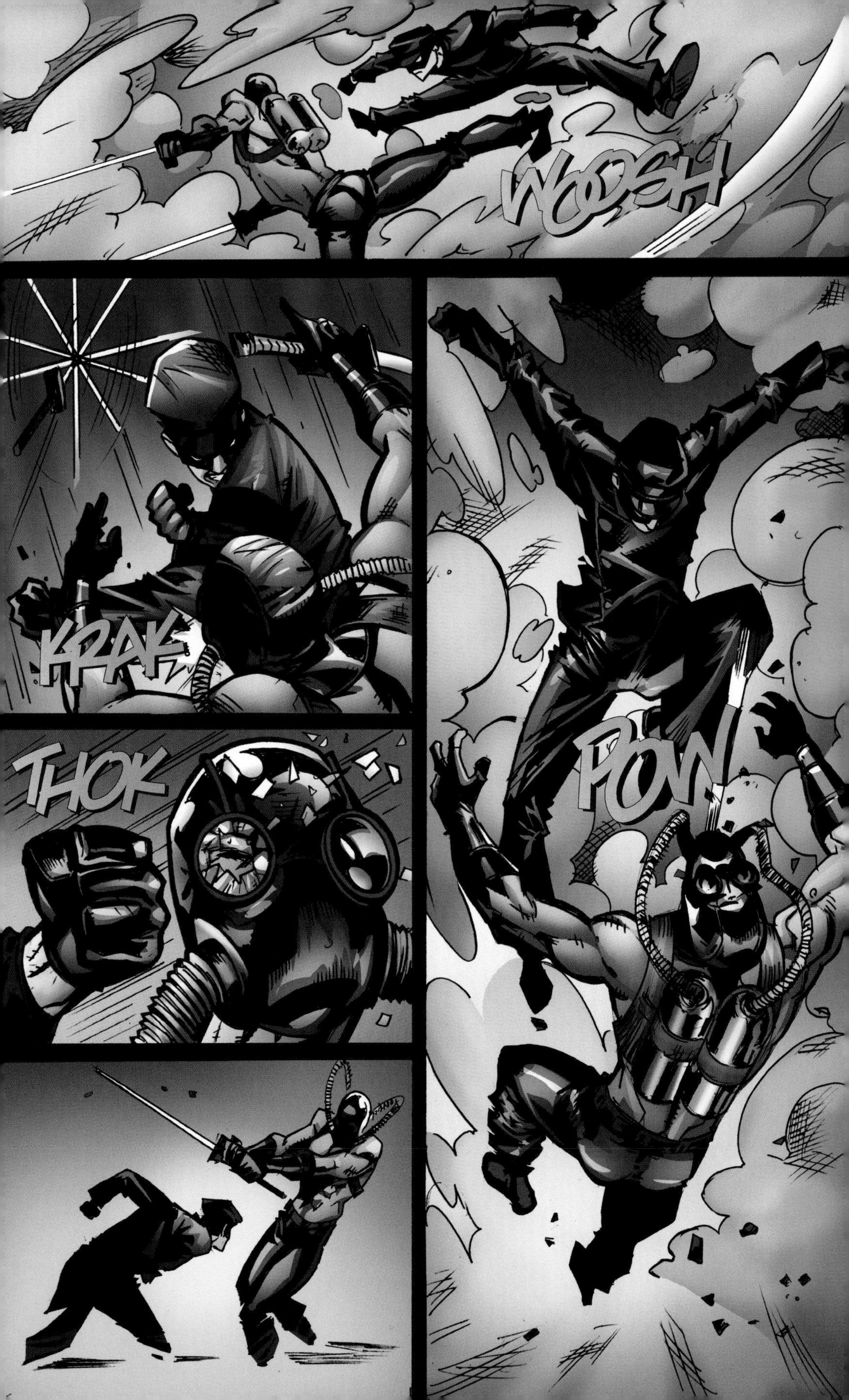
WOOSH
KRAK
THOK
POW

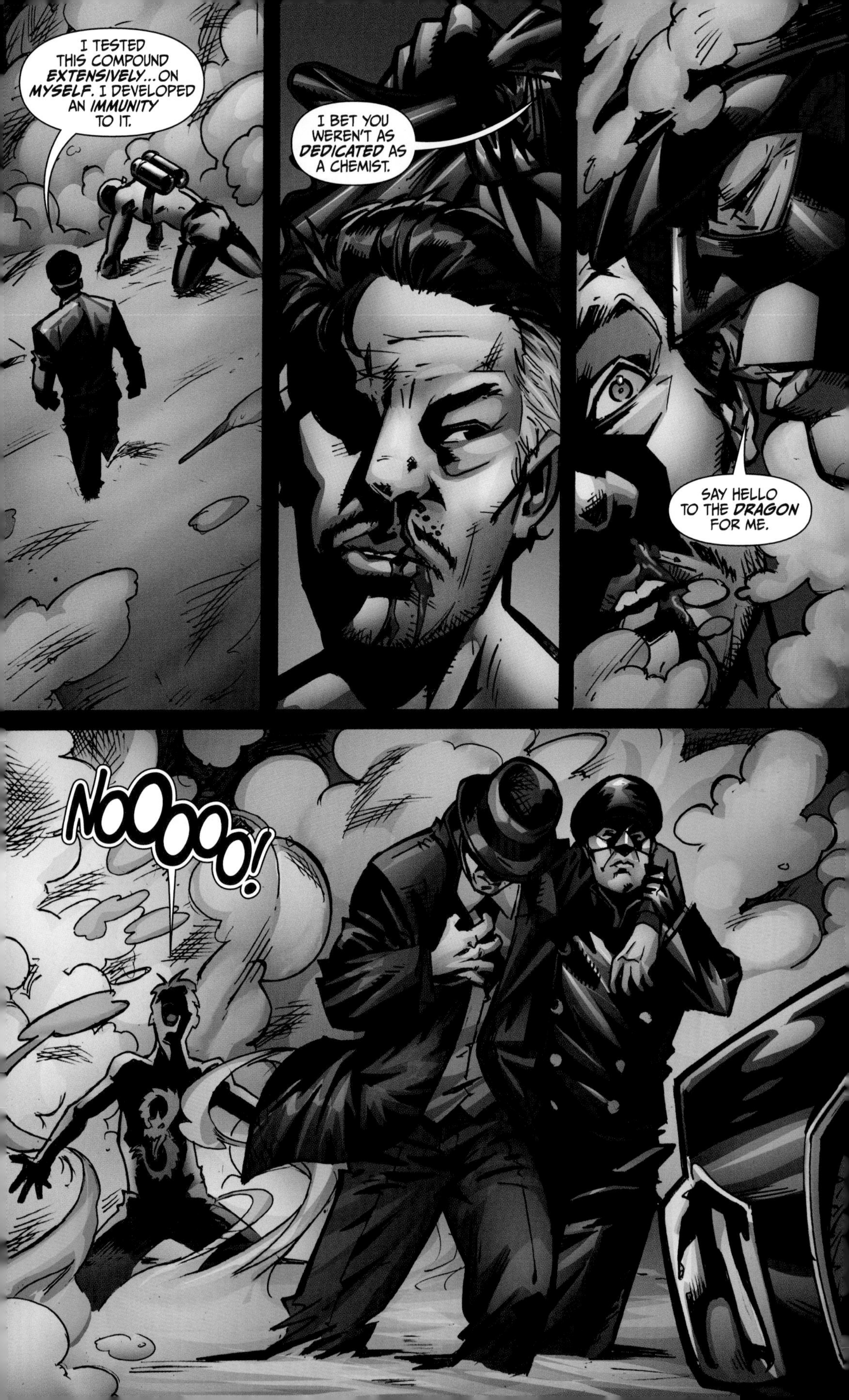
I TESTED THIS COMPOUND EXTENSIVELY... ON MYSELF. I DEVELOPED AN IMMUNITY TO IT.
I BET YOU WEREN'T AS DEDICATED AS A CHEMIST.
SAY HELLO TO THE DRAGON FOR ME.
NOOOOOO!

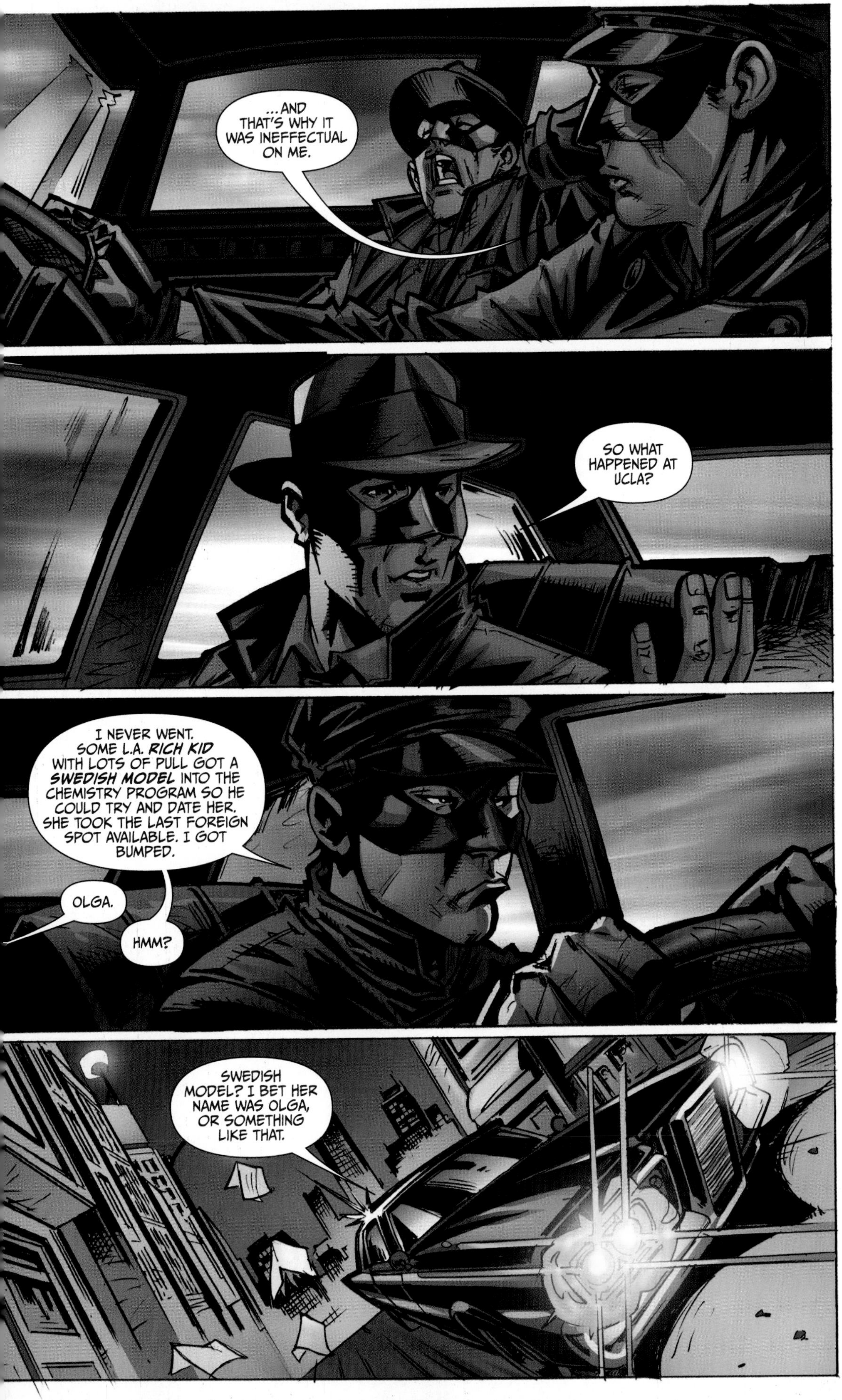
...AND THAT'S WHY IT WAS INEFFECTUAL ON ME.
SO WHAT HAPPENED AT UCLA?
I NEVER WENT. SOME L.A. RICH KID WITH LOTS OF PULL GOT A SWEDISH MODEL INTO THE CHEMISTRY PROGRAM SO HE COULD TRY AND DATE HER. SHE TOOK THE LAST FOREIGN SPOT AVAILABLE. I GOT BUMPED.
OLGA.
HMM?
SWEDISH MODEL? I BET HER NAME WAS OLGA, OR SOMETHING LIKE THAT.

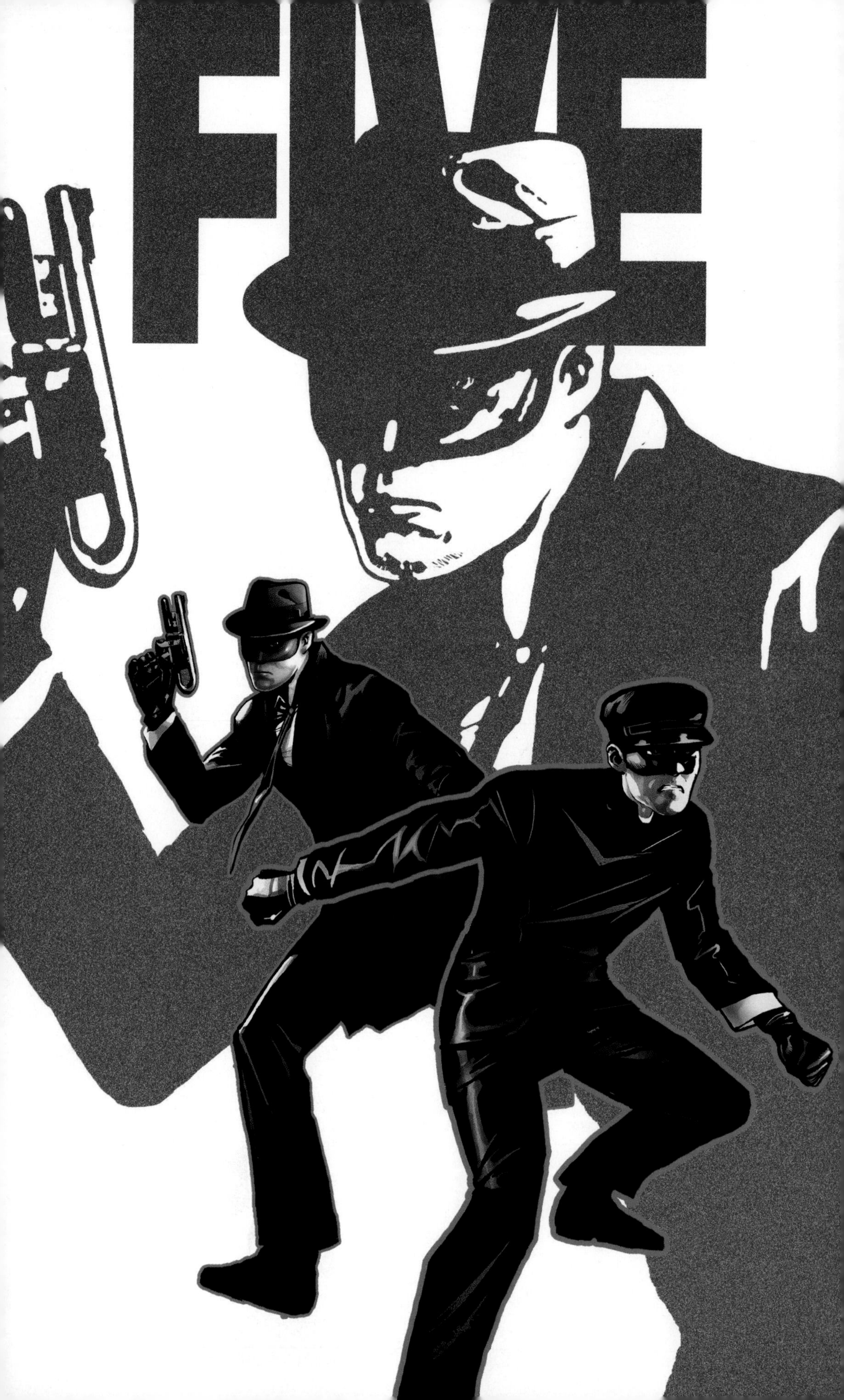
FIVE

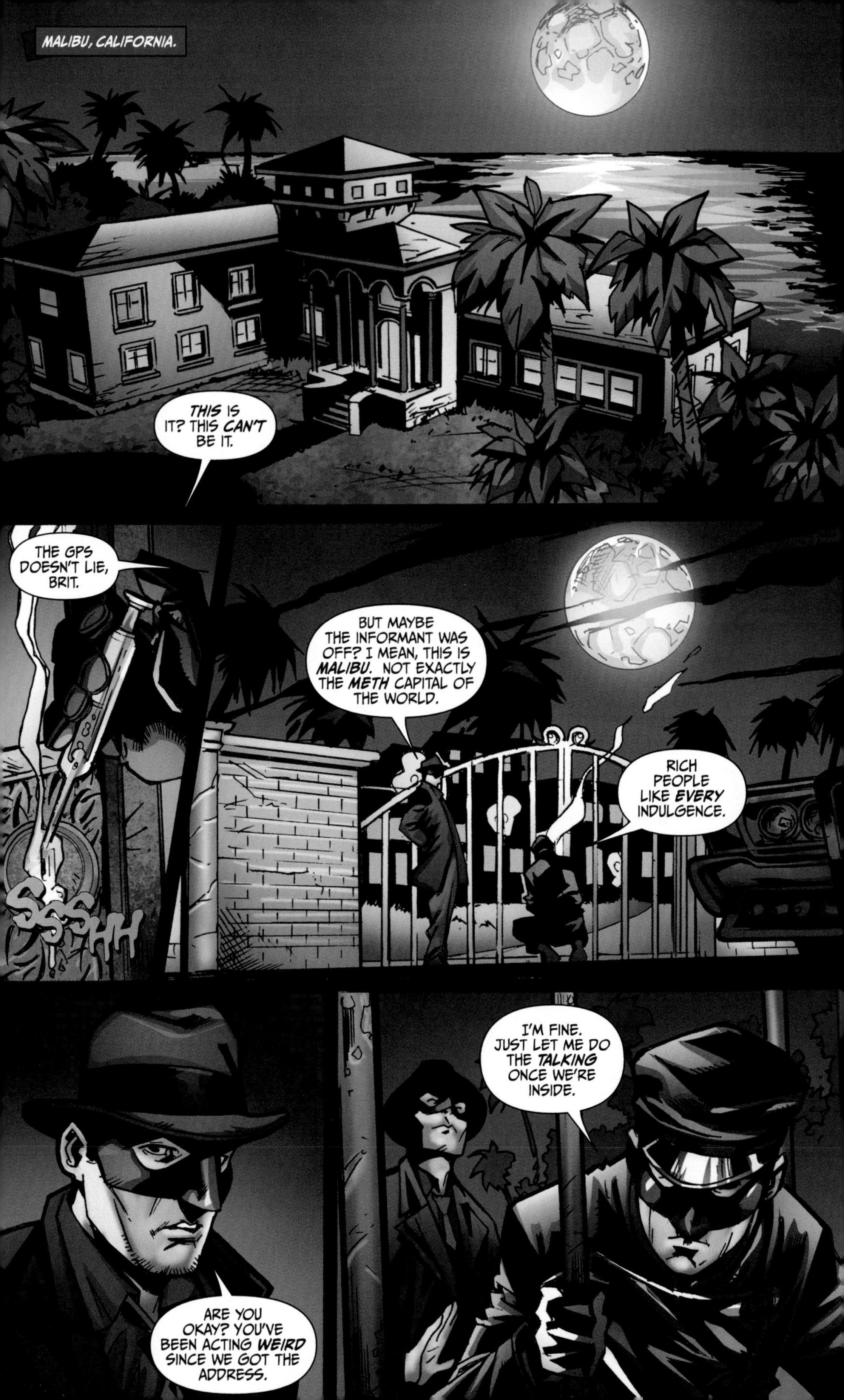
MALIBU, CALIFORNIA.
THIS IS IT? THIS CAN'T BE IT.
THE GPS DOESN'T LIE, BRIT.
BUT MAYBE THE INFORMANT WAS OFF? I MEAN, THIS IS MALIBU. NOT EXACTLY THE METH CAPITAL OF THE WORLD.
RICH PEOPLE LIKE EVERY INDULGENCE.
SSSHH
ARE YOU OKAY? YOU'VE BEEN ACTING WEIRD SINCE WE GOT THE ADDRESS.
I'M FINE. JUST LET ME DO THE TALKING ONCE WE'RE INSIDE.

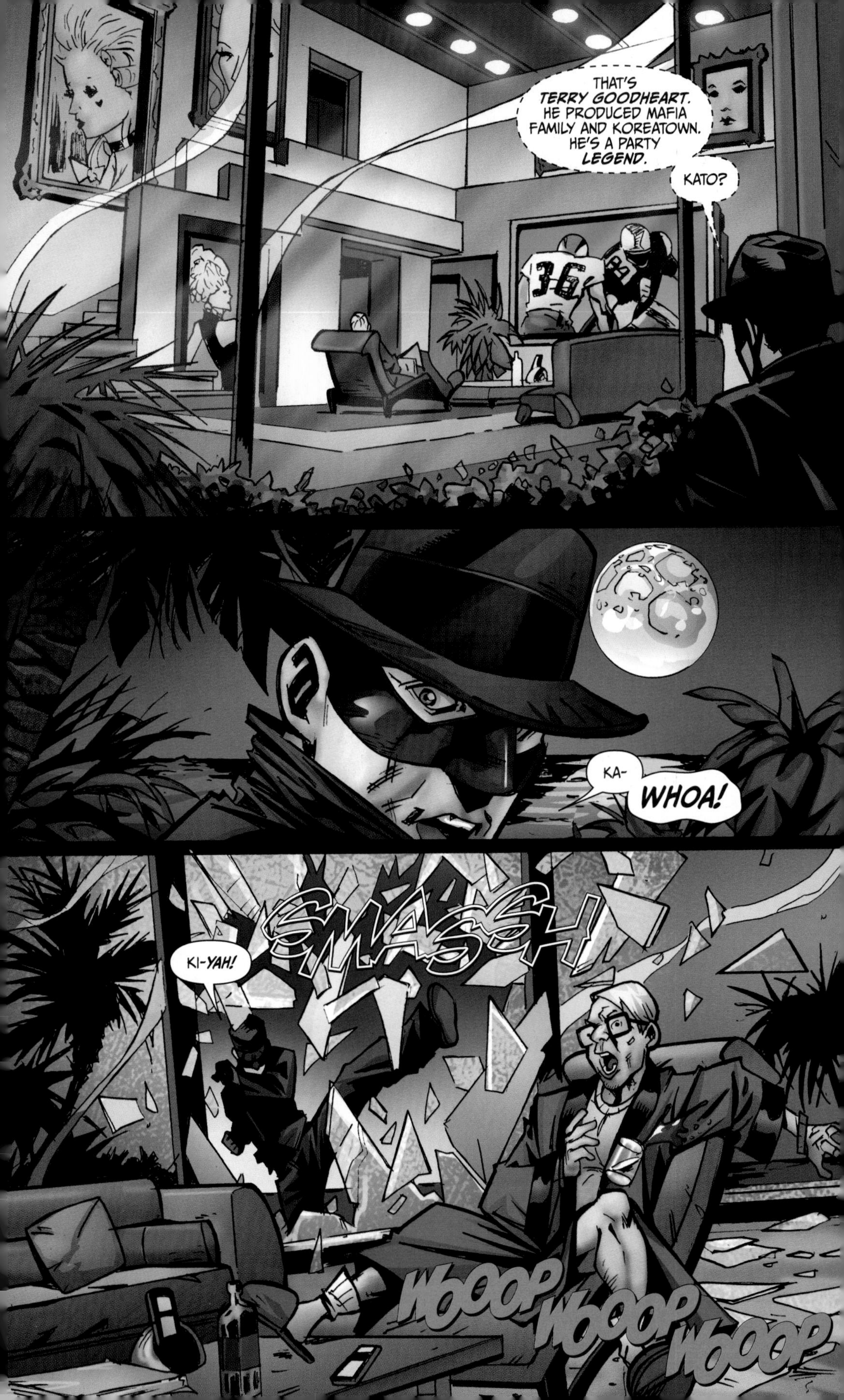
THAT'S TERRY GOODHEART. HE PRODUCED MAFIA FAMILY AND KOREATOWN. HE'S A PARTY LEGEND.
KATO?
36
KA-
WHOA!
SMASH
KI-YAH!
WOOOP WOOOP WOOOP

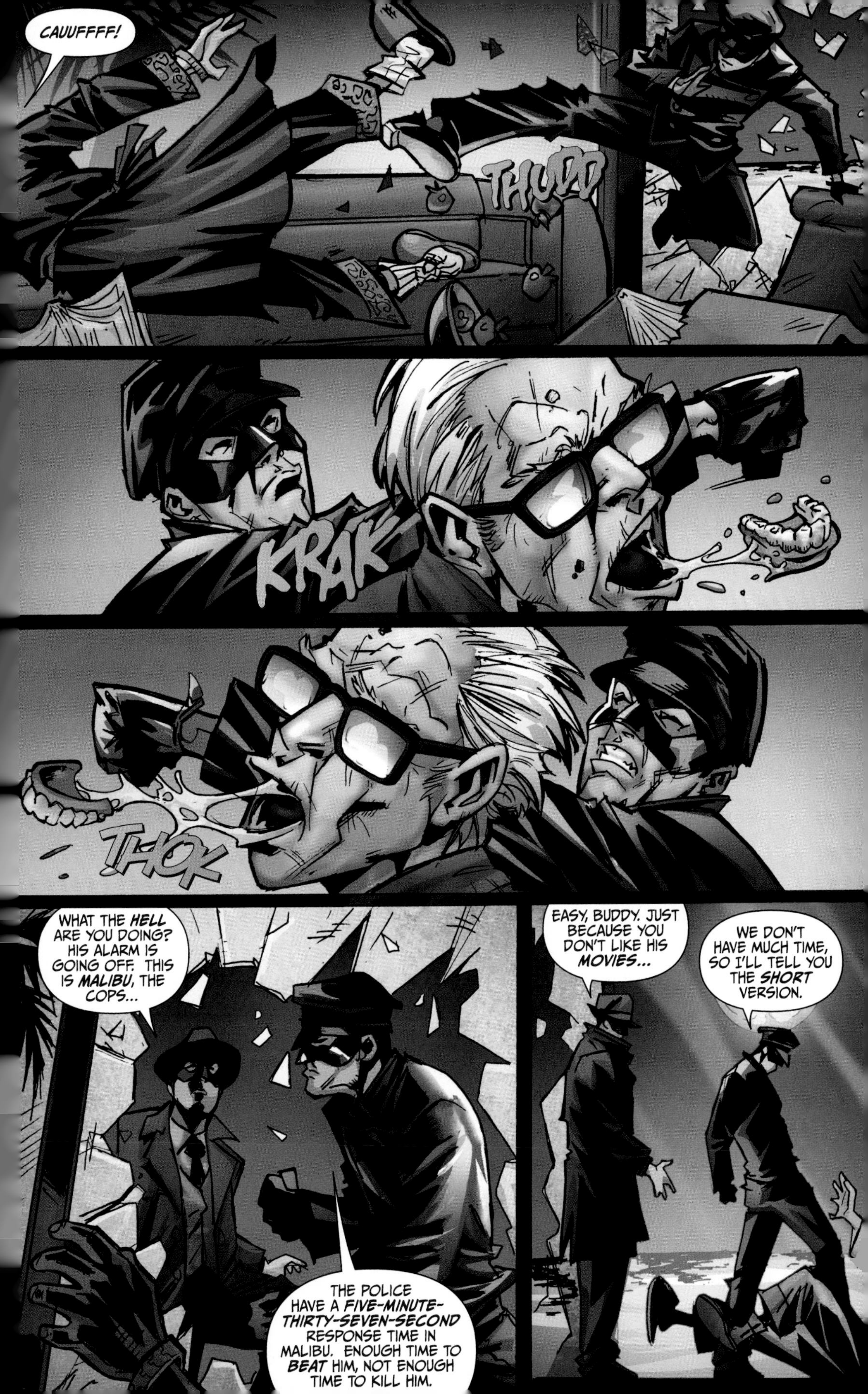
CAUUFFFF!
THUDD
KRAK
THOK
WHAT THE *HELL* ARE YOU DOING? HIS ALARM IS GOING OFF. THIS IS *MALIBU*, THE COPS...
THE POLICE HAVE A *FIVE-MINUTE-THIRTY-SEVEN-SECOND* RESPONSE TIME IN MALIBU. ENOUGH TIME TO *BEAT* HIM, NOT ENOUGH TIME TO KILL HIM.
EASY, BUDDY. JUST BECAUSE YOU DON'T LIKE HIS *MOVIES*...
WE DON'T HAVE MUCH TIME, SO I'LL TELL YOU THE *SHORT* VERSION.

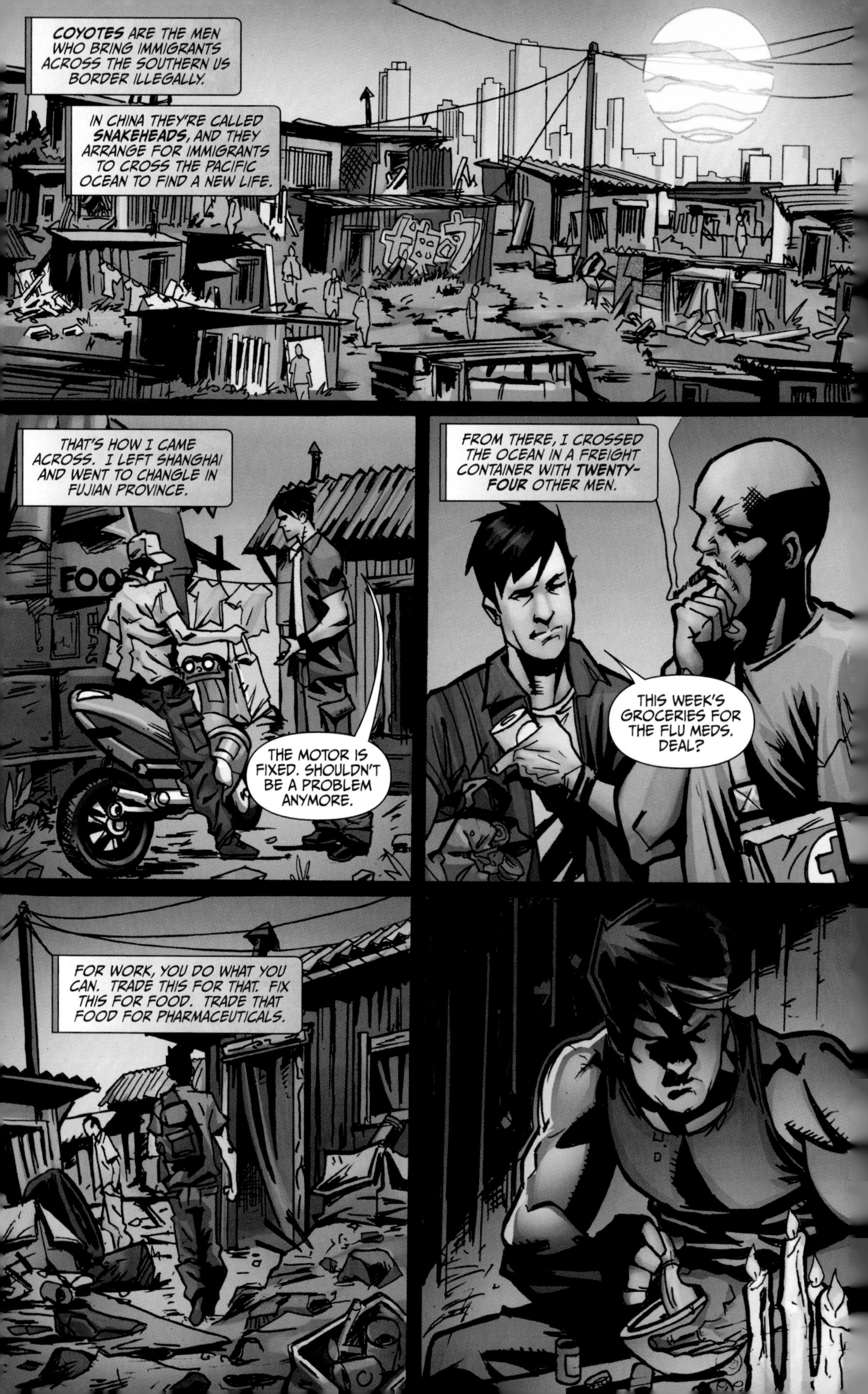
COYOTES ARE THE MEN WHO BRING IMMIGRANTS ACROSS THE SOUTHERN US BORDER ILLEGALLY.
IN CHINA THEY'RE CALLED SNAKEHEADS, AND THEY ARRANGE FOR IMMIGRANTS TO CROSS THE PACIFIC OCEAN TO FIND A NEW LIFE.
THAT'S HOW I CAME ACROSS. I LEFT SHANGHAI AND WENT TO CHANGLE IN FUJIAN PROVINCE.
FOO
THE MOTOR IS FIXED. SHOULDN'T BE A PROBLEM ANYMORE.
FROM THERE, I CROSSED THE OCEAN IN A FREIGHT CONTAINER WITH TWENTY-FOUR OTHER MEN.
THIS WEEK'S GROCERIES FOR THE FLU MEDS. DEAL?
FOR WORK, YOU DO WHAT YOU CAN. TRADE THIS FOR THAT. FIX THIS FOR FOOD. TRADE THAT FOOD FOR PHARMACEUTICALS.

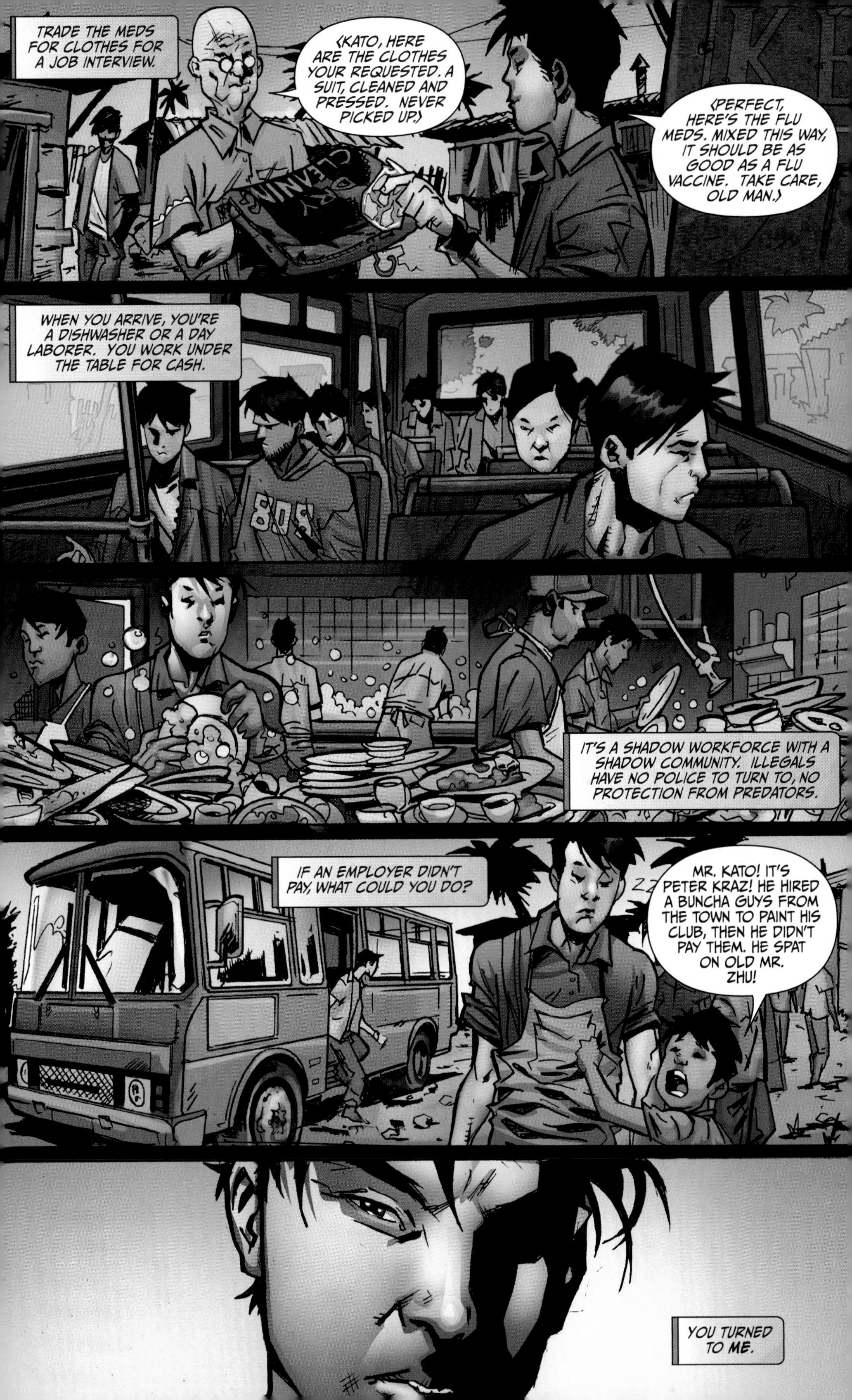
TRADE THE MEDS FOR CLOTHES FOR A JOB INTERVIEW.
‹KATO, HERE ARE THE CLOTHES YOUR REQUESTED. A SUIT, CLEANED AND PRESSED. NEVER PICKED UP.›
‹PERFECT, HERE'S THE FLU MEDS. MIXED THIS WAY, IT SHOULD BE AS GOOD AS A FLU VACCINE. TAKE CARE, OLD MAN.›
WHEN YOU ARRIVE, YOU'RE A DISHWASHER OR A DAY LABORER. YOU WORK UNDER THE TABLE FOR CASH.
IT'S A SHADOW WORKFORCE WITH A SHADOW COMMUNITY. ILLEGALS HAVE NO POLICE TO TURN TO, NO PROTECTION FROM PREDATORS.
IF AN EMPLOYER DIDN'T PAY, WHAT COULD YOU DO?
MR. KATO! IT'S PETER KRAZ! HE HIRED A BUNCHA GUYS FROM THE TOWN TO PAINT HIS CLUB, THEN HE DIDN'T PAY THEM. HE SPAT ON OLD MR. ZHU!
YOU TURNED TO ME.

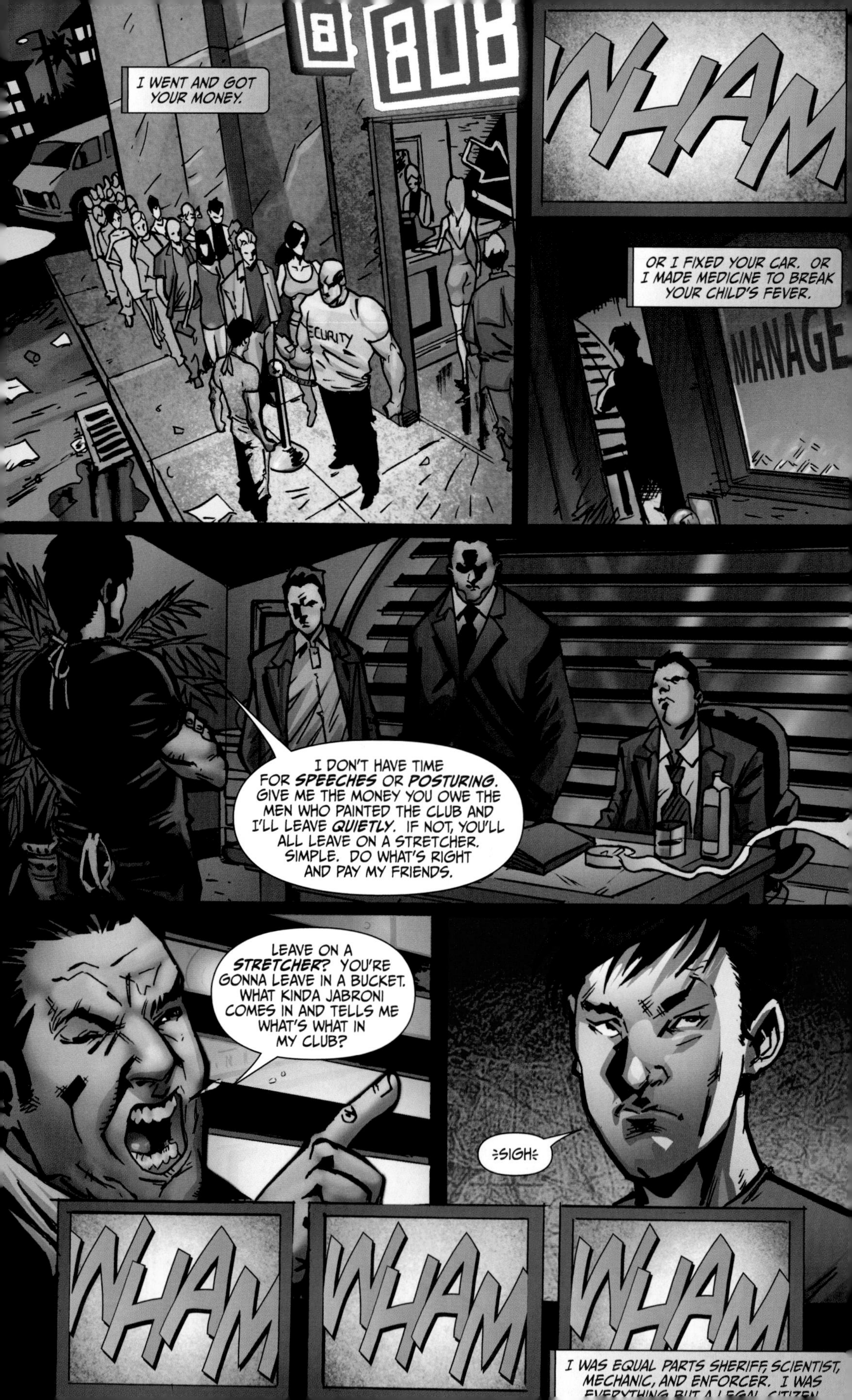
808
I WENT AND GOT YOUR MONEY.
WHAM
OR I FIXED YOUR CAR. OR I MADE MEDICINE TO BREAK YOUR CHILD'S FEVER.
MANAGE
I DON'T HAVE TIME FOR SPEECHES OR POSTURING. GIVE ME THE MONEY YOU OWE THE MEN WHO PAINTED THE CLUB AND I'LL LEAVE QUIETLY. IF NOT, YOU'LL ALL LEAVE ON A STRETCHER. SIMPLE. DO WHAT'S RIGHT AND PAY MY FRIENDS.
LEAVE ON A STRETCHER? YOU'RE GONNA LEAVE IN A BUCKET. WHAT KINDA JABRONI COMES IN AND TELLS ME WHAT'S WHAT IN MY CLUB?
SIGH
WHAM
WHAM
WHAM
I WAS EQUAL PARTS SHERIFF, SCIENTIST, MECHANIC, AND ENFORCER. I WAS

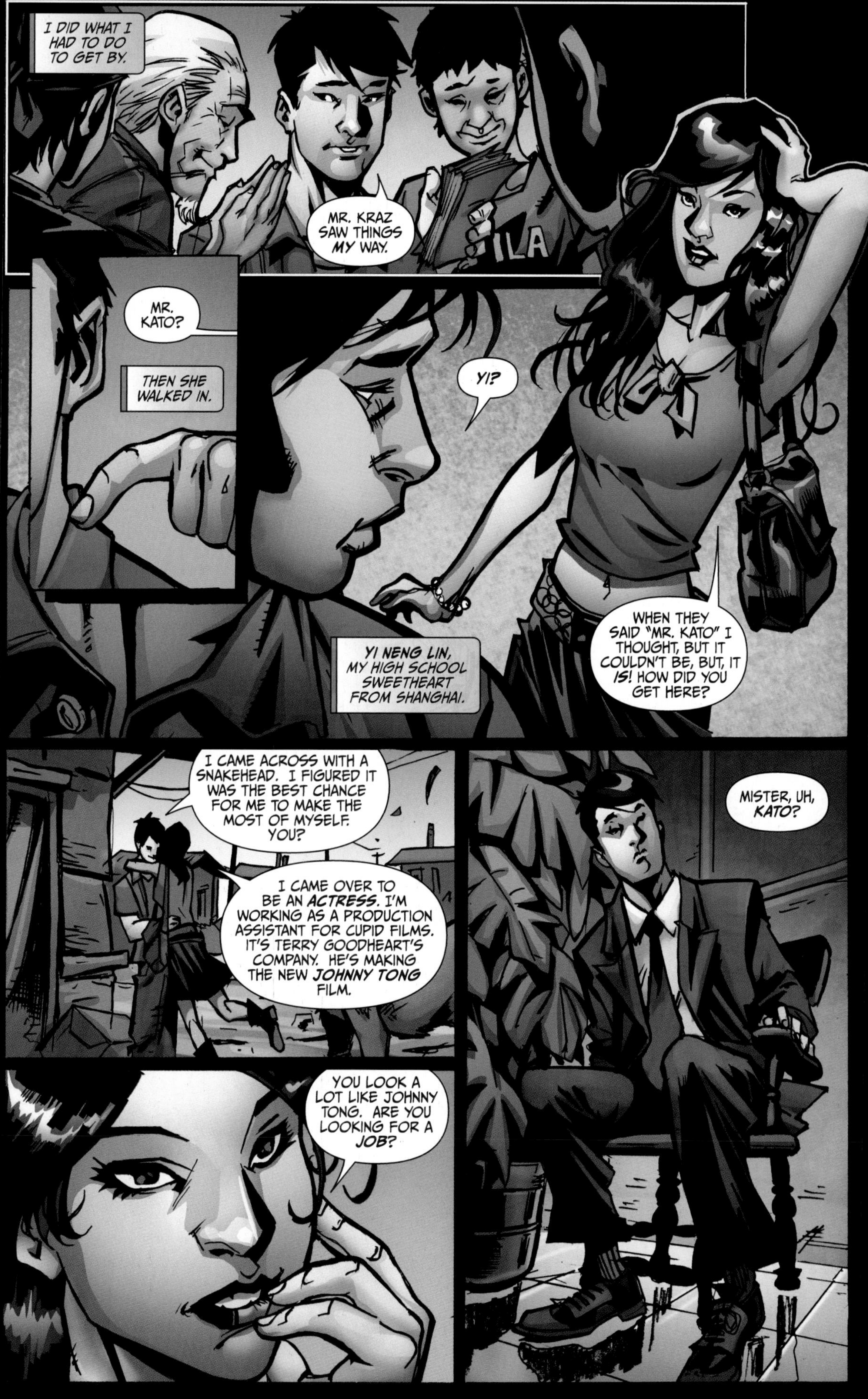

I DID WHAT I HAD TO DO TO GET BY.
MR. KRAZ SAW THINGS *MY* WAY.
MR. KATO?
THEN SHE WALKED IN.
YI?
YI NENG LIN, MY HIGH SCHOOL SWEETHEART FROM SHANGHAI.
WHEN THEY SAID "MR. KATO" I THOUGHT, BUT IT COULDN'T BE, BUT, IT *IS*! HOW DID YOU GET HERE?
I CAME ACROSS WITH A SNAKEHEAD. I FIGURED IT WAS THE BEST CHANCE FOR ME TO MAKE THE MOST OF MYSELF. YOU?
I CAME OVER TO BE AN *ACTRESS*. I'M WORKING AS A PRODUCTION ASSISTANT FOR CUPID FILMS. IT'S TERRY GOODHEART'S COMPANY. HE'S MAKING THE NEW *JOHNNY TONG* FILM.
YOU LOOK A LOT LIKE JOHNNY TONG. ARE YOU LOOKING FOR A *JOB*?
MISTER, UH, *KATO*?

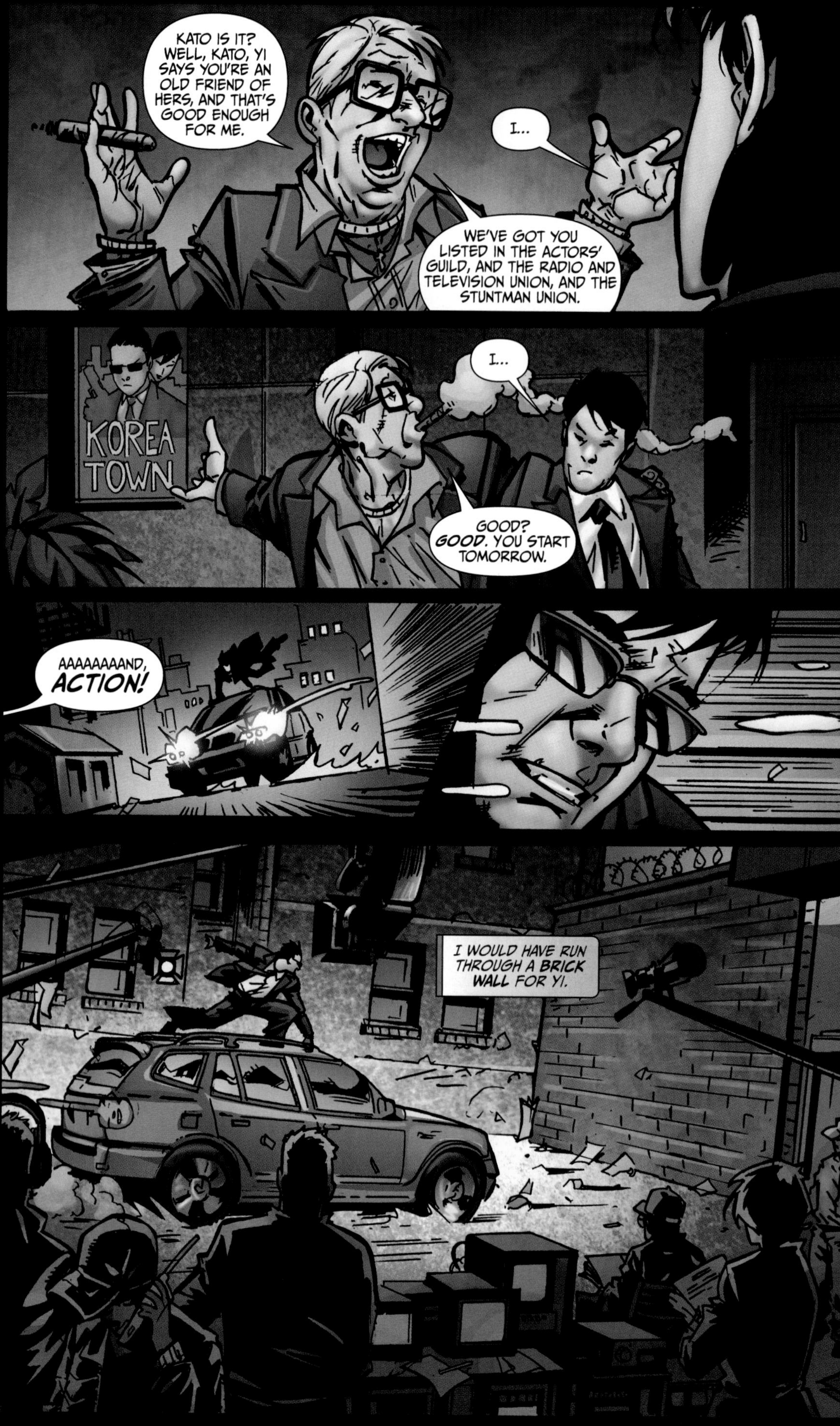
KATO IS IT? WELL, KATO, YI SAYS YOU'RE AN OLD FRIEND OF HERS, AND THAT'S GOOD ENOUGH FOR ME.
I...
WE'VE GOT YOU LISTED IN THE ACTORS' GUILD, AND THE RADIO AND TELEVISION UNION, AND THE STUNTMAN UNION.
KOREA TOWN
I...
GOOD? GOOD. YOU START TOMORROW.
AAAAAAAAND, ACTION!
I WOULD HAVE RUN THROUGH A BRICK WALL FOR YI.

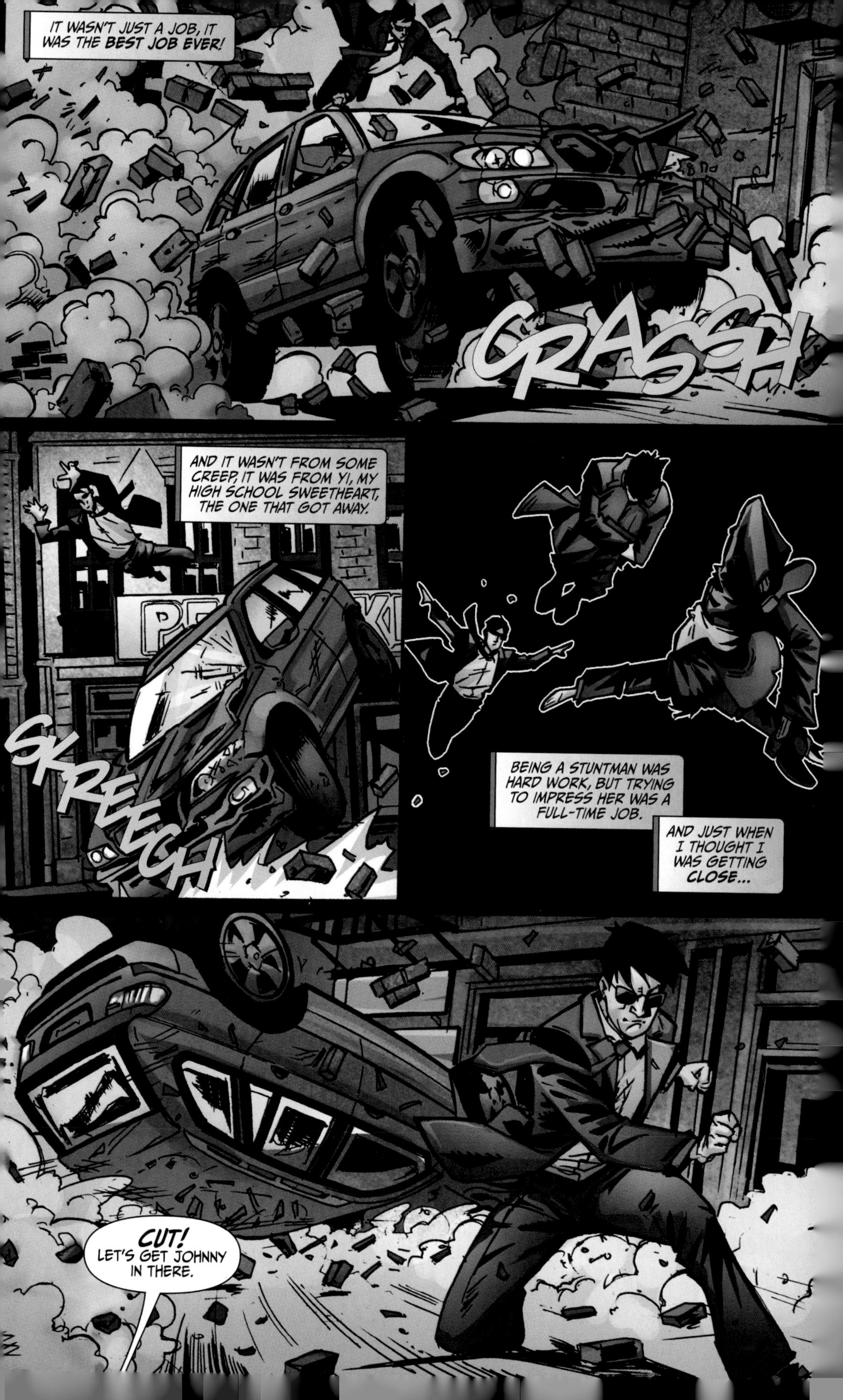
IT WASN'T JUST A JOB, IT WAS THE BEST JOB EVER!
CRASSH
AND IT WASN'T FROM SOME CREEP, IT WAS FROM YI, MY HIGH SCHOOL SWEETHEART, THE ONE THAT GOT AWAY.
SKREEECH
BEING A STUNTMAN WAS HARD WORK, BUT TRYING TO IMPRESS HER WAS A FULL-TIME JOB.
AND JUST WHEN I THOUGHT I WAS GETTING CLOSE...
CUT! LET'S GET JOHNNY IN THERE.

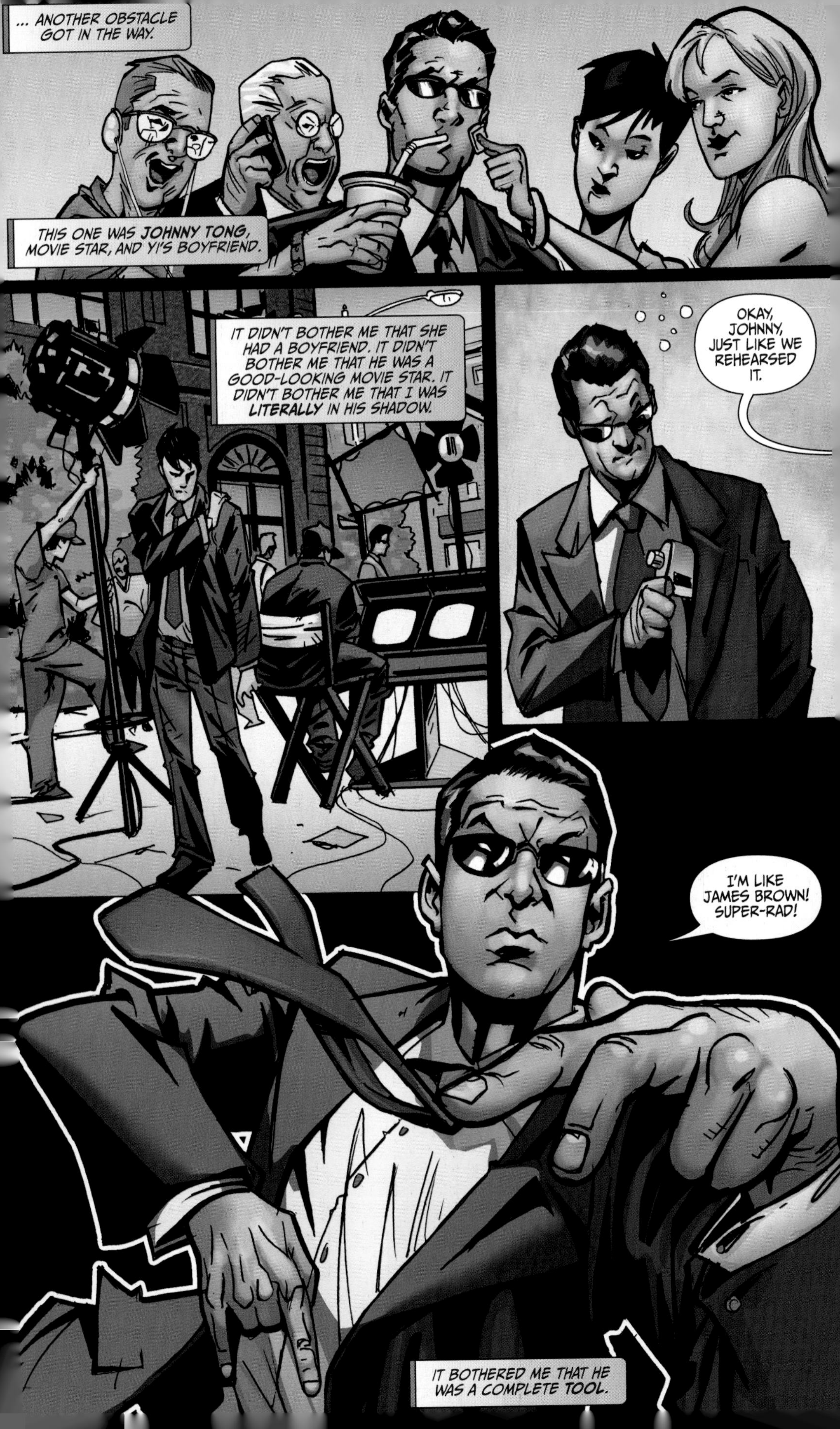
... ANOTHER OBSTACLE GOT IN THE WAY.
THIS ONE WAS JOHNNY TONG, MOVIE STAR, AND YI'S BOYFRIEND.
IT DIDN'T BOTHER ME THAT SHE HAD A BOYFRIEND. IT DIDN'T BOTHER ME THAT HE WAS A GOOD-LOOKING MOVIE STAR. IT DIDN'T BOTHER ME THAT I WAS LITERALLY IN HIS SHADOW.
OKAY, JOHNNY, JUST LIKE WE REHEARSED IT.
I'M LIKE JAMES BROWN! SUPER-RAD!
IT BOTHERED ME THAT HE WAS A COMPLETE TOOL.

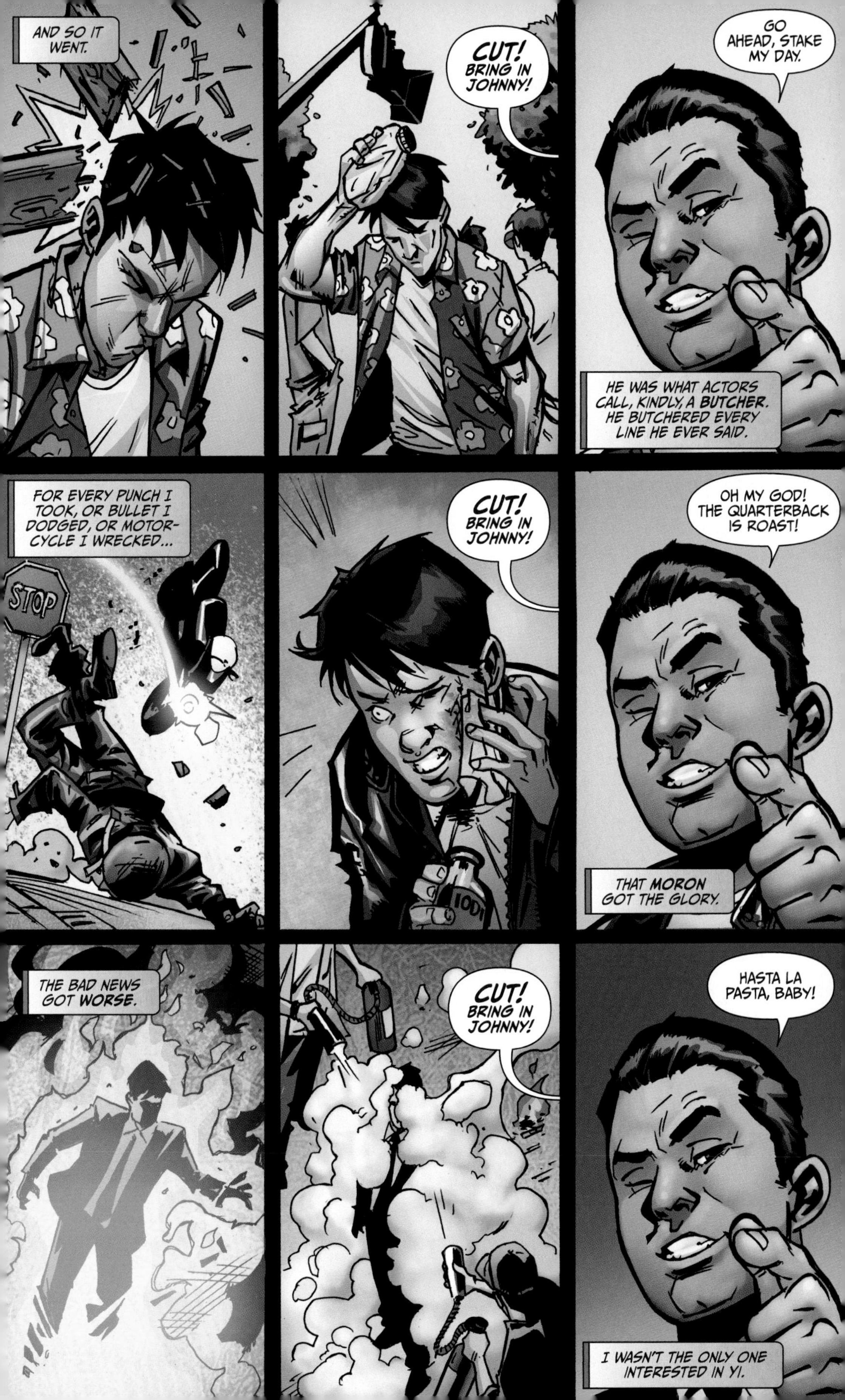
AND SO IT WENT.
CUT! BRING IN JOHNNY!
GO AHEAD, STAKE MY DAY.
HE WAS WHAT ACTORS CALL, KINDLY, A BUTCHER. HE BUTCHERED EVERY LINE HE EVER SAID.
FOR EVERY PUNCH I TOOK, OR BULLET I DODGED, OR MOTOR-CYCLE I WRECKED...
STOP
CUT! BRING IN JOHNNY!
OH MY GOD! THE QUARTERBACK IS ROAST!
THAT MORON GOT THE GLORY.
THE BAD NEWS GOT WORSE.
CUT! BRING IN JOHNNY!
HASTA LA PASTA, BABY!
I WASN'T THE ONLY ONE INTERESTED IN YI.

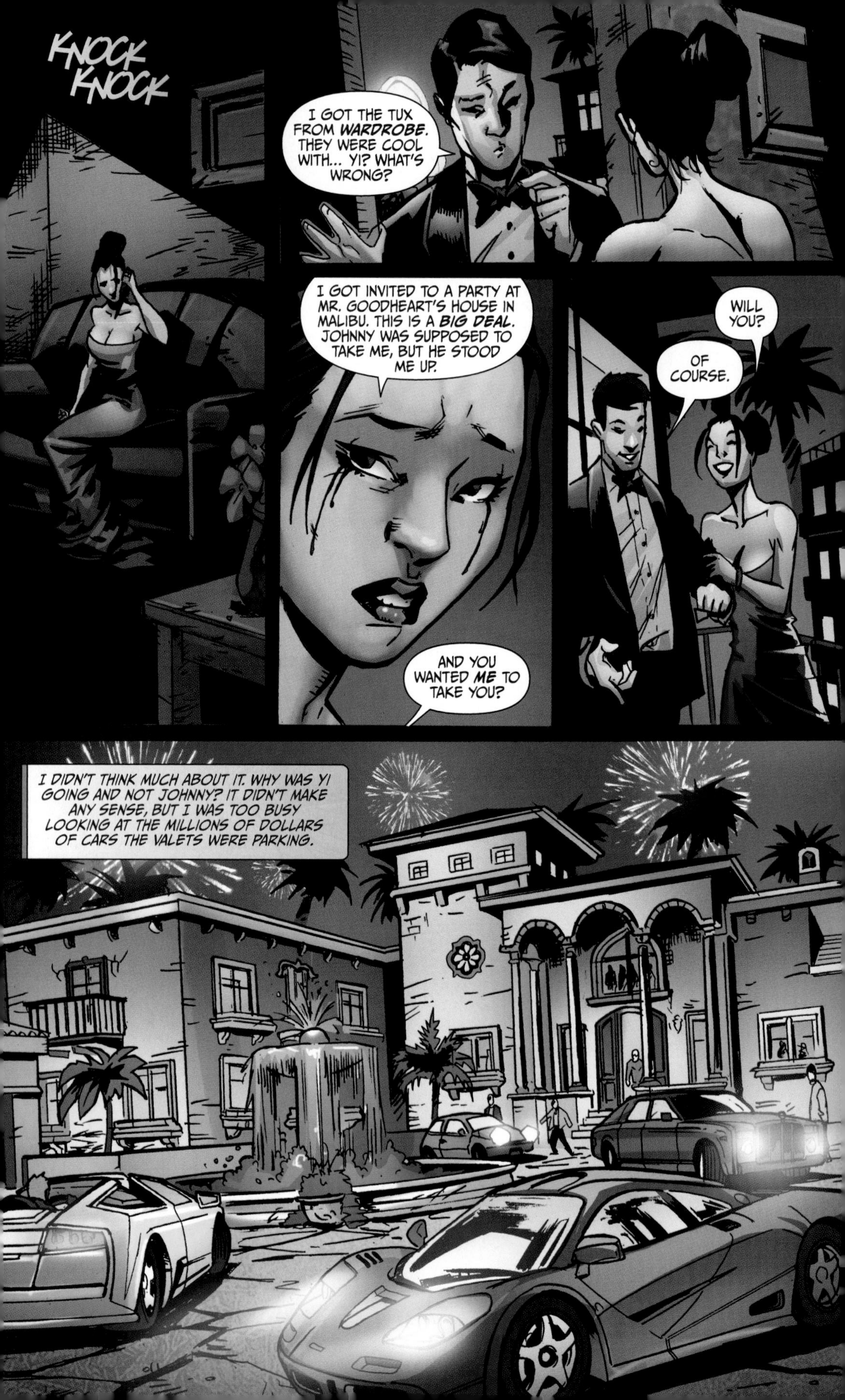
KNOCK KNOCK
I GOT THE TUX FROM WARDROBE. THEY WERE COOL WITH... YI? WHAT'S WRONG?
I GOT INVITED TO A PARTY AT MR. GOODHEART'S HOUSE IN MALIBU. THIS IS A BIG DEAL. JOHNNY WAS SUPPOSED TO TAKE ME, BUT HE STOOD ME UP.
AND YOU WANTED ME TO TAKE YOU?
WILL YOU?
OF COURSE.
I DIDN'T THINK MUCH ABOUT IT. WHY WAS YI GOING AND NOT JOHNNY? IT DIDN'T MAKE ANY SENSE, BUT I WAS TOO BUSY LOOKING AT THE MILLIONS OF DOLLARS OF CARS THE VALETS WERE PARKING.

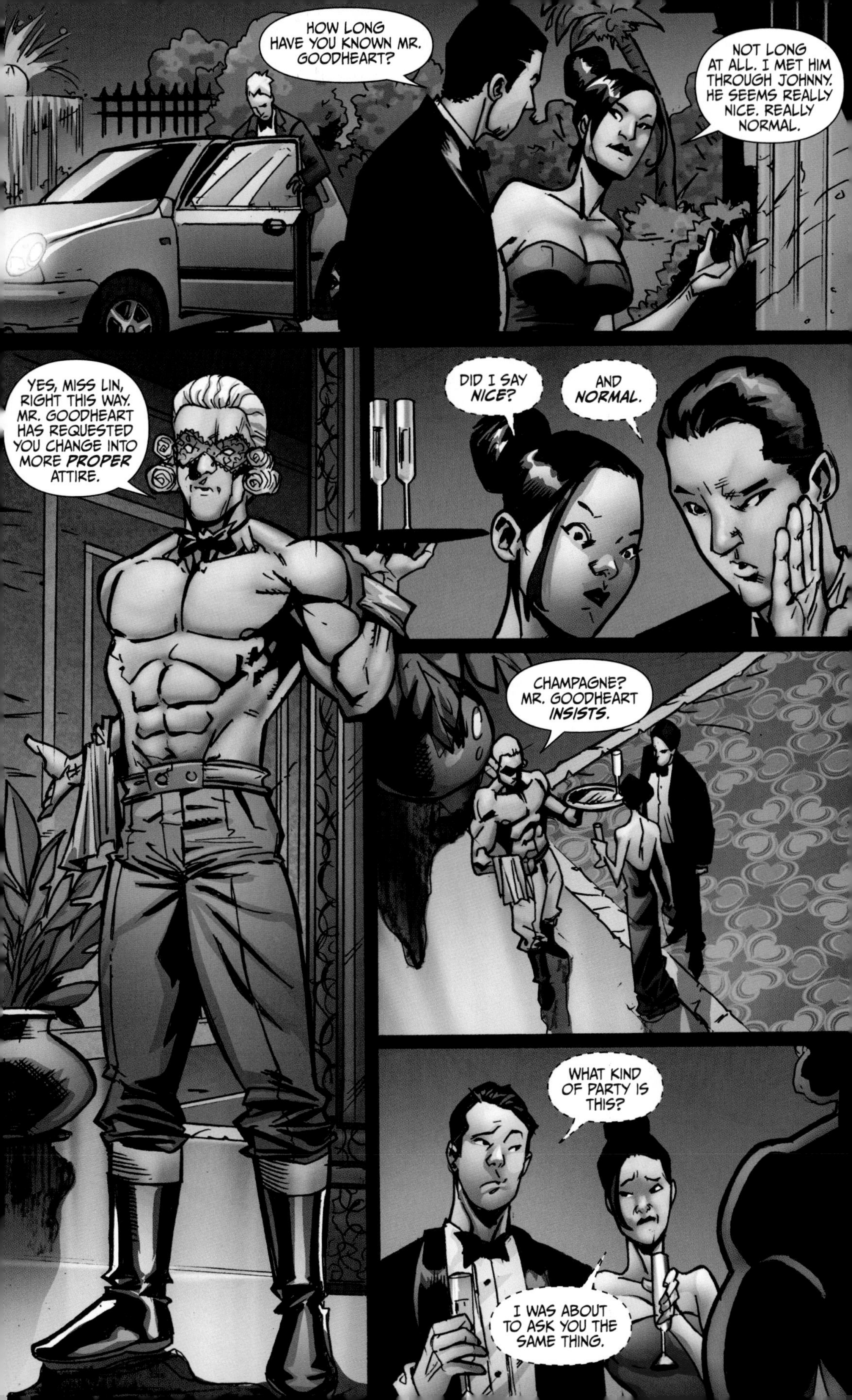
HOW LONG HAVE YOU KNOWN MR. GOODHEART?
NOT LONG AT ALL. I MET HIM THROUGH JOHNNY. HE SEEMS REALLY NICE. REALLY NORMAL.
YES, MISS LIN, RIGHT THIS WAY. MR. GOODHEART HAS REQUESTED YOU CHANGE INTO MORE PROPER ATTIRE.
DID I SAY NICE?
AND NORMAL.
CHAMPAGNE? MR. GOODHEART INSISTS.
WHAT KIND OF PARTY IS THIS?
I WAS ABOUT TO ASK YOU THE SAME THING.

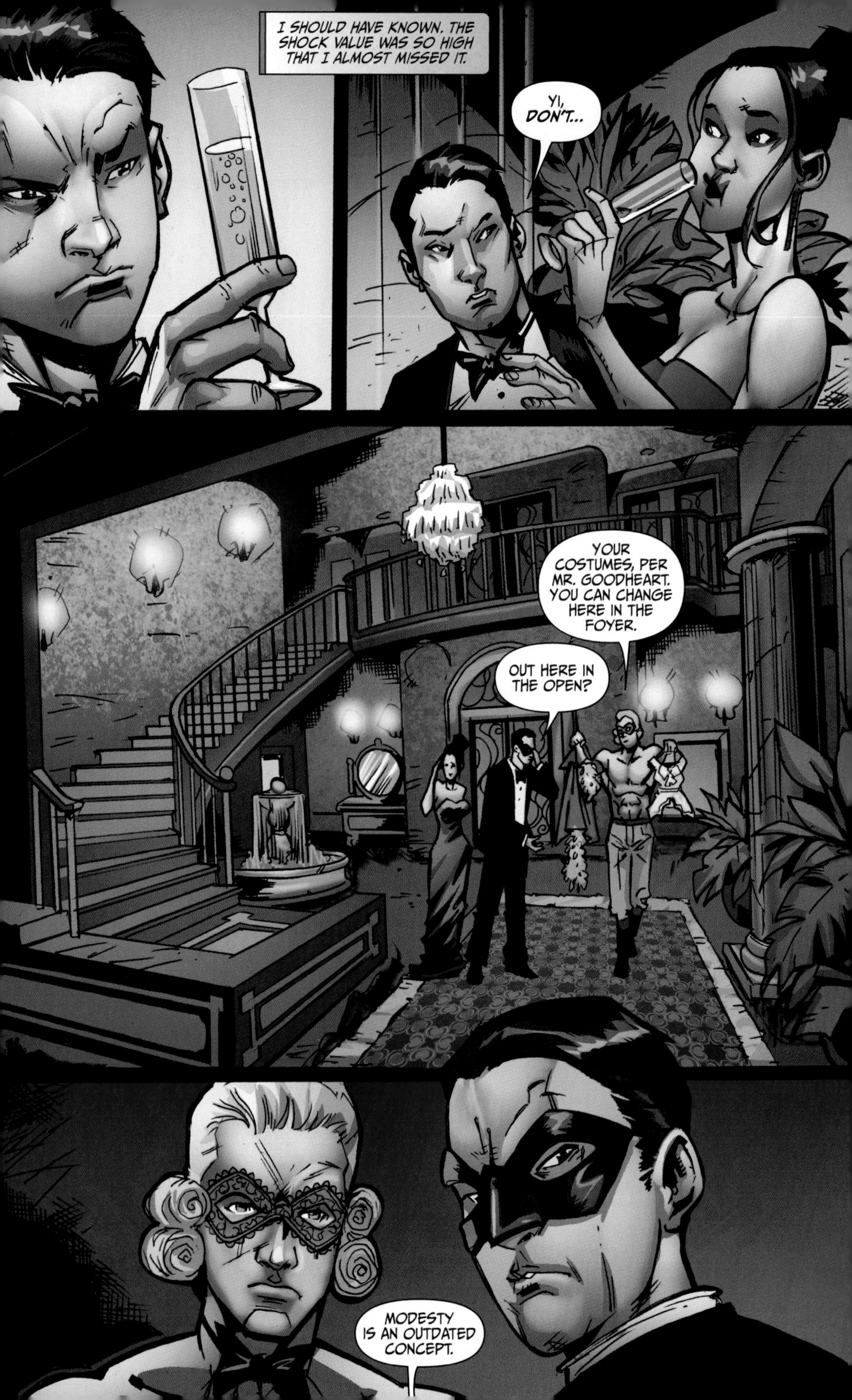
I SHOULD HAVE KNOWN. THE SHOCK VALUE WAS SO HIGH THAT I ALMOST MISSED IT.
YI, DON'T...
YOUR COSTUMES, PER MR. GOODHEART. YOU CAN CHANGE HERE IN THE FOYER.
OUT HERE IN THE OPEN?
MODESTY IS AN OUTDATED CONCEPT.

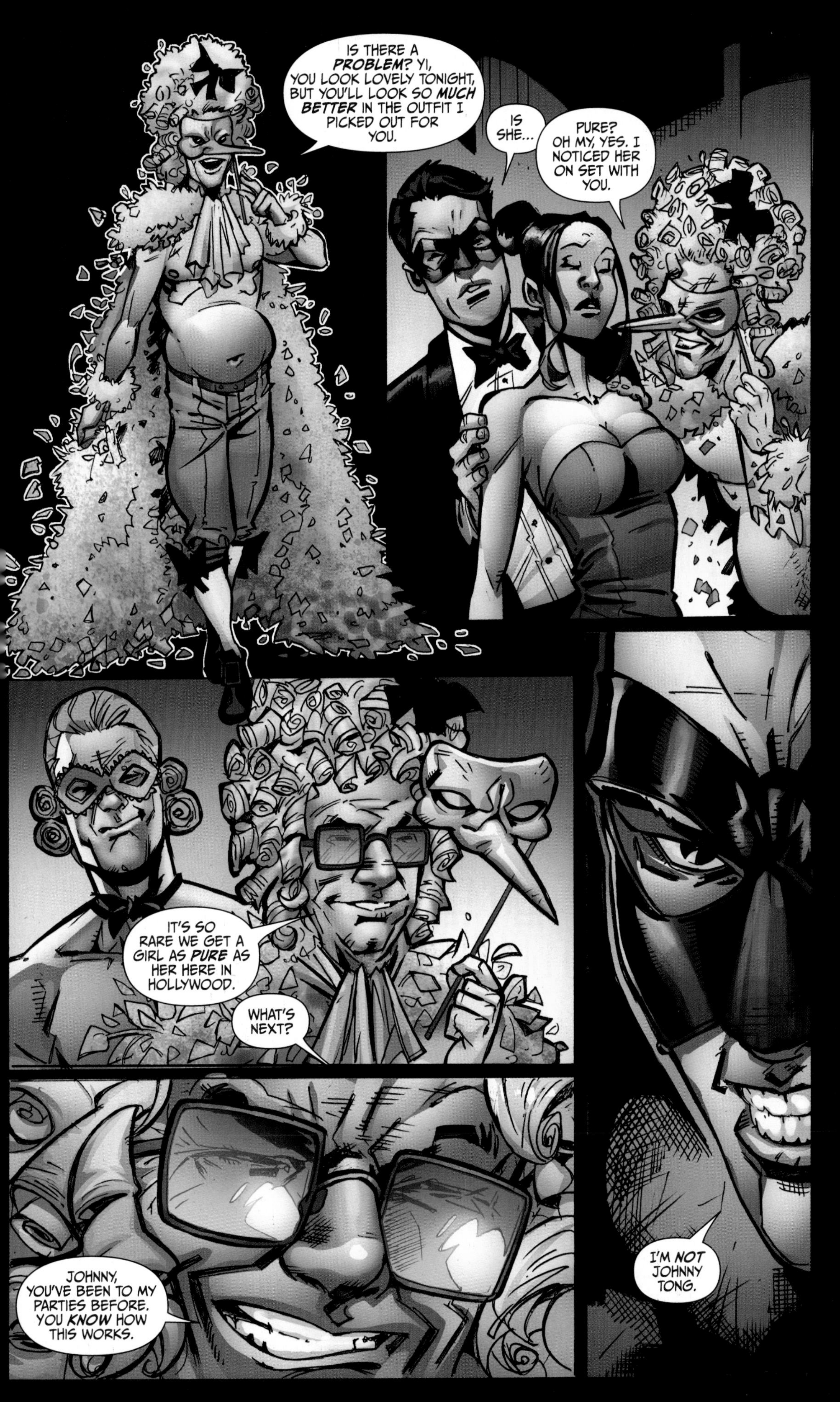
IS THERE A PROBLEM? YI, YOU LOOK LOVELY TONIGHT, BUT YOU'LL LOOK SO MUCH BETTER IN THE OUTFIT I PICKED OUT FOR YOU.
IS SHE...
PURE? OH MY, YES. I NOTICED HER ON SET WITH YOU.
IT'S SO RARE WE GET A GIRL AS PURE AS HER HERE IN HOLLYWOOD.
WHAT'S NEXT?
JOHNNY, YOU'VE BEEN TO MY PARTIES BEFORE. YOU KNOW HOW THIS WORKS.
I'M NOT JOHNNY TONG.

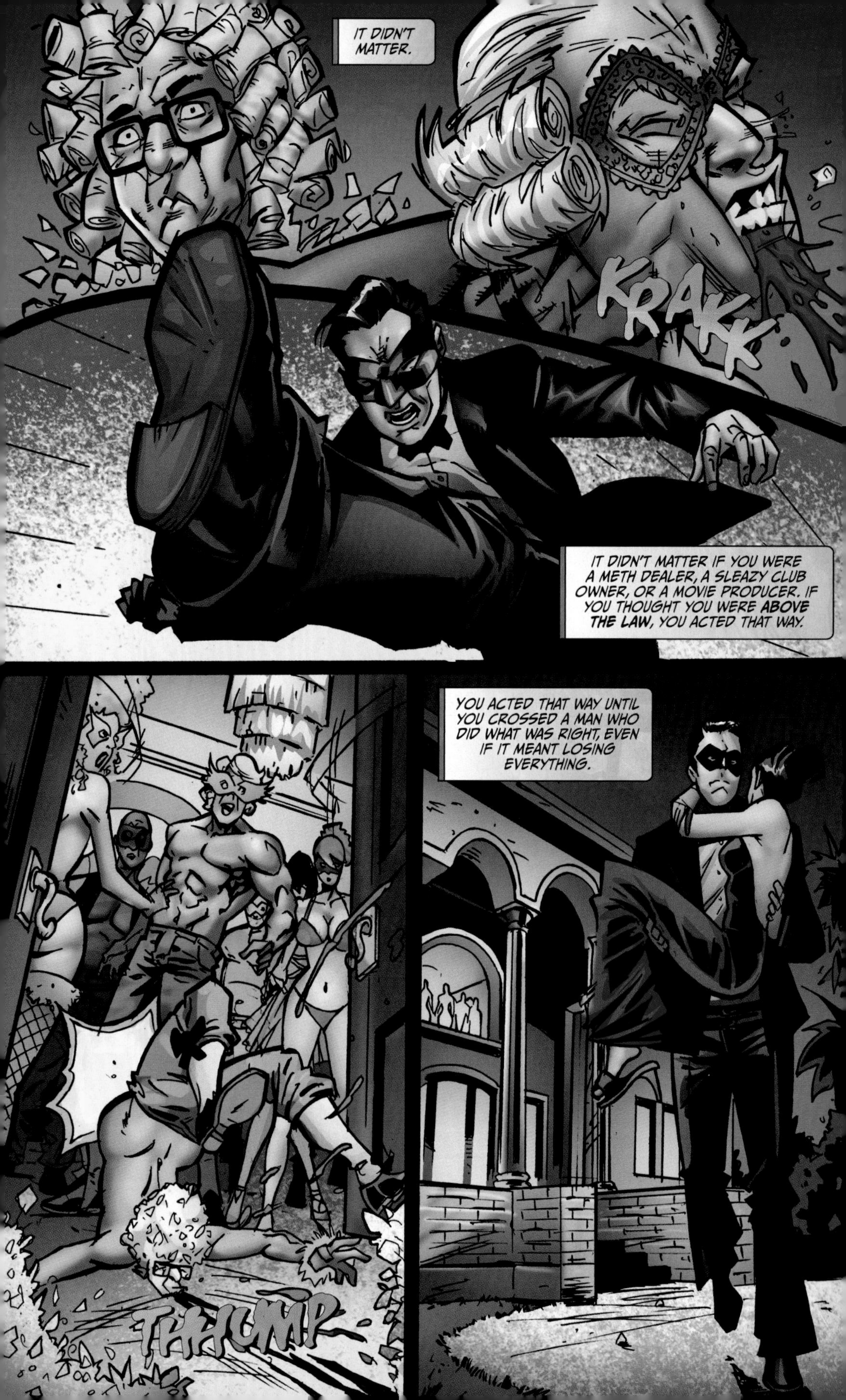
IT DIDN'T MATTER.
KRAKK
IT DIDN'T MATTER IF YOU WERE A METH DEALER, A SLEAZY CLUB OWNER, OR A MOVIE PRODUCER. IF YOU THOUGHT YOU WERE **ABOVE THE LAW**, YOU ACTED THAT WAY.
THHUMP
YOU ACTED THAT WAY UNTIL YOU CROSSED A MAN WHO DID WHAT WAS RIGHT, EVEN IF IT MEANT LOSING EVERYTHING.

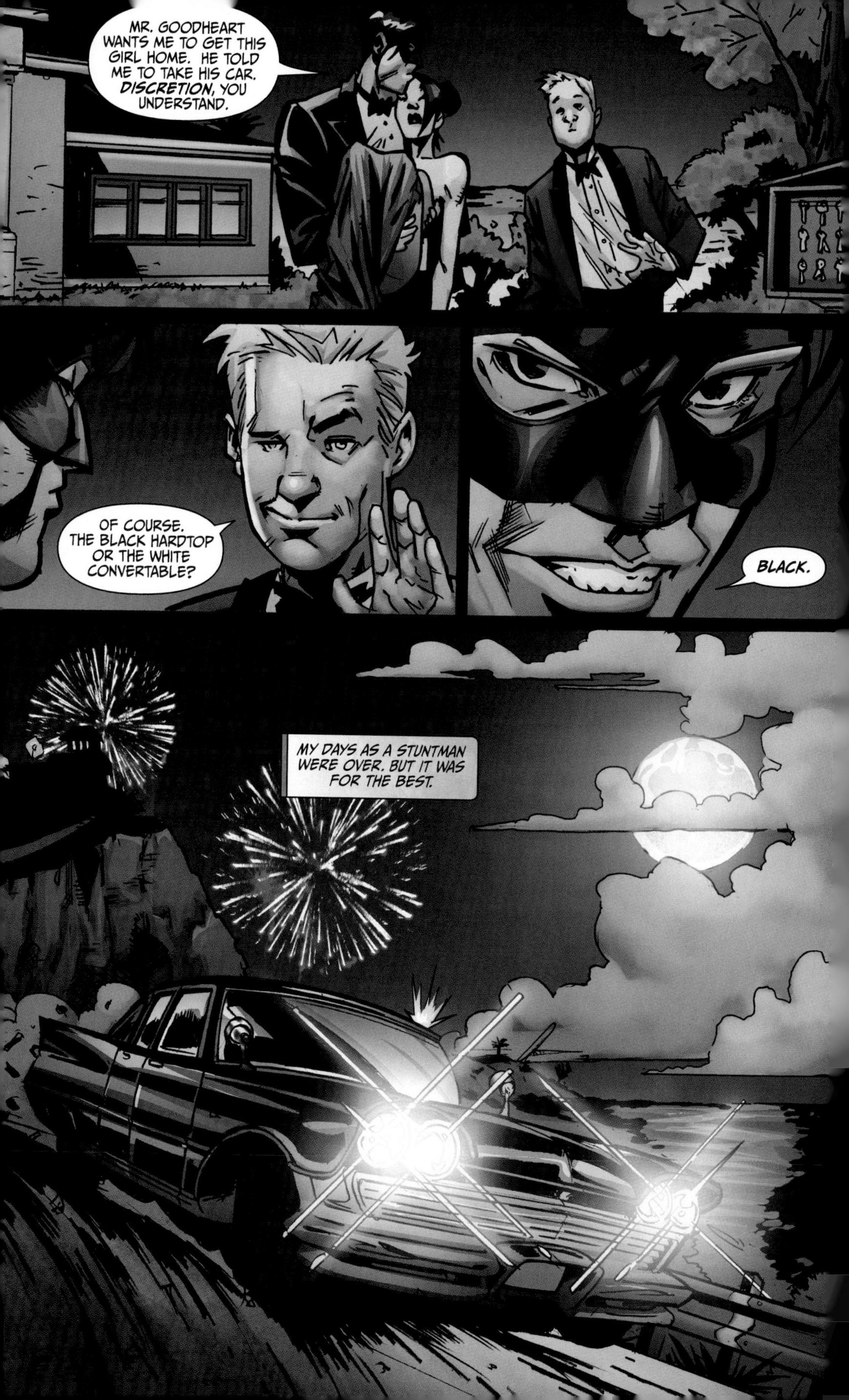
MR. GOODHEART WANTS ME TO GET THIS GIRL HOME. HE TOLD ME TO TAKE HIS CAR. *DISCRETION*, YOU UNDERSTAND.
OF COURSE. THE BLACK HARDTOP OR THE WHITE CONVERTABLE?
BLACK.
MY DAYS AS A STUNTMAN WERE OVER. BUT IT WAS FOR THE BEST.

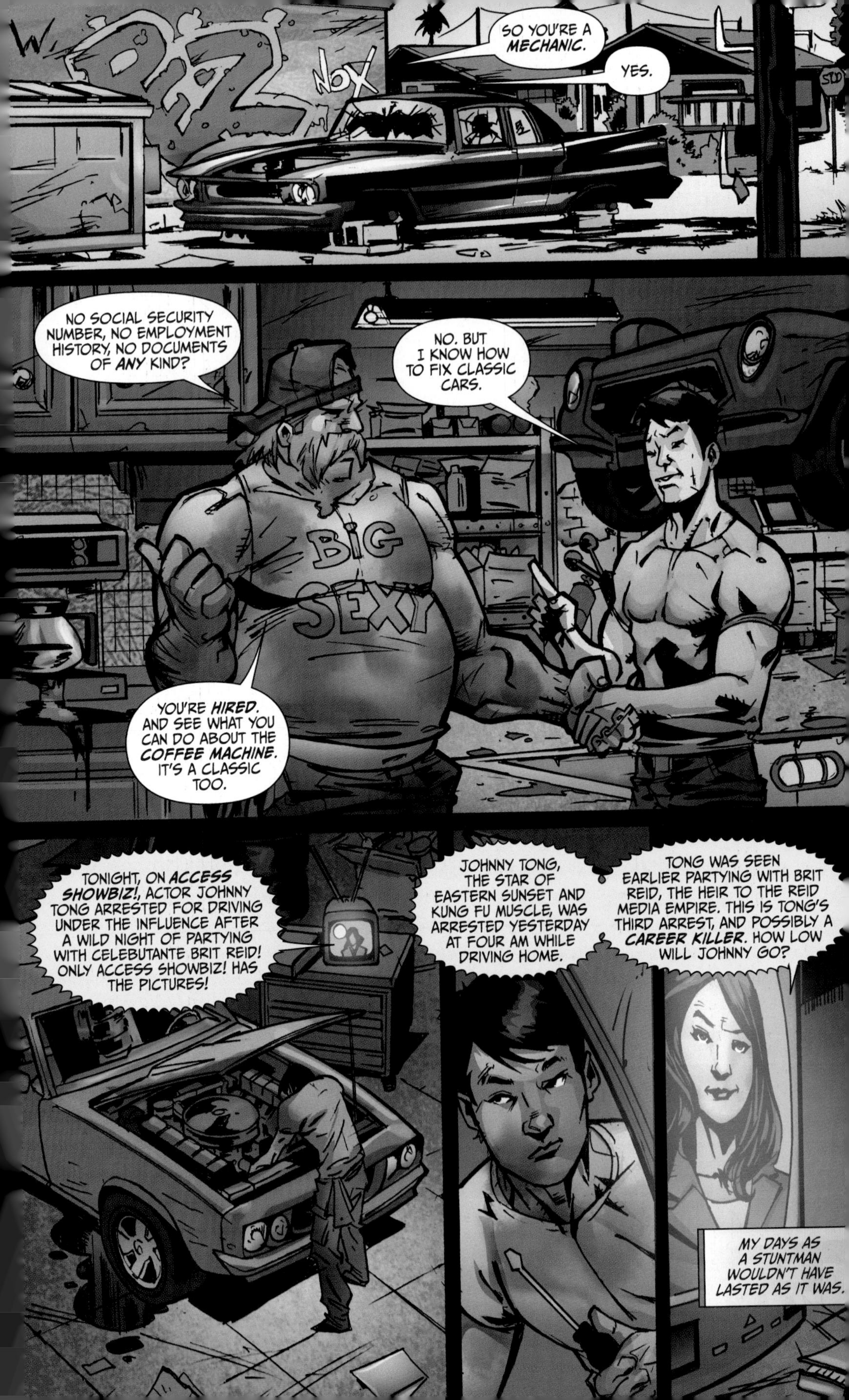
W
NOX
SO YOU'RE A MECHANIC.
YES.
NO SOCIAL SECURITY NUMBER, NO EMPLOYMENT HISTORY, NO DOCUMENTS OF ANY KIND?
NO. BUT I KNOW HOW TO FIX CLASSIC CARS.
BIG SEXY
YOU'RE HIRED. AND SEE WHAT YOU CAN DO ABOUT THE COFFEE MACHINE. IT'S A CLASSIC TOO.
TONIGHT, ON ACCESS SHOWBIZ!, ACTOR JOHNNY TONG ARRESTED FOR DRIVING UNDER THE INFLUENCE AFTER A WILD NIGHT OF PARTYING WITH CELEBUTANTE BRIT REID! ONLY ACCESS SHOWBIZ! HAS THE PICTURES!
JOHNNY TONG, THE STAR OF EASTERN SUNSET AND KUNG FU MUSCLE, WAS ARRESTED YESTERDAY AT FOUR AM WHILE DRIVING HOME.
TONG WAS SEEN EARLIER PARTYING WITH BRIT REID, THE HEIR TO THE REID MEDIA EMPIRE. THIS IS TONG'S THIRD ARREST, AND POSSIBLY A CAREER KILLER. HOW LOW WILL JOHNNY GO?
MY DAYS AS A STUNTMAN WOULDN'T HAVE LASTED AS IT WAS.

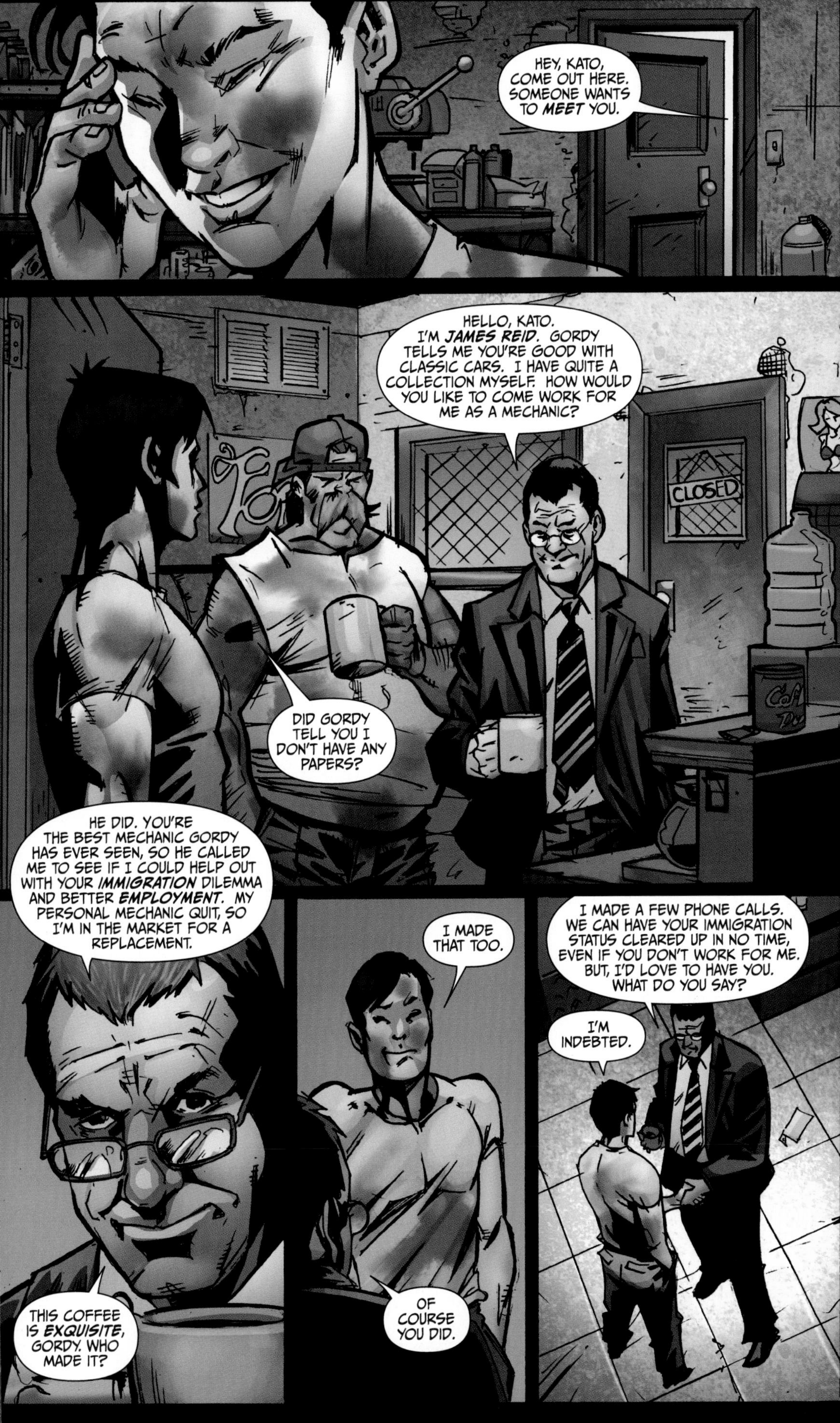
HEY, KATO, COME OUT HERE. SOMEONE WANTS TO MEET YOU.
HELLO, KATO. I'M JAMES REID. GORDY TELLS ME YOU'RE GOOD WITH CLASSIC CARS. I HAVE QUITE A COLLECTION MYSELF. HOW WOULD YOU LIKE TO COME WORK FOR ME AS A MECHANIC?
CLOSED
DID GORDY TELL YOU I DON'T HAVE ANY PAPERS?
HE DID. YOU'RE THE BEST MECHANIC GORDY HAS EVER SEEN, SO HE CALLED ME TO SEE IF I COULD HELP OUT WITH YOUR IMMIGRATION DILEMMA AND BETTER EMPLOYMENT. MY PERSONAL MECHANIC QUIT, SO I'M IN THE MARKET FOR A REPLACEMENT.
THIS COFFEE IS EXQUISITE, GORDY. WHO MADE IT?
I MADE THAT TOO.
OF COURSE YOU DID.
I MADE A FEW PHONE CALLS. WE CAN HAVE YOUR IMMIGRATION STATUS CLEARED UP IN NO TIME, EVEN IF YOU DON'T WORK FOR ME. BUT, I'D LOVE TO HAVE YOU. WHAT DO YOU SAY?
I'M INDEBTED.

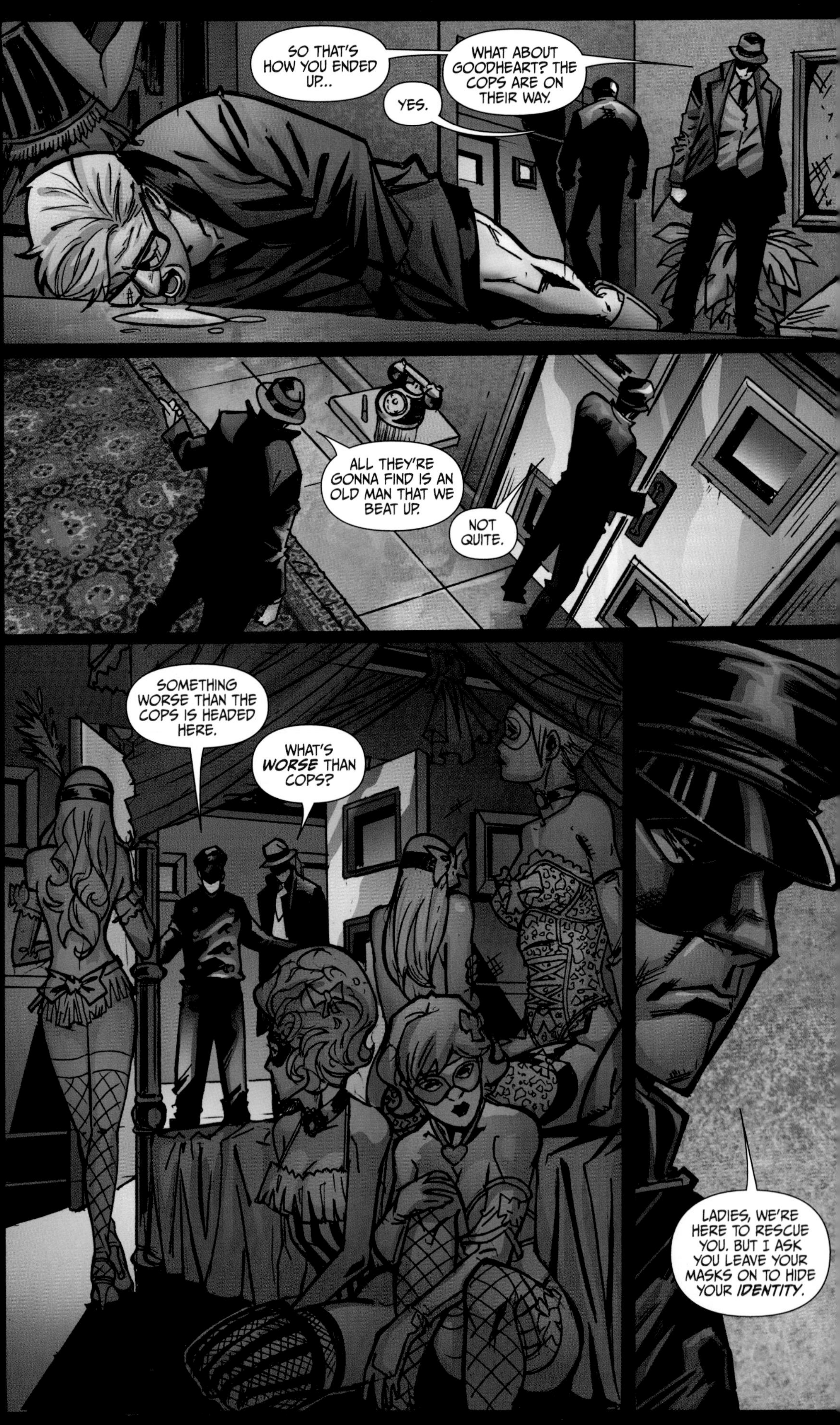
SO THAT'S HOW YOU ENDED UP...
YES.
WHAT ABOUT GOODHEART? THE COPS ARE ON THEIR WAY.
ALL THEY'RE GONNA FIND IS AN OLD MAN THAT WE BEAT UP.
NOT QUITE.
SOMETHING WORSE THAN THE COPS IS HEADED HERE.
WHAT'S **WORSE** THAN COPS?
LADIES, WE'RE HERE TO RESCUE YOU. BUT I ASK YOU LEAVE YOUR MASKS ON TO HIDE YOUR ***IDENTITY***.

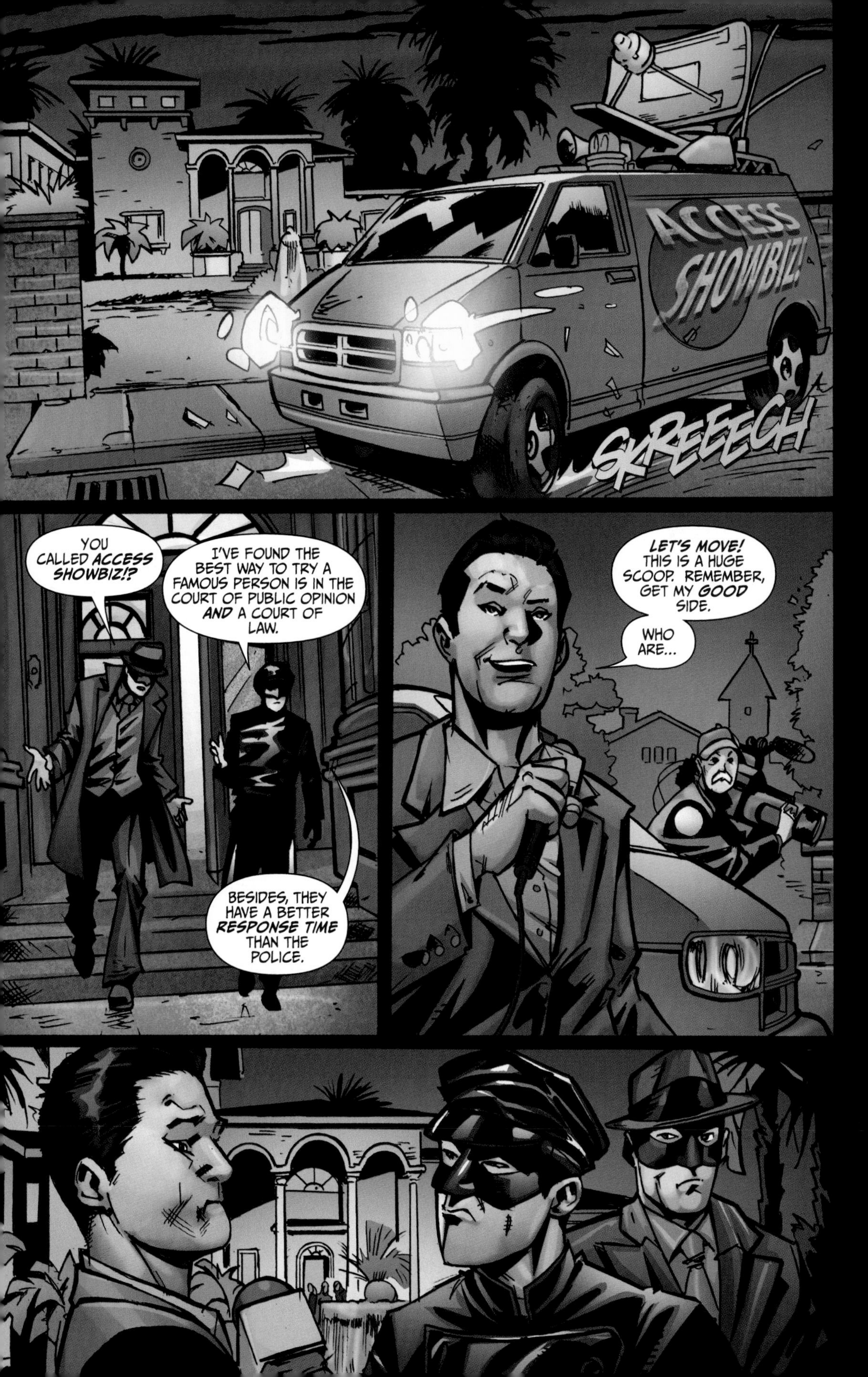
ACCESS SHOWBIZ!
SKREEECH
YOU CALLED ACCESS SHOWBIZ!?
I'VE FOUND THE BEST WAY TO TRY A FAMOUS PERSON IS IN THE COURT OF PUBLIC OPINION AND A COURT OF LAW.
BESIDES, THEY HAVE A BETTER RESPONSE TIME THAN THE POLICE.
LET'S MOVE! THIS IS A HUGE SCOOP. REMEMBER, GET MY GOOD SIDE.
WHO ARE...

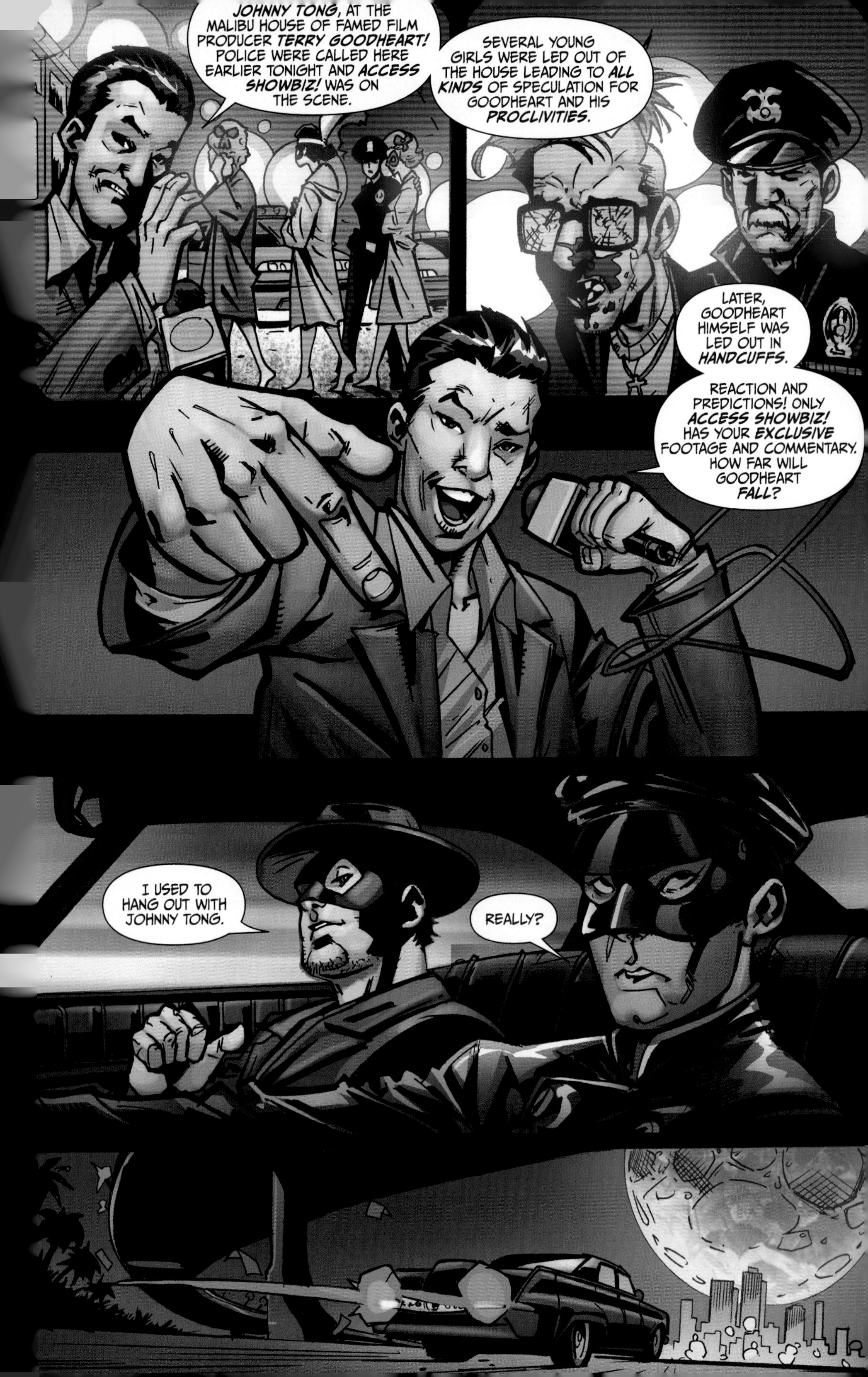
JOHNNY TONG, AT THE MALIBU HOUSE OF FAMED FILM PRODUCER TERRY GOODHEART! POLICE WERE CALLED HERE EARLIER TONIGHT AND ACCESS SHOWBIZ! WAS ON THE SCENE.
SEVERAL YOUNG GIRLS WERE LED OUT OF THE HOUSE LEADING TO ALL KINDS OF SPECULATION FOR GOODHEART AND HIS PROCLIVITIES.
LATER, GOODHEART HIMSELF WAS LED OUT IN HANDCUFFS.
REACTION AND PREDICTIONS! ONLY ACCESS SHOWBIZ! HAS YOUR EXCLUSIVE FOOTAGE AND COMMENTARY. HOW FAR WILL GOODHEART FALL?
I USED TO HANG OUT WITH JOHNNY TONG.
REALLY?

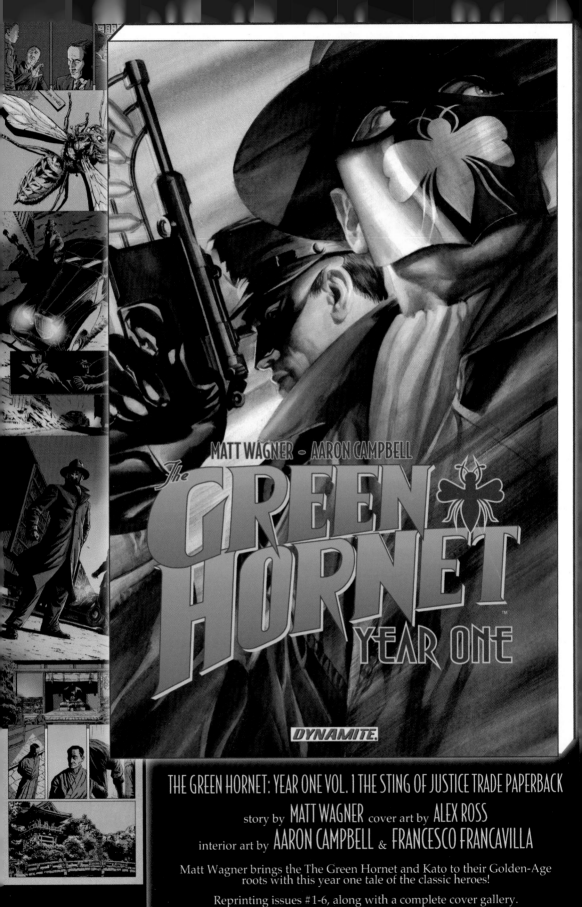

MATT WAGNER - AARON CAMPBELL

The GREEN HORNET
YEAR ONE

DYNAMITE.

THE GREEN HORNET: YEAR ONE VOL. 1 THE STING OF JUSTICE TRADE PAPERBACK

story by MATT WAGNER cover art by ALEX ROSS

interior art by AARON CAMPBELL & FRANCESCO FRANCAVILLA

Matt Wagner brings the The Green Hornet and Kato to their Golden-Age
roots with this year one tale of the classic heroes!

Reprinting issues #1-6, along with a complete cover gallery.